ASIAN AMERICAN ELDERS IN THE TWENTY-FIRST CENTURY

ASIAN AMERICAN ELDERS IN THE TWENTY-FIRST CENTURY

KEY INDICATORS OF WELL-BEING

Ada C. Mui and Tazuko Shibusawa

COLUMBIA UNIVERSITY PRESS   NEW YORK

COLUMBIA UNIVERSITY PRESS
Publishers Since 1893
New York   Chichester, West Sussex

Library of Congress Cataloging-in-Publication Data

Mui, Ada C., 1949–
   Asian American elders in the twenty-first century : key indicators of well-being / Ada C. Mui
and Tazuko Shibusawa.
      p. cm.
   Includes bibliographical references and index.
   ISBN 978-0-231-13590-0 (cloth : alk. paper)—ISBN 978-0-231-50974-9 (e-book)
   1. Older Asian Americans—Social conditions—21st century.   2. Older Asian Americans—
Services for—History—21st century.   3. Quality of life—United States.   I. Shibusawa,
Tazuko.   II. Title.

   HV1465.M83 2008
   362.6089'95073—dc22   2008024365

Columbia University Press books are printed on permanent
and durable acid-free paper.

This book is printed on paper with recycled content.
Printed in the United States of America

c 10 9 8 7 6 5 4 3 2 1

My husband, Peter H. Mui, and son, Isaiah W. Mui

—A.M.

My parents, Masahide and Fusako Shibusawa

—T.S.

CONTENTS

TABLES

PREFACE

AMERICAN SOCIETY is at a critical juncture: policy makers, practitioners, families, and individuals are forced to face the urgent issues that result from expanding ethnic diversification and an aging population. In recent years, gerontological research that focuses on ethnic and cultural diversity has been emerging as a discipline with the potential to shape public policies as well as health and social service programs. However, more work needs to be done to formulate precise and effective recommendations.

In the next decade, the Asian American growth rate is projected to outpace that of whites, blacks, Native Americans, and Hispanics. The number and proportion of Asian Americans sixty-five or older will increase at an even faster rate than the Asian American population as a whole. Despite the rapid increase in the Asian American elderly population, empirically based research with this group has been limited, both nationally and regionally. Furthermore, much of the work that has been done assumes that the study subjects are homogeneous, whereas the Asian American population is in fact diverse, representing more than thirty groups with different national origins. The large surveys that place all Asian Americans in a single category do not allow for an understanding of differences based on nationality or ethnicity.

The aim of this book is to provide information on Asian American elders and their quality-of-life issues. We address the void in the existing body of gerontological literature by presenting empirical findings on the key indicators of psychosocial well-being among this population. Our data are based on the U.S. Census 2000 and the Asian American Elders in New York City (AAENYC) Study, 2000, the very first regional probability sample of Asian American elders in the United States. Data on quality-of-life issues of the six largest groups (Chinese, Filipino, Indian, Japanese, Korean, and Vietnamese) are presented and discussed by addressing their (1) physical health, (2) mental health, (3) acculturation, (4) intergenerational relationships, (5) utilization of social and health services, and (6) productive activities.

The book examines eight areas in the lives of Asian American elders. Chapter 1 presents the historical and sociological background of Asian immigrants to the U.S. The research methodology of the AAENYC Study is discussed in chapter 2, and data from that study is examined in light of the U.S. Census 2000 and the New York City 2000 Census. Chapter 3 looks at the health of Asian American elders and the effects of cultural influences, everyday life stresses, and cultural ways of coping with health-related issues. Mental health indicators are presented in chapter 4, with a focus on depression and life satisfaction. Traditional Asian values regarding family relationships and eldercare, in addition to the extent to which current Asian elders uphold these values, are discussed in chapter 5. Chapter 6 considers the actual state of family relationships and social network support, and examines factors associated with intergenerational exchanges. Utilization of formal services is reviewed in chapter 7, where we also examine help-seeking behaviors and factors associated with the use of community-based, in-home, and health services. Using productive aging as a framework, chapter 8 analyzes factors associated with volunteerism and grandparent caregiving among Asian American elders. In chapter 9 we present the implications of the findings of our study for developing elder-friendly environments responsive to the needs of Asian American elders.

We are indebted to the Asian American Federation of New York and the Brookdale Center on Aging of Hunter College for their generous collaboration in the study. The opinions expressed in this book, however, are those of the authors and should not be attributed to the collaborating organizations. We would like to express our appreciation to our research assistants: Dooyeon Kang, Duy D. Nguyen, Ruchika Bajaj, Elsa Lee, and Isaiah Mui. We also wish to thank Mercedes Del Rosario for her research and editorial assistance. A special appreciation goes to Jim Runsdorf for reviewing portions of the manuscript. We are also grateful to our reviewers for their insightful and valuable feedback. Last but not least, we would like to express our deepest gratitude to the Asian American elders who participated in this study.

ASIAN AMERICAN ELDERS IN THE TWENTY-FIRST CENTURY

1

UNDERSTANDING ASIAN AMERICAN ELDERS
Historical, Political, and Sociocultural Contexts

ASIAN AMERICANS ELDERS comprise one of the fastest-growing groups of ethnic elders in the United States. According to the U.S. Census 2000, more than eight hundred thousand Asians aged sixty-five and older reside in the United States (U.S. Census Bureau 2001). The population of Asian American elders increased by 78 percent between 1990 and 2000, and this number is projected to increase to close to 7 million by 2050 (Federal Interagency Forum on Aging-Related Statistics 2004; U.S. Census Bureau 1990, 2000). In contrast to Asian Americans, the non-Hispanic, white elderly population is projected to grow by only 74 percent in the next twenty-five years (U.S. Department of Health and Human Services, Administration on Aging, 2005).

Despite the rapid increase in the Asian American elderly population, empirically based research with this group has been limited on both the national and regional levels. Included among the twenty-four groups of Asian national origin classified in the U.S. Census 2000 are Asian Indian, Bangladeshi, Cambodian, Chinese, Filipino, Hmong, Indonesian, Japanese, Korean, Laotian, Malaysian, Pakistani, Sri Lankan, Taiwanese, Thai, and Vietnamese (U.S. Census Bureau, 2002). The nationalities that comprise the largest Asian groups, for individuals reporting only one race, are Chinese (25.4%), Filipino (19.3%), and Asian Indian (17.6%) (U.S. Department of Health and Human Services 2001).

The majority of Asian American elders, with the exception of Japanese, were born outside the United States. Table 1.1 presents the demographic characteristics of Asian American elders by nationality, nativity, and year of immigration, based on the U.S. Census 2000. Over 90 percent of the Filipino, Indian, Korean, and Vietnamese elders, and 88 percent of the Chinese elders were born outside the United States. In contrast, only 30 percent of the Japanese

TABLE 1.1 Demographic Characteristics: Asian Population Age 65 and Over, Census 2000

	CHINESE[1]	FILIPINO	INDIAN	JAPANESE	KOREAN	VIETNAMESE	TOTAL
n =	11,202	8,233	2,947	8,326	3,180	2,681	36,569
Proportion of Asian elders (%)	30.60	22.5	8.1	22.8	8.7	7.3	
Mean age	74.1	73.9	72.3	74.5	73.1	72.7	73.8
(SD)	(6.9)	(6.9)	(6.3)	(6.7)	(6.6)	(6.6)	(6.8)
Age (over 75)[2],[****] (%)	41.0	39.9	30.7	35.5	44.7	32.3	39.7
Gender (female)[2],[****] (%)	54.1	58.3	50.4	63.9	62.1	51.5	57.5
Foreign-born[2],[****] (%)	86.7	91.5	95.7	28.0	93.8	97.4	76.52
U.S. citizen[2],[****] (%)	71.5	75.2	50.5	93.0	64.7	59.3	74.0
Arrived after age 60[2],[4],[****] (%)	34.9	34.7	43.0	5.4	30.2	43.6	34.0
Years in the U.S.[3]	23.6	23.6	17.4	39.7	21.2	14.8	23.2
(SD)	(16.4)[a]	(16.7)[a]	(12.3)[b]	(13.9)[c]	(11.5)[d]	(9.6)[e]	(16)
Age at immigration[3]	50.4	50.4	54.8	32.0	51.7	57.8	50.1
(SD)	(16.8)[a]	(16.5)[a]	(14.0)[b]	(13.1)[c]	(13.7)[d]	(10.8)[e]	(16.5)

Note: Figures reflect analyses of Census 2000 PUMS data, 5% file, extracted from IPUMS-USA (Integrated Public Use Microdata Series –USA). ANOVA statistics with Tukey's post hoc multiple comparisons were used to test the differences among means.

[1] Chinese include Taiwanese.
[2] Chi-square statistics were used.
[3] Excludes those married, with spouse not present.
[4] Calculated for foreign-born population, $n = 27{,}761$.
[*] $p < .05$.
[****] $p < .0001$.

[a],[b],[c],[d],[e] Means with the different letters are significantly different at less than the .05 level in the same variable.

elders were born in the United States. A typical immigrant in the United States arrives before reaching middle age, attracted largely by better employment opportunities than are available in the home country. Many Asian elders, however, immigrated after age sixty to live with their adult children. For example, more than 30 percent of Chinese, Korean, and Filipino elders and close to 43 percent of Indian and Vietnamese elders immigrated after age sixty (U.S. Census Bureau 2001).

Asian immigrants in the U.S. are often categorized as Asian and Pacific Islanders (API). However, following the U.S. Census 2000, which presented "Native Hawaiian and Other Pacific Islanders" as separate racial categories, we use the term "Asian American" in this book. The term "Asian American" was coined in the 1960s by the late historian and social activist Yuji Ichioka during an era when Asians, influenced by the Civil Rights movement, came together to resist discrimination and oppression (Zhou and Lee, 2004). In contrast to the word "Oriental," which carries derogatory connotations having been imposed in the late 1800s by those in power to discriminate against Asians, the term "Asian American," chosen by Asian Americans, is a neutral expression that acknowledges the hybrid nature of the group it designates. Using the term "Asian American" as a racial category is significant because race has a profound impact on the lives of ethnic elders and their families in the United States. As Thomas contends, ignoring race minimizes the consequences of racism on physical and mental health (Thomas 2001).

Though the term "Asian American" is important sociopolitically, the term should not be taken to deny the heterogeneity of Asian Americans based on national origin, social class, and gender (Lowe 1991). Variations exist even within the many national groups. The majority of Chinese elders are from the People's Republic of China (PRC) or Taiwan and speak Mandarin, Cantonese, Taiwanese, and dialects such as Toishanese and Fujianese. A sizable number that come from Cambodia, Indonesia, Laos, Singapore, and Vietnam are ethnically Chinese. As is well known, Indian elders represent a highly diversified nation with at least six different major ethnic groups, thirty-three languages (Das 2002), and many religions including Buddhism, Christianity, Hinduism, Islam, Janism, Judaism, Sikhism, and Zoroastrianism (Rastogi and Wadhwa, 2006). Filipino elders come from an archipelago made up of seven thousand islands with 150 different languages (Tucker 1998). Frequently, however, elders from Southeast Asia are grouped in one category when the reality is that, although Cambodians, Laotians, Hmongs, and Vietnamese, for example, share national boundaries, historically Vietnam was heavily influenced by China and Mahayana Buddhism, and the cultures of Laos and Cambodia were influenced by Hinduism and Theravada Buddhism (Jenkins et al. 1996). Moreover, not all Asian immigrants come directly from their home countries to the United States. For instance, according to Park (1997), more than forty-thousand Koreans who originally immigrated to countries in South America have moved to the United States.

HISTORICAL BACKGROUND OF ASIANS IN THE UNITED STATES

PRE-1965 IMMIGRANTS

The current demographic characteristics of Asian American elders are strongly associated with U.S. immigration policies. The first Asian immigrants to arrive in the United States came from China, the Philippines, Korea, India, and Japan starting in the mid-1800s through the early 1900s. The majority came in response to labor demands (Segal 2002). Many Chinese Americans worked in the gold mines, and others were recruited as laborers on the transcontinental railroad. Japanese and Koreans first migrated to Hawaii to work on plantations and then moved to the West Coast (Ichioka 1988; K. Park 1997). The Filipinos came to the United States as early as 1763 on Spanish galleons and established a settlement in New Orleans. Known as Manila Men, these Filipinos founded the first large-scale shrimp fishery on the Gulf Coast (Cordova 1983). Other Filipinos began migrating to Hawaii in the 1900s to work on plantations (Posadas 1999). The Sikhs from Punjabi were among the first groups to emigrate from South Asia, prompted by a British law in India forbidding them to own arable land. The Sikhs had originally settled in Canada but immigrated to the United States because of anti-Indian sentiments. They entered through San Francisco and eventually settled as farmers in central California (Mazumdar 1984).

Asian immigrants first came to the United States during an era of intense anti-Asian sentiments. During the 1880s and 1920s more than 27 million European immigrants arrived in the United States. The Asian population, however, because of exclusionary policies, remained small, representing less than 5 percent of the immigrant population (Zhou and Gatewood 2000). The 1790 Naturalization Law limited citizenship to people who were white, preventing

Asians from gaining U.S. citizenship. The 1882 Chinese Exclusion Act, one of the first restrictive U.S. immigration laws, banned Chinese from immigrating to the United States. This act was not repealed until 1943, when China became a wartime ally of the United States (M. G. Wong 1986). The Chinese Exclusion Act was followed by the Immigration Act of 1917. Also known as the Asiatic Barred Zone Act, this legislation banned immigration from India, Siam, Indochina, Afghanistan, Arabia, and parts of Siberia. Asian Indians, originally considered to be white, had gained citizenship. However, a 1923 Supreme Court decision determined that Asian Indians were Caucasians but not "free white persons" and therefore were not eligible for citizenship. As a result of this legislation, Indians who had gained naturalization before 1923 were stripped of their citizenship (Mazumdar 1984). Not until 1946, when a new immigration bill allowed an annual quota of one hundred Indian immigrants, were Indians allowed to come to the U.S. (Das 2002).

The first wave of Korean immigrants to the U.S. arrived in Hawaii in 1903 to work in the plantations. Many were brought to replace Japanese laborers who had gone on strike in the cane fields (Park 1997). Immigration from Korea, however, was short-lived. At the time, Korea was occupied by Japan, and in 1905 the Japanese government placed a ban on Korean immigration to the United States. It is estimated that seven thousand Koreans entered the United States during this period (Okihiro 2001). Immigration from Japan was curtailed following the Gentlemen's Agreement of 1907–1908. This legislation, however, allowed families of those already in the U.S. to immigrate, which led to women arriving as "picture brides" from Japan as well as Korea. Marriages were arranged by proxy between men who were in the United States and women who were in their home country. Approximately eleven hundred Korean women immigrated to Hawaii and the mainland as picture brides (Yu, Choe, and Han 2002). The exact number of Japanese women who entered as picture brides is unknown. Records indicate that by 1920, in San Francisco alone, twenty thousand picture brides had been processed on Angel Island, which had served as an immigration and quarantine station (Lucaccini 1996). These women, along with their husbands and children, established the foundations of the first Japanese American and Korean American communities in the United States.

Early Asian immigrants also faced segregation laws, such as the 1913 Alien Land Law prohibiting Asians who were ineligible for citizenship from owning land in the United States. Asians were also subject to segregation laws that prohibited their children from attending schools with whites, and to anti-miscegenation laws banning them from marrying whites (Hing 1993).

The National Origins Quota Act of 1921 imposed a quota system and restricted the number of new immigrants from a given country to 3 percent of the people of the national origin group that were already in the U.S. in 1910 (M. G. Wong 1986). Finally, the Immigration Act of 1924, the Johnson-Reed Act, reduced each country's quota to 2 percent of those immigrants already in the United States. China, Japan, and Korea received no quota, and the 1924 Immigration Act effectively ended immigration from those countries. Filipinos were not subjected to these laws because the Philippines were under U.S. colonial rule. The Tydings-McDuffie Act of 1934, however, acknowledged the Philippines as a commonwealth and changed the status of Filipinos in the U.S. from colonial subjects to citizens of an autonomous nation. As a result, Filipinos also became aliens ineligible for U.S. citizenship (Posadas 1999).

The exclusionary immigration laws were lifted for Asian women following World War II. The War Brides Act was enacted in 1945 to allow spouses and adopted children of U.S. servicemen to immigrate. It is estimated that between 1947 and 1964 more than seventy-two thousand women, mostly from Japan and Korea, immigrated under this law (Simpson 1998; R. Wong 2007). The McCarren-Walter Act of 1952 abolished national origin requirements and allowed one hundred people per year to immigrate from Pacific and Asian countries.

POST-1965 IMMIGRANTS

Because of the exclusionary immigration policies, there was little immigration from Asia to the United States between the 1920s and the 1960s. It was not until the Immigration and Nationality Act of 1965, which abolished national quotas and national origin, race, and ancestry as a basis for denying immigration to the U.S., that Asians began to immigrate again. Immigrants were admitted based on three criteria: (1) family reunification, (2) occupational immigration, and (3) refugees and those seeking asylum from political persecution. Since 1980, Asians have comprised 43 percent of the total number of immigrants to the United States (M. G. Wong 1986). The following is a brief summary of post-1965 immigration of the six ethnic groups—Chinese, Filipino, Indian, Japanese, Korean and Vietnamese—that are the focus of this book.

CHINESE. The Chinese constitute the largest subgroup of Asian Americans and the second-largest immigrant group in the United States following Mexican Americans. According to the U.S. Census 2000, the Chinese population grew by 48 percent from 1.6 million in 1990 to nearly 2.5 million in 2000 (U.S. Census Bureau 2001). Chinese immigration to the United States increased after 1965 because of separate quotas for people from the People's Republic of China (PRC), Taiwan, and Hong Kong. The U.S. began to admit immigrants from the PRC in 1979, after diplomatic ties were established between the two countries. Post-1965 immigrants from China mostly came from urban areas. About half of those who immigrated between 1966 and 1975 were students, professionals, and white-collar workers (Takaki 1989). Another half were low-wage earners who worked for garment sweatshops and small businesses (Lee 1997). It is important to acknowledge a group of undocumented immigrants from the rural areas of China who are victims of human trafficking and human rights violations. A large number are from Fujian Province and work in restaurants and garment factories that ignore labor codes (Kwong 1997). Currently cities with large Chinese American populations include New York, San Francisco, Los Angeles, and Houston (U.S. Census Bureau 2001). In addition to these concentrations in large cities, smaller pockets of Chinese Americans are dispersed in rural towns, often university towns, throughout the United States. A large number of elders in the Chinese community immigrated to be with their family members.

FILIPINOS. Until the 1960s the Filipinos were mostly concentrated in Hawaii, where the majority worked on plantations (Posadas 1999). Following the Immigration Act of 1965, a new group of Filipinos, with professional backgrounds, moved to the United States (Wolf 1997). In the 1970s and 1980s Filipina immigrants had the highest percentage of professionals compared to other native and foreign-born women (Cabezas, Shinagawa, and Kawaguchi 1986). In the early 1970s most Filipinos in the mainland lived in California. Since then, the Filipinos have moved to other states including Illinois, New York, Texas, New Jersey, Pennsylvania, and Michigan. The majority of Filipino Americans live in metropolitan areas, such as Honolulu, Chicago, New York, Jersey City, and Seattle. The number of Filipinos in the United States continues to grow: the population increased from 1.4 million to 1.85 million between 1990 and 2000. It is important to note that the Immigration Act of 1990 featured an important provision, allowing about 150,000 Filipinos who served in the U.S. military during World War II to gain U.S. citizenship (Posadas 1999).

INDIANS. The initial Indian immigrants who arrived after 1965 were mostly professionals, including physicians, scientists, and academics, as well as students (Pettys and Balgopal 1998). It is estimated that 85,000 scientists, engineers, and physicians emigrated from India between 1966 and 1977 (Subramanian 2007). Since the 1970s there has been an increase in the number of Indian women immigrants. There has also been growing diversity among the Indian population since the mid-1980s as earlier groups began to sponsor their relatives to immigrate to the United States. Currently the Indian immigrant group is the third-largest Asian American ethnic group in the United States, following the Chinese and Filipinos. According to the U.S. Census 2000, there are close to 1.7 million Indians in the United States, and the states with Indian populations of more than sixty thousand are California, Texas, New York, New Jersey, and Illinois. Indians comprise the largest Asian American ethnic group in New Jersey, the second-largest after the Chinese in New York. The states of California, Illinois, Michigan, New Jersey, New York, Ohio, Pennsylvania, and Texas accounted for 70 percent of the Indian population in the 1990s (Das 2002). Indians have the highest median family income among all groups in the United States (U.S. Census Bureau 2004).

JAPANESE. Japanese Americans are the only Asian group that decreased in population in the past decade (U.S. Census Bureau, 2004). This decrease is due to low immigration rates from Japan and high rates of out marriages. According to the U.S. Census 2000, 70 percent of Japanese American elders were born in the United States. Japanese elders in the U.S. are categorized into groups according to their immigration history and are identified as such. Currently, the oldest group of Japanese American elders is composed of the second generation, known as *Nisei*, which means "second generation," and new immigrants are known as *Shin Issei*, which means "first generation." Among *Nisei*, there are two subgroups: *Nisei* who grew up in the United States and those known as *Kibei Nisei*, who were sent back to be educated in Japan as children. The *Kibei Nisei* tend to be less acculturated to the United States, preferring to speak Japanese, and share similarities with immigrants arriving later from Japan (*Shin Issei*). A growing number of third-generation Japanese Americans, known as *Sansei* and belonging to the baby boom generation, are entering older adulthood (Shibusawa, Lubben, and Kitano 2001). Japanese Americans have the longest average life span among all ethnic groups in the United States (McCormick et al. 1996).

KOREANS. Korean Americans rank as the fifth-largest Asian group in the United States, with a population of more than 1 million, according to the U.S. Census 2000. California is the state with the largest Korean American population (33%), followed by New York (12%). Prior to 1965 there were about ten thousand Koreans in the United States (Takaki 1989). Between 1970 and 1988 the population grew to nearly half a million (Min 1990). Many of the initial post-1965 immigrants were medical professionals such as physicians, pharmacists, and nurses, who entered under special provisions of the immigration law, which encouraged the immigration of professionals with skills in short supply in the United States (Min 1990). More recent immigrants from Korea are concentrated in retail and service industries. In the 1980s one-third of Korean immigrant families were engaged in small businesses, and have the highest rate of self-employment among any ethnic group (Lee 2007). It is also important to note that there are more than one hundred thousand Korean adoptees in the United States (Huh and Reid 2000).

VIETNAMESE. According to the U.S. Census 2000, more than 1.1 million U.S. residents identified themselves as Vietnamese. Among Asian Americans, the Vietnamese along with Cambodians, Laotians, and Hmong are the least likely to marry outside their ethnic group, and have the largest percentage of people who identify themselves as belonging to only one ethnicity (U.S. Census Bureau 2002). The first wave of immigration from Vietnam occurred after the end of the Vietnam War in 1975. People who had close ties to Americans or who worked for the South Vietnamese government left Vietnam during the spring of 1975 immediately following the war (Gold 1992). These Vietnamese were generally highly skilled and educated, and were airlifted by the U.S. government to refugee centers in the United States. The second wave of immigration began in 1978 and continued until the early to mid-1980s. Those who left Vietnam during this era are known as "boat people," because they fled in small fishing boats to escape the Communist regime, reeducation camps, or forced evacuation to "new economic zones" (Gold 1992). These people suffered extreme hardships, remaining in the harsh conditions of refugee camps for many years. Half of those who tried to escape are thought to have perished during their exit from Vietnam. During the third wave of immigration that took place between the mid-1980s and 2000, more than five hundred thousand Vietnamese refugees immigrated to the United States. Among those who immigrated in the mid- to late 1980s were survivors of reeducation camps who were permitted to leave Vietnam and join their families in the United States (Gold 1992). A subgroup of this wave of immigrants, the ethnic Chinese, was descended from Chinese who had immigrated to Vietnam centuries earlier (Gyory 2000). The proportion of adults sixty-five and older is 5 percent, quite small compared to other Asian immigrant groups (Leung and Boehnlein 2005).

ASIAN ELDERS: A LIFE COURSE PERSPECTIVE

This book is based on a cross-sectional study in which elders were interviewed about their current life situation at a single point in time. Thus the data do not include information about their past life experiences. It is important, however, to consider the lives of Asian American elders from a life course perspective. Life course theory views human development and aging as a lifelong process and stresses the importance of understanding the contexts that shape this process (Bengston, Burgess, and Parrott 1997). These contexts include socially and culturally defined life-cycle stages and the timing at which an elder progressed through these stages. Another important aspect to consider is the influence of historical and social events in the life of an elder and the timing of these events (Elder, Johnson, and Crosnoe 2003). Table 1.2, the Life Course Chart, presents the historical and social events that occurred for Chinese, Filipino, Indian, Japanese, Korean, and Vietnamese elders born in 1930.

As seen in table 1.2, Asian elders have lived through different periods of historical turmoil. Chinese elders born in the 1930s spent their early childhood years during the Japanese military occupation and their adolescent years in the civil war between the Nationalists and the Communists following the defeat of Japan in World War II. Some Chinese fled to Taiwan, and others stayed behind to witness Mao Zedong proclaim the establishment of the People's Republic of China in 1949. People of this generation who remained in China spent their young adulthood under various land reforms and Mao's economic program known as the Great Leap Forward, an attempt to transform China from an agricultural economy to an industrial communist society (Becker 1996). This resulted in a famine that killed 20–40 million people (Becker 1996). During their thirties and forties, they experienced the Cultural Revolution and the destruction of old establishments by the Red Guards, a group largely composed of youth carrying out communist policies.

TABLE 1.2 Life Course: Global and National Events in the Life of a Person Born in 1930

PERIOD	U.S./ASIAN AMERICAN	CHINA	PHILIPPINES	INDIA	JAPAN	KOREA	VIETNAM
1930s **Age: 0–10**	**1929** Great Depression **1939–45** World War II	**1931** Japan invasion of Manchuria **1934** Long March **1937–45** Second Sino-Japanese War	**1906-34** First major immigration wave to the U.S. **1934** Tydings-McDuffie Act: Annual immigration quota cut to 50 persons; Filipinos in the U.S. reclassified as "Aliens"	**1800s** Occupation by Great Britain **1930–31** Civil Disobedience Movement led by Mahatma Gandhi	**1931** Japan invasion of Manchuria	Japan continues Korean occupation, which started in **1905**	**1930** Ho Chi Minh forms Indochinese Communist Party (ICP)
1940s **Age: 10–20** Childhood, early to mid-adolescence	**1942** Internment of 120,000 Japanese Americans **1945** War Brides Act: Immigration of an estimated 200,000 Asian women married to U.S. servicemen	**1945** Chinese wives of American citizens allowed to immigrate **1947** Kuomintang retreats to Taiwan **1949** People's Republic of China established; Mao Zedong becomes Chinese Communist Party Chairman	**1944–46** Allied forces in the Philippines **1946** Independent Republic of the Philippines established	**1944** Japanese invasion along the Indian-Burmese border **1946** Indian Citizenship Bill (token annual quota of 100 immigrants to the U.S.) **1947** Independence; country partitioned into India and Pakistan	**1941** Attack on Pearl Harbor **1941–42** Invasion of the Philippines, Thailand, the Dutch East Indies, and British India **1945** The U.S. drops atomic bombs on Hiroshima and Nagasaki; Japan surrenders	**1945** Korea is divided	**1946–54** Indo-China War; Vietnam is divided into two separate countries at the 17th Parallel. Geneva Accord gives control of North Vietnam to Communist Party causing approximately one million anti-Communists to flee to South Vietnam

(continued)

TABLE 1.2 (*continued*)

PERIOD	U.S./ASIAN AMERICAN	CHINA	PHILIPPINES	INDIA	JAPAN	KOREA	VIETNAM
	1948 California repeals law banning interracial marriages		1946 Filipino Naturalization Bill allows Filipinos to become U.S. citizens. 1947 Military Bases Agreement with U.S.	1947 Second wave of immigration of South Asians to the U.S. begins	1945–47 45,000 war brides admitted to the U.S. 1946 U.S. occupies Japan		
1950s Age: 20–30	1952 Relatives of Asian immigrants allowed to immigrate to the U.S. 1952 The McCarran-Walter Act repeals the 1790 Naturalization Law racial restrictions 1959 Hawaii becomes the fiftieth state 1959 Vietnam War begins	1950 Treaty with USSR forming an alliance 1951–52 Land reform and redistribution of land 1953–57 First Five-Year Plan 1958–60 Great Leap Forward	1951 The Republic of the Philippines signs peace treaty with Japan. Post–WWII war brides to U.S.	1950 India becomes a republic	1952 End of U.S. occupation; First-generation Japanese gain the right to become naturalized U.S. citizens 1956 Japan joins the United Nations Late 1950s–70s Economic growth	1950 North Korea invades South Korea 1950–53 The Korean War; Korea is divided into North Korea and South Korea 1953 The second wave of Korean immigration to the U.S.	1955 Ngo Dinh Diem appointed Premier of South Vietnam; the U.S. provides direct support 1957 Troops from North Vietnam invade South Vietnam 1959 Family code prohibits legal separation and divorce

	United States	China	Philippines	India	Japan	Korea	Vietnam
1960s **Age: 30–40**	1965 Immigration Act of 1965 eliminates "national origin" quotas		1960s Immigration Act of 1965 draws many Filipino professionals to the U.S.; the annual immigration quota increases to 20,000 1965 Ferdinand Marcos becomes president	1962 India loses border war with China 1964 Prime Minister J. Nehru dies 1965 India-Pakistani War 1965 Second wave of immigration to U.S. begins 1966 Indira Gandhi becomes prime minister	1964 Tokyo Olympics	1960 Student protest; Syngman Rhee steps down as president 1961 General Park Chung Hee organizes military coup, establishes and later becomes president 1968 Third wave of immigration to the U.S.	1964 U.S. Congress passes the Gulf of Tonkin Resolution authorizing use of force in Vietnam 1965 The U.S. begins bombing North Vietnam; U.S. combat troops land in Da Nang 1968 The Tet Offensive; massacre at My Lai
1970s **Age: 40–50**	1975 End of Vietnam War	1972–76 End of the Era of Mao Zedong 1978 The U.S. Congress passes Taiwan Relations Act 1978 Deng Xiaoping assumes power	1972 President Marcos declares Martial Law under Proclamation 1081 1973 A new constitution gives Marcos absolute powers	1974 India conducts its first nuclear test explosion 1975–77 A state of emergency is declared and 1,000 political opponents are imprisoned; compulsory birth control program is introduced	1972 Okinawa is returned to Japan	1979 President Chung Hee Park is assassinated	1973 U.S. troops leave Vietnam 1975 End of the Vietnam War The first wave of Vietnamese, Cambodians, Hmong, and other Southeast Asians arrive in the U.S. 1976 Socialist Republic of Vietnam is established

(continued)

TABLE 1.2 (continued)

PERIOD	U.S./ASIAN AMERICAN	CHINA	PHILIPPINES	INDIA	JAPAN	KOREA	VIETNAM
		1979 The PRC and the U.S formally exchange diplomatic recognition of the border war between Vietnam and China 1979 U.S. begins to admit immigrants from the PRC					1978 The second wave of Southeast Asian refugees enter the U.S. 1978–79 Vietnam overthrows the Khmer Rouge government in Cambodia
1980s Age: 50–60		1980 Trial of the Gang of Four 1987 and 1988 Riots in Lhasa (Tibet) 1988 China increases diplomatic exchanges to 134 countries 1989 Tiananmen Square protests	1982 Martial law lifted 1983 Opposition leader Benigno Aquino is assassinated 1986 Corazon Aquino forms a new government Late 1980s–early 1990s Filipino labor export; 500,000 citizens work outside the country	1984 Indira Gandhi is assassinated; Rajiv Gandhi succeeds as prime minister	1982 Honda, the automobile company, opens its first U.S. plant 1988 President Ronald Reagan signs the Civil Liberties Act, authorizing $125 billion in reparations to Japanese American survivors of WW II internment camps	1980 Military coup by General Chun Doo Hwan 1987 Violent student demonstrations 1988 Seoul Olympics 1988 National elections; Roh Taewoo becomes President	1980s Second wave of refugees from the Hill Tribes of Laos immigrates to the U.S. By 1980, 1 million people have immigrated from Vietnam because of political conflict 1987 The third wave of Vietnamese immigration to the U.S. begins

1990s Age: 60–70					
1997 Hong Kong returned to China	1990 Immigration Reform Act, U.S. citizenship offered to 20,000 Filipino WW II veterans 1992 Subic Bay U.S. naval base returned, ending U.S. military presence in the Philippines	1991 Rajiv Gandhi is assassinated 1992 Widespread Hindu-Muslim riots 1998 India carries out nuclear tests	1997 The Japanese economy experiences severe recession	1992 Los Angeles riots 1997 IMF Crisis (Asian Economic Crisis) impacts nation 1998 Daejung Kim elected President	1994 The U.S. lifts its thirty-year trade embargo on Vietnam

2000s Age: 70–80		
2001 Beijing elected to hold 2008 Summer Olympics	2000 Celebration of the birth of India's billionth citizen	2001 9/11 Terrorist attacks

Sources: C. Agatucci, Central Oregon Community College. China: Timeline 5: Republican & Communist China (1912–present), retrieved April 2006 from, http://web.cocc.edu/cagatucci/classes/hum210/tml/ChinaTML/chinatml5.htm; C. Agatucci, Central Oregon Community College, India: Timelines, Sources and Resources, retrieved April 2006 from, http://web.cocc.edu/cagatucci/classes/hum210/tml/IndiaTML/indiatml4.htm; BBC News: Timeline India, Retrieved April, 2006 from, http://news.bbc.co.uk/1/hi/world/south_asia/country_profiles/1155813.stm; BBC News: Timeline: Vietnam, retrieved April 2006 from, http://news.bbc.co.uk/1/hi/world/asia-pacific/country_profiles/1243686.stm; S. Chan, *Asian Americans: An Interpretive History* (Boston: Twayne, 1991); CNN Interactive: India & Pakistan: Fifty years of independence, retrieved April 2006 from, http://www.cnn.com/WORLD/9708/India97/india/timeline/; S. Das, Loss or gain? A saga of Asian Indian immigration and experiences in America's multi-ethnic mosaic, *Race, Gender & Class* 9, no. 1 (2002): 131–155; Japanese American National Museum. Historical Timeline of Japanese American, retrieved April 2006 from, http://www.janm.org/projects/inrp/english/time_us.htm; Korean American Museum, Korean American History, retrieved April 2006 from, http://www.kamuseum.org/community/base.htm; Library of Congress, Federal Research Division, Country Studies: Philippines, retrieved April 2006 from, http://lcweb2.loc.gov/frd/cs/cshome.html; Library of Congress, Federal Research Division, Country Studies: Vietnam, retrieved April 2006 from, http://lcweb2.loc.gov/frd/cs/vntoc.html#vn0004; S. Mazumdar, Punjabi agricultural workers in California, 1905–1945, in L. Cheng and E. Bonachich, eds., *Labor Immigration under Capitalism: Asian Workers in the United States before World War II*, pp. 549–578 (Berkeley: University of California Press, 1984); Northern Illinois University Center for Southeast Asian Studies, Vietnam: Timeline of Events to 1974, Retrieved April 2006 from, http://www.seasite.niu.edu/crossroads/russell/vntimeline.htm; B. Posadas, *The Filipino Americans* (Westport, Conn.: Greenwood, 1999); U. A. Segal, *A Framework for Immigration: Asians in the United States* (New York: Columbia University Press, 2002); R. Takaki, *Strangers from a Different Shore: A History of Asian Americans* (Boston: Little, Brown, 1989); M. G. Wong, Post-1965 Asian immigrants: Where do they come from, where are they now, and where are they going? *Annals of the American Academy of Political and Social Science* 487 (1986): 150–168; G. Yeo, ed., *Curriculum in Ethnogeriatrics*, Stanford Geriatric Education Center, retrieved April 2006 from, http://www.stanford.edu/group/ethnoger/index.html.

Korean elders born in the 1930s also spent their childhood under Japanese occupation, and experienced the Korean War and the subsequent partition of their country into South and North Korea during their young adulthood. Later they experienced the rapid transformation of their country from an agrarian society to an industrial society and the growth of a new middle class (K. Park 1997; S.-J. Park and Kang 2007).

Japanese elders who grew up in Japan spent their childhood years under the extreme nationalism that led to World War II, while their Japanese American counterparts who grew up in the United States were incarcerated in internment camps during the war. The Indians of this generation spent their childhood years in India under the occupational rule of Great Britain. They also witnessed the independence of their nation and its division into Pakistan and India during their adolescence. The Vietnamese elders born in the 1930s spent their childhood years under the French colonial occupation of their country, witnessed their country divided into South and North Vietnam during their adolescence, and lived through the Vietnam War (or the "American War," as it is known in Vietnam) during their thirties and forties. Many Vietnamese elders were exposed to traumatic events as a result of the Vietnam War. Many lost family members during and after the war, and those who escaped Vietnam in fishing boats were subjected to attacks by pirates, and many women were victims of sexual assaults. As refugees, they were placed in camps for stays averaging two years, where they suffered severe physical and emotional distress including lack of food and water, overcrowded living conditions, and persecution by camp personnel (Mollica, Wyshak, and Lavelle 1987).

As this historical background illustrates, Asian elders have lived through many disruptive events, and it is important to understand how these events have shaped their current lives. Studies of Vietnamese and other Southeast Asian refugees report high rates of psychological trauma (Shapiro et al. 1999). Many Asian elders who were born and grew up in the United States also lived through extremely stressful events. For example, the internment experience during World War II has left an indelible mark on the lives of Japanese Americans (Nagata 1993). Despite the growing interest in the impact of traumatic events on children and adults, few studies have focused on trauma among older adults. Very little is known about the negative interactions between unresolved distal and recent trauma, on the one hand, and stressors associated with aging, on the other. Research on long-term psychological effects of trauma have been limited to studies with Holocaust survivors (Joffe et al. 2003) and military veterans (Schnurr et al. 2002). These studies suggest that external and internal resources can diminish in later life, and that prior trauma can be reactivated. Delayed onset, reemergence, or exacerbation of symptoms and behaviors associated with posttraumatic stress may appear during the aging process.

Conditions in late life not only are related to past events but are also associated with access to education, labor, and health care in earlier stages of life. Inequities experienced in earlier life are usually intensified later in life (Dannerfer 2003). Different sociohistorical periods provide different opportunity structures and social roles for individuals with varying personal characteristics. These opportunities and roles, in turn, determine the particular life events that people experience and the adaptive resources with which they respond to these events. Opportunity structures refer to the various restrictions that prevailing society places on individuals with certain personal attributes, thus reducing their life chances. Asian elders who were born and grew up in the United States experienced different episodes of discrimination throughout the course of their lives. The accumulation of these multiple disadvantages can have negative effects on their aging process. The majority of elders from rural areas of Asia had limited access to education, reducing their opportunities for employment in the United States.

Health status among elders is frequently associated with nutrition and access to health care in earlier life. Early developmental experiences such as malnutrition may influence chronic physical conditions in later life (Hertzman 2004). Research suggests that a lifetime of deficits such as low-paying jobs and inadequate resources translates into poor physical and mental health among Asian elders (Mui 1993).

IMMIGRATION AND THE LIFE COURSE

The life stage at which people immigrate influences their subsequent life experiences. People who immigrate during young adulthood usually migrate at the beginning of their career and during their child-bearing years. Those who immigrate before mid-adulthood have a work history, and many come with their children in search of new opportunities. Older adults who immigrate usually do so to be with their adult children. The current cohort of Asian elders includes those born in the United States, those who immigrated during young and middle adulthood, and those who immigrated after age sixty. Although immigrants of all ages face stressors such as loss of a familiar environment, support systems, and identity and status, researchers suggest that it is more difficult to adjust to a new environment in late adulthood than in young adulthood (Angel et al. 1999; Kim, Kim, and Hurh 1991; Q. K. Le 1997; Phua, Kaufman, and Park 2001). Older immigrants are thought to be less capable of meeting the demands of acculturation, such as learning a new language and adapting to new surroundings, than those who immigrate earlier in life.

Life stage transitions follow an age-graded timetable, which marks the time when individuals typically enter and exit specific stages (Hagestad and Neugarten 1985). Transitions such as getting married or entering the workforce are evaluated as being on time if they take place during culturally determined ages and off time if they do not. When role transitions occur off time, individuals and families can experience psychological distress (Hagestad and Neugarten 1985). Immigrating to a new country in late life counters the normal transitions in aging. As people age, they are expected to ease out of their work and career, to find new meaning in life while adjusting to various physical limitations posed by the physical conditions of aging. Elders who immigrate in late life not only have to go through life-cycle challenges, but they also have to cope with the process of acculturating to a new environment. Stressors that accompany immigration, such as language barriers, altered social and financial resources, fear of racial discrimination, and feelings of helplessness, can have negative impacts on psychological well-being. (Angel et al. 1999; Tsai and Lopez 1997). The concept of "multiple jeopardy" contends that occupying several disadvantaged positions, such as racial minority status, lack of language proficiency, and low-income status, may increase the risk of negative outcomes in old age (P. T. P. Wong and Ujimoto 1998).

RISKS AND RESILIENCY

While it is important to recognize the challenges of Asian elders who face the effects of cumulative disadvantages, it is equally important to examine their strengths and the ways in which they adjust to mainstream culture, navigate through the formal service systems, and cope with changes in their family relationships. Resilience among older adults has been defined as their capacity to withstand or endure difficulties and to recover or thrive in the face of disruptive life challenges (Hardy, Concato, and Gill 2004; Ryff et al. 1998). The notion of resiliency also includes the way in which individuals gain positive outcomes from a stressful event by fostering positive adaptation (Luthar, Cicchetti, and Becker 2000).

The consequences of stressful factors in an elder's life are often mediated by protective or adaptive factors. Protective factors found in individuals include previous life experience, personality, optimism, coping skills, religiosity/spirituality, and self-rated health (Ong and Bergeman 2004). Positive attitudes toward acculturation, reasons for and conditions of emigration, and having a sense of coherence are also considered individual protective factors among immigrants (Ying et al. 1997). Family and community resources that serve as protective factors for elders include social support from family, friends, and neighbors; availability of community services; religious affiliation; and cultural influences (Ong and Bergeman 2004). Socioeconomic status, economic security, and the receptiveness of the host society are also important resources. These strengths and resources enable individuals and their families to respond successfully to crises and persistent challenges, and to recover and grow from those experiences (Walsh 2004). In this book, we examine intergenerational relationships, social support, psychological well-being, and involvement with family and social activities as sources of resilience among Asian American elders.

2

RESEARCH METHOD AND DEMOGRAPHIC PROFILES OF ASIAN AMERICAN ELDERS

DATA SOURCES AND SAMPLE

THE EMPIRICAL DATA for this book were derived from the Asian American Elders in New York City (AAENYC) survey conducted in 2000 (Mui et al. 2006; Ryan, Mui, and Cross 2003). This chapter discusses the research methodology used in that survey and the demographic characteristics of the six Asian elderly groups studied. Data from the U.S. Census 2000 and the New York City Census 2000 on these six national origin groups are also presented as a basis for comparison (U.S. Census Bureau 2000, 2004).

In 2000 the Asian American Federation of New York (AAFNY) and its research team conducted the AAENYC survey with the objective of establishing a benchmark for measuring and evaluating changes in the quality of life and care of Asian American elders in New York City and other urban communities (Ryan et al. 2003). The study involved Asian American elders aged sixty-five and over who identified themselves as having come from one of the six nations with the largest group of Asian-born elders in the United States (China, Korea, the Philippines, India, Vietnam, and Japan). In a collaborative effort by the AAFNY and a research team from Harris Interactive Research, Inc., the Harris team performed sampling, data collection, and data processing on behalf of the AAFNY. The sample was drawn from a 1990 U.S. Census list of more than 5,785 block groups, or primary sample units (PSUs), in the five boroughs of New York City, ranked according to the percentage of Asian households recorded in the 1990 Census. A cut-off was made when the census block groups represented 70 percent of all Asians sixty-five and older listed in the 1990 Census. The final sample included sixty block groups that met the inclusion criteria.

The survey used an area-probability sample that was designed to give each eligible population member or household in the area a known chance of being interviewed. Using a street map and specially designed listings, trained bilingual interviewers went to a randomly designated point in the area and listed housing units. From each of the 60 selected block groups, 100 to 150 households were selected. In each selected household, a short screening interview was administered to assure eligibility for the survey. Selected households had a person sixty-five or older and a member of one of the six national origin groups under study. Interviews were completed only in eligible households; In case of incomplete interviews, the interviewers recorded the reasons. Fact-to-face interviews were conducted with 407 Asian American elders, at the elders' residences, between February 2 and May 31, 2000. The interviews were an average of 1.5 hours in length, and the completed survey included 84.3 percent of the eligible participants.

Interviewers were guided by a bilingual interviewing manual and instructions designed to minimize systematic errors and increase inter-rater reliability. Interviews were conducted in English, Chinese, Pilipino (a language popularly known as Tagalog), Hindi, Korean, and Vietnamese. To ensure that questions were culturally accurate and conceptually and linguistically consistent, panels of bilingual professionals prepared the questionnaires in English and then translated them into each of the languages. Participants were asked the questions in English or the ethnic language of choice. Most participants chose their own ethnic language, but all Japanese elders chose the English questionnaire.

TRAINING OF INTERVIEWERS AND THE DATA-COLLECTION PROCESS

Interviewers were trained for two days before they began fieldwork. The training included explanations and instructions concerning the different types of questions to be used, an orientation on the use of the interviewing manual, and instructions for administering each question. The training sessions and manuals covered general research, interviewing, and sampling procedures. The sessions included discussions of the interviewer's role in motivating respondents to reply fully to the questions; the need for interviewers to communicate to respondents and maintain confidentiality about responses to questions and about the study itself; the requirement that interviewers maintain a neutral attitude and appearance; and methods that interviewers could use to prevent eligible participants from refusing to be interviewed.

Sampling-related issues included instructions on how to locate respondents, list households in a selected PSU, and record attempts to interview. Interviewers also were instructed on the importance of varying the time of day and days of the week when they attempted or conducted interviews, the maximum number of attempts they should make at each household for screening and interviewing purposes, and ways to handle building-access issues and other community problems.

To reinforce their skills training, the interviewers were taught to play the role of an interviewee and complete the questionnaires themselves. Role-playing was used to demonstrate appropriate techniques to probe for responses, assure the absence of communication bias, and illustrate proper ways for interviewers to introduce themselves and prevent or reverse refusals. Interviewers were provided with two letters from the AAFNY home office designed to elicit cooperation from respondents and, where necessary, from building owners and managers. The letters stated the purpose of the study, the identity of the study sponsor, and the importance of participation. Letters directed toward respondents were written in English, Chinese, Korean, Hindi, Vietnamese, or Pilipino, as appropriate for the respondents' ethnic group.

QUALITY OF THE DATA AND SAMPLING VARIATION

Returned questionnaires were checked for completeness and accuracy by Harris Interactive Research, Inc. Those with significant errors or large proportions of missing data were set aside and removed from the survey. Typically, incomplete survey forms account for less than 1 percent of surveys reviewed. The overall results of surveying a sample of a given population generally are not an exact representation of the population but are subject to sampling variation. The magnitude of this variation is affected both by the number of interviews involved and the percentage of the population that was sampled. The range of sampling variation that applies to percentage results for this type of survey is usually small (Ryan et al. 2003); the sampling variation reflects a 95 percent probability that the survey results differ by plus or minus a certain number of percentage points that would have been obtained had interviews been conducted with all persons in the population that was sampled. The size of the potential sampling error varies with both the size of the sample and the percentage of people who give a particular answer. Sampling error is only one way in which a survey may vary from the findings that would have resulted had the entire population under study been interviewed. The procedures used by the Harris research team, however, were designed to minimize such errors. With such errors kept to a minimum, statistical significant differences were found within the Asian national origin groups. However, because of the small size of each sample group, these findings should be interpreted with caution, although the implications of the findings are noteworthy, especially for developing group-specific policy and program recommendations. The following sections of this chapter examine the sociodemographic characteristics of the six Asian national origin groups.

AGING POPULATION DATA BY RACE AND ETHNICITY IN THE U.S. CENSUS 2000

Data on race have been collected ever since the first U.S. decennial census in 1790. In the most recent census, information was collected on six major races: white; black, or African American; American Indian or Alaska Native; Asian; Native Hawaiian or Other Pacific Islander; and some other race (U.S. Census Bureau 2004). The federal government considers race and Hispanic origin as separate groupings. Accordingly, questions on race and Hispanic origin were asked of every individual in the U.S. Census 2000, with answers based on self-report. The six racial groups can be divided into two broad categories: people who reported only one race and those who classified themselves in more than one of the six racial categories. Those who indicated one race only are referred to as the *race alone population*. In the U.S. Census 2000 classification system, a respondent reporting his or her race as being from one or more of the detailed Asian groups (such as Vietnamese, Korean, or Japanese) but no non-Asian race would be included in the single-race Asian population, identified as *Asian alone*. Those who reported a specified race and one or more other major races are referred to as the *race in combination* population. The option of reporting multiple races did not exist prior to the U.S. Census 2000.

In the U.S. Census 2000 (see table 2.1 and figures 2a, 2b, and 2c), the term "Asian" refers to individuals with origins in the peoples of the Far East, Southeast Asia, or the Indian subcontinent. In many census reports, analyses are based on twelve detailed groupings by nationality or ethnicity: *Asian Indian, Korean, Cambodian, Laotian, Chinese, Pakistani, Filipino, Thai, Hmong, Viet-*

namese, Japanese, and the residual category *Asian other.* As of 2000, the U.S. Asian population consisted of 11.9 million people, representing 4.2 percent of the total population. Five Asian groups in the United States each numbered 1 million or more: Asian Indian, Chinese, Filipino, Korean, and Vietnamese. Together, these groups accounted for approximately 80 percent of the U.S. Asian population. The Chinese population was the largest group, representing about 24 percent, followed proportionately by the Filipino, Asian Indian, Vietnamese, and Korean populations. The Japanese, Cambodian, Hmong, Laotian, Pakistani, and Thai groups together accounted for approximately an additional 15 percent, and the residual category *Asian other* accounted for about 5 percent of the total U.S. Asian population.

The question on race in the U.S. Census 2000 differed from the previous census in several ways. In addition to the new option of selecting multiple races, the 1990 *Asian or Pacific Islander* category was separated into two new categories, *Asian* and *Native Hawaiian or Other Pacific Islander.* Consequently the U.S. Census 2000 data on race are not directly comparable to data in the 1990 or earlier censuses, and caution must be used when using these data to interpret changes in the racial composition of the U.S. population over time. It should be noted that the findings discussed in this book are based on the U.S. Census 2000 alone.

TABLE 2.1 Population Age 65 and Over, the U.S. Census 2000, 2003 Estimates, and 2050 Projections

RACE AND HISPANIC ORIGIN	2000 CENSUS[a]		2003 ESTIMATES[b]		2050 PROJECTIONS[c]	
	Number	Percent	Number	Percent	Number	Percent
Non-Hispanic White alone	30,405,538	83.5	29,597,559	82.3	344,206	61.1
Black alone	2,822,950	8.1	3,011,410	8.4	10,401,575	12
Asian alone	800,795	2.3	954,967	2.6	6,776,033	7.8
All other races alone or in combination	503,466	1.1	398,551	1.1	2,328,390	2.7
Hispanic (of any race)	1,733,591	5.0	2,034,994	5.6	15,178,025	17.2
Total	36,266,340	100	35,997,481	100	35,028,229	100

Sources: (a) U.S. Census Bureau 2001; (b) and (c) Federal Interagency Forum on Aging-Related Statistics 2004.

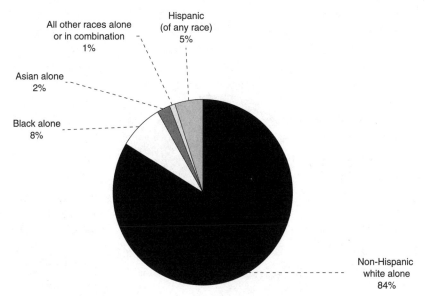

FIGURE 2a. Population Age 65 and over, Census 2000

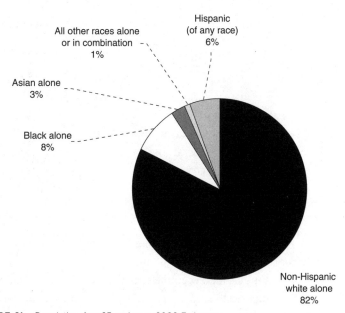

FIGURE 2b. Population Age 65 and over, 2003 Estimates

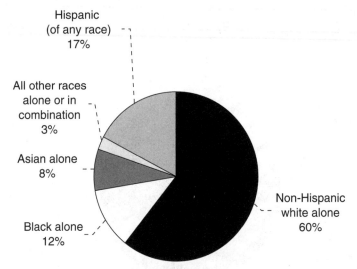

Hispanic
(of any race)
17%

All other races
alone or in
combination
3%

Asian alone
8%

Black alone
12%

Non-Hispanic
white alone
60%

FIGURE 2c. Population Age 65 and over, 2050 Projections

U.S. CENSUS 2000 AGING DATA COMPARED
TO AAENYC SURVEY DATA

The six Asian national origin groups in this study represent 94.4 percent of all Asian American elderly groups accounted for in the U.S. Census 2000, and 96 percent of those in the New York City Census 2000 (see table 2.2; U.S. Census Bureau 2000). The sampling frame of the AAENYC survey included all the geographical areas with high concentrations of Asian American elders, and the sample size was chosen to include a predetermined number of respondents from each of the six Asian American elderly groups. But because the sample was small, the proportion of the Chinese, Filipino, Japanese, and Vietnamese groups each was less than its probable actual proportion of the population (see table 2.2). By contrast, the Indian and Korean groups were proportionally overrepresented. Because of both over- and under-representation, the size of each group in both absolute numbers and relative to the others was an artifact of the study design.

Survey results based on small samples of national origin groups may be subject to large sampling error (Kerlinger and Lee 1999). The magnitude of the sampling error here is shown by comparing the AAENYC data to the U.S. Census 2000 data. Chinese elders accounted for slightly over 25 percent of the AAENYC sample compared to 29.5 percent in the U.S. Census 2000; whereas Koreans comprised 8.5 percent of Asian American elderly in the U.S. Census

2000, they made up 24.6 percent of the AAENYC sample. Similarly, nearly a quarter of this study sample was Indian compared to 8.3 percent in the U.S. Census 2000. The Filipino population makes up 20.5 percent of Asian American elderly in the U.S. Census 2000, but it accounts for only 12.8 percent in this study sample. Our sample had about 6 percent Japanese, which is less than one-third of the 20.1 percent represented in the U.S. Census 2000. Vietnamese elders represented 7.3 percent of Asian Americans in the U.S. Census 2000 but made up only 6 percent of our study sample.

Differences were also found in proportional representation between the 2000 New York City Census and the U.S. Census 2000 data specific to the same location. The U.S. Census 2000 showed that nearly two-thirds (65%) were Chinese compared to approximately 25 percent in this sample. Koreans compose just less than 10 percent of Asian Americans in the 2000 New York City Census but accounted for nearly one-quarter (24.6%) of the study sample. Similarly, the Indian population in this study made up one-quarter of the total sample, more than twice that of the same population (12%) in the U.S. Census 2000 in New York City. The proportion of the Filipino residents in this study was also nearly twice that in the 2000 New York City Census, constituting 13 percent of this sample compared to 7 percent. Whereas our sample contained approximately 6 percent Japanese, the U.S. Census 2000 in New York City reflected about 2 percent of the total Asian population as Japanese. Finally, the Vietnamese group was proportionately six times greater in this sample (6%) than the Vietnamese group in the New York City Census 2000, which made up only 1 percent of the total Asian population.

Nonetheless, there are evident similarities in the U.S. Census 2000 data, the New York City Census 2000 data, and the AAENYC survey sample data. The AAENYC survey resembles both the national U.S. Census 2000 and the 2000 New York City Census data, showing the Chinese elderly as the largest group (25.8%, 29.5%, and 64.8%, respectively); similarly, the Vietnamese group comprised the smallest segment in each case, accounting for between 1 percent in the New York City Census 2000 data and 7.3 percent in the U.S. Census 2000 national data. In the AAENYC survey and the New York City Census 2000 data, the Indian population represented the second-largest group (24.6% and 11.6%, respectively). The U.S. Census 2000 national data differs in showing Filipinos to be the second-largest national origin group, accounting for 20.5 percent of Asian elders; however, in the AAENYC survey, the Filipino population is closely ranked as the third-largest population, accounting for 12.8 percent of the sample.

TABLE 2.2 Comparisons between the AAENYC Survey Data and the U.S. Census 2000 Aging Data

	CHINESE (n=105)	FILIPINO (n=52)	INDIAN (n=100)	JAPANESE (n=25)	KOREAN (n=100)	VIETNAMESE (n=25)	OTHER 0	TOTAL (N=407)
AAENYC Study sample (N=407)	25.8%	12.8%	24.6%	6.1%	24.6%	6.1%	0%	100%
New York City Census 2000 Aging data (N=56,855)	38,333	4,121	6,838	1,117	5,870	576	2,329	59,184
Percent	64.8	7.0	11.6	1.9	9.9	1.0	3.9	Total of six groups=56,855; 96% of all Asian elders in New York City
U.S. Census 2000 Aging data (N=755,661)	235,995	164,798	66,834	161,288	68,505	58,241	45,134	800,795
Percent	29.5	20.5	8.3	20.1	8.5	7.3	5.6	Total of six groups=755,661; 94.4% of all Asian elders in U.S. Census 2000

Source: U.S. Census Bureau 2000.

Because the Filipino, Japanese, and Vietnamese elderly groups each had fewer than a hundred respondents in the AAENYC survey, findings relating to these populations should be viewed as suggestive, requiring further research to ascertain the degree to which the survey results may be generalized. Percentage calculations based on these small population samples may suggest differences that are more dramatic than warranted, and comparisons with other Asian nationality groups may not be appropriate. Further, because this study was based on Asian Americans living in New York City's most densely populated block groups, findings may be more indicative of characteristics of those who live in such areas than of their counterparts who are more dispersed.

Despite the study limitations, this first landmark study of Asian American elders provides a useful set of exploratory data relating to the groups investigated. The data give a portrait of each group's sociodemographic characteristics and economic well-being, as well as physical health, health-related quality of life, mental health status, and stressful life events. The research also summarizes perceived, unmet needs, the quality and quantity of informal supports, and the availability of intergenerational assistance. Also described are factors relating to immigration, acculturation, and utilization of medical care in the home and in the community, as well as issues concerning work, leisure, volunteering, grandparental caregiving, and family values.

DEMOGRAPHIC COMPARISON BETWEEN THE U.S. CENSUS 2000 AND THE AAENYC SURVEY

GENDER DISTRIBUTION

Approximately 57.5 percent of Asian elders aged sixty-five and older in the United States 57.5 percent are female. The AAENYC survey data on gender differ slightly from this average, with females comprising 56 percent of respondents (Mui et al. 2006). However, gender distribution within the six subgroups in the present study differs markedly from the national picture (see table 2.3). In the AAENYC survey, the Indian and Vietnamese groups had a disproportionate level of male respondents—62 percent and 64 percent, respectively. Although the U.S. Census 2000 and the AAENYC survey exhibited a similar proportion of Chinese female respondents, with 54.1 percent and 56.2 percent, respectively, in the two datasets, the Filipino and Korean U.S. Census 2000 data reflect fewer female respondents than do the AAENYC

TABLE 2.3 Sociodemographic Comparisons between the AAENYC Survey and the U.S. Census 2000 Aging Data (reported as %)

	CHINESE	FILIPINO	INDIAN	JAPANESE	KOREAN	VIETNAMESE	TOTAL
Gender (female)							
Census 2000	54.1	58.3	50.4	63.9	62.1	51.5	57.5
Survey sample	56.2	67.3	38.0	52.0	74.0	36.0	56.0
Age (M, SD)							
Census 2000	74.1 (6.9)	73.9 (6.9)	72.3 (6.3)	74.5 (6.7)	73.1 (6.6)	72.7 (6.6)	73.8 (6.8)
Survey sample	75.1(7.1)	73.2(6.6)	70.3(4.2)	70.9(4.7)	72.3 (6.1)	68.8(3.5)	72.4(6.2)
Age 75+							
Census 2000	41.0	39.9	30.7	35.5	44.7	32.3	39.7
Survey sample	47.6	42.3	17.0	24.0	37.0	8.0	32.9
U.S. citizen (yes)*							
Census 2000	71.5	75.2	50.5	93.0	64.7	59.3	74.0
Survey sample	67.3	59.9	19.4	32.2	54.4	8.0	46.1
Length of stay in U.S. (M, SD)*							
Census 2000	23.6 (16.4)	23.6 (16.7)	17.4 (12.3)	39.7 (13.9)	21.2 (11.5)	14.8 (9.6)	23.2 (16.0)
Survey sample	26.2(14.8)	18.9(14.6)	21.2(12.7)	30.8(10.1)	16.3(8.1)	7.0(3.0)	20.8(13.2)
Living alone							
Census 2000	16.3	9.1	6.8	24.4	20.7	8.6	15.6
Survey sample	32.4	3.9	3.0	28.0	25.0	24.0	18.9
Marital status (married)							
Census 2000	57.4	50.7	54.5	58.4	52.8	49.3	54.9
Survey sample	53.3	51.9	62.0	40.0	29.0	68.0	49.4

Education*							
Less than high school							
Census 2000	49.0	40.3	44.9	25.8	44.9	66.3	42.3
Survey sample	1.0	14.3	11.1	8.0	10.3	21.7	8.6
High school							
Census 2000	17.1	18.4	15.1	43.2	23.0	15.2	23.6
Survey sample	98.0	51.0	64.7	8.0	86.6	78.3	74.3
Post–high school							
Census 2000	33.9	41.3	40.0	31.0	32.1	18.5	34.1
Survey sample	1.0	34.7	26.3	84.0	3.1	0	17.1
Public benefits							
RECEIVING SSI*							
Census 2000	15.9	17.6	15.6	3.3	18.7	36.6	14.8
Survey sample	36.2	27.4	8.3	12.2	64.1	79.4	36.7
RECEIVING SOCIAL SECURITY							
Census 2000	49.6	50.0	32.6	83.0	44.4	24.8	53.7
Survey sample	29.1	51.3	52.9	77.8	66.9	0	48.0
EMPLOYMENT STATUS (NOT EMPLOYED)*							
Census 2000	89.9	83.6	83.0	85.4	86.7	90.9	86.7
Survey sample	100	97.6	88.8	96.1	98.8	100	88.5

Source: U.S. Census Bureau 2000.
* Statistical differences between the Survey sample and the U.S. Census data of these variables were found ($p < .05$).

survey data. In the U.S. Census 2000, 58.3 percent of Filipinos and 62.1 percent of Koreans were female compared to 67.3 percent of Filipinos and 74 percent of Koreans in the AAENYC survey. Japanese elders in the U.S. Census 2000 reflected a greater proportion of females than any other group, with 63.9 percent females, compared to Indian elders with 50.4 percent females. In the AAENYC survey, nearly three-quarters of Korean respondents were female, a proportion nearly double that of females in the Indian group (38%) and more than double that in the Vietnamese group (36%).

AGE DISTRIBUTION

The mean age of respondents in the two datasets was similar, with the U.S. Census 2000 showing a mean age of 73.8 years, and the AAENYC survey reflecting a slightly younger group, with a mean age of 72.4 (Mui et al. 2006). In both datasets, less than half of the respondents were seventy-five or older; in the U.S. Census 2000, 39.7 percent of respondents were in this category compared to 32.9 percent in the AAENYC survey. The oldest group in the U.S. Census 2000 was the Japanese, with a mean age of 73.1; in the AAENYC survey, the oldest respondents were Chinese, with a mean age of 75.1. In both datasets, the Vietnamese were younger, ranking youngest in the AAENYC survey (mean = 68.8) and next-to-youngest in the U.S. Census 2000 (mean = 72.7). The Indian group was also among the younger ethnic groups in both datasets: in the AAENYC survey, it was the next-to-youngest group, with a mean age of 70.3; in the U.S. Census 2000, it was the youngest group, with a mean age of 72.3. The greatest age difference between the U.S. Census and the survey was in the Japanese group, with the U.S. Census 2000 group an average of 4.5 years older than the AAENYC survey group. The Vietnamese group in the U.S. Census 2000 (mean age = 72.7) was also older, with a nearly three-year mean difference. The Filipino and Korean groups, with mean ages of 73.9 and 73.1, respectively, in the U.S. Census 2000, were the closest in age in the U.S. Census and the survey, but older in the census as well, with mean differences of 0.7 and 0.8 years, respectively.

U.S. CITIZENSHIP

The AAENYC survey and the U.S. Census 2000 reported different results on the question of U.S. citizenship. All six populations in the U.S. Census 2000 showed a higher percentage of U.S. citizens than did the AAENYC survey, and the differences between the two datasets were statistically significant in that there was less than a 5 percent chance that they could have been randomly achieved. Among the six groups studied, the U.S. Census 2000 indicated the highest rate of citizenship in the Japanese population, at 93 percent, compared to 32.2 percent for the same population in the AAENYC survey. The Indian population in the U.S. Census 2000 had the lowest rate of citizenship, at 50.5 percent, in contrast to 19.4 percent for those in the AAENYC survey. The largest contrast between datasets was among the Vietnamese: in the AAENYC survey, 8 percent reported having U.S. citizenship, whereas in the U.S. Census 2000, 59.3 percent reported U.S. citizenship, a sevenfold difference between the two. The datasets also differ not only in the proportional rates of citizenship within each group but in the ranking of groups within each survey: in the U.S. Census 2000, the Japanese had the highest level of citizenship, followed, respectively, by the Filipino, Chinese, Korean, Vietnamese, and Indian groups; in the AAENYC survey, the Chinese had the highest level of citizenship (67.3%), followed, respectively, by the Filipino, Korean, and Japanese groups, who reported U.S. citizenship rates of 59.9 percent, 54.4 percent, and 32.2 percent, respectively (Mui et al. 2006).

LENGTH OF STAY IN THE UNITED STATES

On the other hand, pronounced differences between datasets were not found in the mean length of stay in the United States: in both the U.S. Census 2000 and the AAENYC survey, the Japanese group had the longest average period of residence in the United States (39.7 and 30.8 years, respectively), followed by the Chinese group (23.6 and 26.2 years, respectively); in both datasets, the Vietnamese group had the shortest average length of stay in the United States (14.8 and 7 years, respectively). The length of stay of the Chinese population was closest in the two datasets, with their average length of stay differing by only 2.6 years in the two datasets. The Vietnamese group, however, reflected the largest proportional difference between the two datasets, with the average length of stay reported in the U.S. Census 2000 more than double that found in the AAENYC survey. For the six groups overall, the mean length of stay in the United States was similar in the two datasets but somewhat longer in the U.S. Census 2000 (23.2 years) than in the AAENYC survey (20.8 years) (Mui et al. 2006).

LIVING ARRANGEMENTS

In both the AAENYC survey and the U.S. Census 2000, most respondents said that they did not live alone, and most reported being married. The U.S. Census 2000 reflected 6.8 percent and 20.7 percent, respectively, of respondents who reported living alone in the Indian and Korean groups; the AAENYC survey showed 3 percent and 32.4 percent of respondents who reported living alone in the Indian and Chinese groups, respectively. In both datasets, members of the Indian population reported the lowest incidence of living alone. In the U.S. Census 2000, the Indian group was followed by the Vietnamese, Filipino, and Chinese groups, of whom 8.6 percent, 9.1 percent, and 16.3 percent, respectively, reported living alone; in the AAENYC survey, 3.9 percent of the Filipino group reported living alone, less than 1 percent more than the Indian group. Compared to the Filipino and Indian groups, the Vietnamese, Korean, and Chinese groups in the AAENYC survey indicated higher rates of people living alone, with 24.0 percent, 25.0 percent, and 32.4 percent, respectively, reporting that they lived alone. Nearly twice as many Chinese in the AAENYC survey (16.3%) reported living alone as did their counterparts in the U.S. Census 2000 (32.4%), and more than twice as many in the Filipino and Indian populations in the U.S. Census 2000 reported living alone (9.1% and 6.8%) as did their counterparts in the AAENYC survey (3.9% and 3.0%, respectively). The Vietnamese, on the other hand, were found to have almost three times as many people living alone in the AAENYC survey than in the U.S. Census 2000.

MARITAL STATUS

Slightly more respondents in the U.S. Census 2000 reported being married than in the AAENYC survey, with an average for all groups of 54.9 percent (U.S. Census 2000) and 49.4 percent (AAENYC survey). The Vietnamese group had the highest rate of marriage in the AAENYC survey, with 68 percent, whereas the U.S. Census 2000 showed the same group as having the lowest rate of marriage, with 49.3 percent. In the U.S. Census 2000, 52.8 percent of Koreans reported being married, and just over half as many (29%) reported being married in the AAENYC survey. In both datasets, the Chinese and Filipino groups reported a similar proportion of the population as being married: the U.S. Census 2000 showed a 57.4 percent rate of married Chinese compared to 53.3 percent in the AAENYC survey, and a 50.7 percent rate of married Filipinos compared to 51.9 percent in the AAENYC survey. Next to the Vietnamese group, the highest percentages of reported married respondents in the AAENYC survey were in the Indian, Chinese, and Filipino groups (62%, 53.3%, and 51.9%, respectively) (Mui et al. 2006). In the U.S. Census 2000, being married was reported most frequently in the Japanese group (58.4%), followed by the Chinese (57.4%), Indian (54.5%), Korean (52.8%), and Filipino (50.7%) groups.

EDUCATIONAL LEVEL

To determine the educational level of respondents in both datasets, three levels were considered: less than a high school education, high school completion, and any level of post–high school education. Based on these three criteria, the differences between datasets are statistically significant. On average, nearly five times as many Asian American elders reported having less than a high school education in the U.S. Census 2000 as in the AAENYC survey. In the AAENYC survey, 8.6 percent of respondents reported not having complete high school compared to 42.3 percent in the U.S. Census 2000. Most notably, although only 1 percent of Chinese in the AAENYC survey had less than a high school education, nearly half (49%) of Chinese in the U.S. Census 2000 reported the same. In four of the five remaining ethnic groups, the AAENYC survey showed a threefold or greater rate of high school completion. In the Indian population, 44.9 percent had less than a high school education in the U.S. Census 2000 compared to 9.1 percent in the AAENYC survey. Of the Japanese in the AAENYC survey, 8 percent had less than a high school education in contrast to 25.8 percent of those in the U.S. Census 2000, where the Japanese nonetheless had the smallest proportion among the six Asian populations with less than a high school education. The difference between the two datasets was more than quadruple among the Korean population: 44.9 percent had not completed high school in the U.S. Census 2000, and 10.3 percent reported the same in the AAENYC survey. In both datasets, the Vietnamese group reported the largest proportion of the six populations with less than a high school education (66.3% in the U.S. Census 2000 and 21.7% in the AAENYC survey). For the Filipino group, the U.S. Census 2000 showed 40.3 percent who had not completed high school compared to 14.3 percent in the AAENYC survey.

With the exception of the Japanese group, a similar educational profile is found when high school completion is used as a defining criterion. An average of 23.6 percent of Asian American elders in the U.S. Census 2000 reported having completed high school, while more than triple that amount (74.3%) did so in the AAENYC survey. Among the Chinese, nearly all (98%) reported having completed high school in the AAENYC survey in contrast to 17.1 percent in the U.S. Census 2000; in the Filipino group, 18.4 percent reported having a high school education in the U.S. Census 2000, but 51 percent did so in the AAENYC survey. More than five times as many Vietnamese in the AAENYC survey reported high school completion than in the U.S. Census 2000, 78.3 percent and 15.2 percent, respectively; and among Koreans, 86.6 percent in the AAENYC survey reported having finished high school, while 23.0 percent in the U.S. Census 2000 reported having done so. Similarly, in the Indian group more than four times as many in the AAENYC survey reported having a high school education than in the U.S. Census 2000 group: 64.7 percent and 15.1 percent, respectively.

In contrast to the other Asian groups, the Japanese in the U.S. Census 2000 reported having completed high school five times more than those in the AAENYC survey (43.2% compared to 8%). This trend, however, did not hold when post–high school education was considered: in the AAENYC survey, 84 percent of Japanese had some post–high school education compared to 31 percent in the U.S. Census 2000.

On average, almost exactly twice as many Asian American elderly respondents in the AAENYC survey as those in the U.S. Census 2000 reported that they had some level of post–high school education (34.1% vs. 17.1%). In considering those with less than a high school education, the ratio of Chinese who reported not having finished high school in the U.S. Census 2000 was forty-nine times greater than their counterparts in the AAENYC survey. In considering post–high school education, that imbalance was reversed: nearly thirty-four times as many Chinese in the U.S. Census 2000 reported having had post–high school education as those in the AAENYC survey (33.9% and 1.0%, respectively). In the AAENYC survey, the Japanese had the greatest level of post–high school education, with 84 percent; in the U.S. Census 2000, the Filipinos reported the highest level of post–high school education (41.3%), followed by the Indians (40%). In the AAENYC survey, no Vietnamese reported more than a high school education; 1 percent of the Chinese and 3.1 percent of the Koreans in the dataset reported more than a high school education. In contrast, the Indian, Filipino, and Japanese groups reported far higher rates of post–high school education, with 26.3 percent, 34.7 percent, and 84.0 percent, respectively (Mui et al. 2006). In the U.S. Census 2000, however, the contrast between groups was not as sharp. Vietnamese elders reported the lowest proportion with more than a high school education with 18.5 percent, followed by the Japanese (31.0%), Korean (32.1%), Chinese (33.9%), Indian (40.0%), and Filipino (41.3%) populations.

PUBLIC BENEFITS

With the exception of the Indian population, a greater proportion of respondents in the AAENYC survey than in the U.S. Census 2000 reported receiving Supplemental Security Income (SSI). As with educational levels, citizenship, and length of stay in the United States, these differences were statistically significant. In the AAENYC survey, 79.4 percent of Vietnamese reported receiving SSI, whereas less than half (36.6%) in the same group reported doing so in the U.S. Census 2000. Similarly, more than twice as many Filipino respondents in the AAENYC survey, and nearly twice as many Indian respondents, reported receiving SSI compared to their counterparts in the U.S. Census 2000. The contrast between datasets is greatest among the Japanese: 12.2 percent of them reported receiving SSI in the AAENYC survey compared to 3.3 percent of their counterparts in the U.S. Census 2000.

In the U.S. Census 2000, a slim majority of those in the six groups (53.7%) reported receiving Social Security, whereas in the AAENYC survey a slim minority (48.0%) reported receiving the same benefit. This difference was not statistically significant, however, and was skewed by results from the Vietnamese population in the AAENYC survey, none of whom reported receiving Social Security. By contrast, nearly one-quarter (24.8%) of Vietnamese in the U.S. Census 2000 reported receiving Social Security. In the two datasets, a similar proportion of the Filipino group reported receiving Social Security (exactly half of those in the U.S. Census 2000 compared to 51.3 percent in the AAENYC survey). In both datasets, smaller percentages of the Vietnamese reported receiving Social Security than any other group, whereas higher percentages of the Japanese reported receiving Social Security benefits than any other group (83% in the U.S. Census 2000 and 77.8% in the AAENYC survey). More Chinese in the U.S. Census 2000 reported receiving Social Security than in the AAENYC survey (49.6% compared to 29.1%), and fewer among the Indian population in the U.S. Census 2000 (32.6%) reported receiving Social Security benefits than did their counterparts in the AAENYC survey (52.9%) (Mui et al. 2006).

ADAPTATION AND ACCULTURATION CHARACTERISTICS

IMMIGRATION EXPERIENCES

Table 2.4 presents data on the migration experience, linguistic challenges, and financial status of the Asian American elderly sample in the AAENYC survey. Findings show that the median age at immigration was fifty-four, indicating that migration to the United States often occurred late in life (Mui et al. 2006). The Japanese were the single exception, with a median age of forty at immigration. Nearly two-thirds of all elders in the sample came to join family members already in the United States, and one-quarter came for employment. More than one-third of the Asian elders still said they were homesick and would to return to their home country if they had a choice. Japanese and Chinese elders were much more likely than other groups to be homesick (72% and 60%, respectively).

Nearly half the AAENYC survey sample reported that they were American citizens. A similar proportion had permanent-resident status, and 10 percent had other visas or refused to answer the question. Among the six ethnic groups, large differences in reported citizenship status were found: two-thirds (66.67%) of the Chinese and six in ten (60%) of the Filipinos were citizens compared to 19 percent of the Indian group and only 8 percent of the Vietnamese group.

LANGUAGE PROFICIENCY

Table 2.4 also summarizes the level of language proficiency in the AAENYC survey sample (Mui et al. 2006). Results indicate that an inability to speak English suggests difficulty in negotiating life, at least outside the local community where the native language may not predominate. As with the other key indicators, the six groups varied markedly in whether and how well they spoke English. Every person in the Vietnamese group reported his or her ability to speak English as either "not too well" or "not well at all"; the same was true of over 93 percent of the Chinese elders. A substantial majority (83%) of Korean respondents reported the same proficiency level as did the Vietnamese and Chinese, followed by 55 percent of the Indian respondents and 40 percent of the Japanese group, while only 11.5 percent of the Filipino elders reported such levels of proficiency.

Given that only a minority reported the ability to speak English well, the availability and capacity of other members in the same household who speak

English well becomes critical. However, the proportion of family members who could not speak English in these Asian American intergenerational families was also relatively high (68%, Vietnamese; 38%, Chinese; 29%, Korean). Most of those in the Chinese group reported no ability to read (78.1%) or write (82.9%) in English, and this was the highest such level among the six groups. Vietnamese elders followed the Chinese group, with 72 percent and 75 percent, respectively, reporting no ability to read or write in English. None of the Vietnamese, less than 2 percent of the Chinese, and 4 percent of the Koreans reported the ability to read or write English very well. The picture for the Filipino group, however, is nearly the exact opposite: less than 2 percent reported no ability to read or write in English. On the other hand, 51.9 percent reported reading and half reported writing very well in English. Less than half as many Japanese elders (24%) reported the ability to read or write in English quite well, and 36 percent reported the ability to read and write some English. A smaller, but similar proportion of Indian respondents reported the ability to read very well (20%) or somewhat (25%) and to write very well (18%) or somewhat (27%).

These findings suggest that most Asian American elders in the sample were at risk of linguistic isolation. The concept of "linguistic isolation" was developed in the 1990 Census (Siegel, Martin, and Bruno 2001), which attempted to estimate the number of households that might need help to communicate with government or social service organizations in the event of an emergency or crisis. The high rates of linguistic isolation may become barriers to effective communication or access to medical and social services (Siegel, Martin, and Bruno 2001). Asian elders may not be able to obtain help if they live in those linguistically isolated households where no one can speak English. The next chapter examines the role of linguistic isolation on the health status and health-related quality-of-life issues of Asian elders.

ECONOMIC STATUS

In terms of financial security, the findings of the AAENYC survey showed that the Asian American elderly sample was very similar to other survey research respondents and that they were not comfortable in reporting income figures (Mui et al. 2006). Among the Chinese, Filipino, and Korean groups, less than three-quarters reported this information. Of those who disclosed financial information, the Filipinos and Vietnamese reported median household incomes below $6,000; the Korean and the Chinese groups reported income in a range of $6,000 to $8,500, and the Indian group reported income between $10,000 and $12,500. Japanese elders were at a relative advantage compared to the others, with a reported median income of $15,000 to $25,000. Since the income variable had considerable missing data, Medicaid coverage was used as a proxy measure of the elderly sample's financial status in the statistical analyses of other chapters. Even though Medicaid entitlement may not be a precise measure of economic resources, it reflects the means testing and income related to federal poverty guidelines as eligibility requirements. As to how the elders perceive their economic well-being, expressed in terms of perceived financial adequacy, 24 percent of the Vietnamese elders indicated that they "can't really get by," followed by the Filipino (18%), Chinese (17%), Indian (13%), Japanese (8%), and Korean (2%) elders. Only 48 percent of our sample received Social Security benefits, a major source of income among the American elderly in general and the single resource that prevents many elders nationwide from being officially classified as living in poverty. Among the six groups, variation in the proportion receiving Social Security was large. None of the Vietnamese, 29 percent of the Chinese, about half the Indians and Filipinos, two-thirds of the Koreans, and more than three-quarters of the Japanese reported receiving Social Security. On average, Asian American elders who immigrated recently are more likely to be poor. Without a substantive work history in the United States, recently immigrated elders are ineligible for Social Security or pension benefits. Since most Asian American elderly respondents immigrated at around age fifty-four, it is not surprising that a much higher proportion of them receive SSI than Social Security benefits.

Similar to the patterns of Social Security and SSI enrollment, most elders in the sample reported participation in government-sponsored health care. An analysis of health insurance coverage shows that 51 percent of respondents reported having Medicare Part A, which covers hospital, skilled nursing, and home health care, and is linked with the Social Security benefit, and 66 percent reported having supplemented their coverage with Medicare Part B to cover physician visits and outpatient services. Of the entire sample, 41 percent reported receiving means-tested Medicaid coverage, a volume only slightly higher than the report of SSI benefits. In contrast, only 14 percent of all these immigrant elders reported having private health insurance coverage. Furthermore, more than one-third (34%) of the sample also reported receiving food stamps. The proportion receiving the poverty-based assistance was very high among the Vietnamese and Koreans (84% and 43%, respectively), intermediate

TABLE 2.4 Acculturation Indicators of the AAENYC Survey Sample (% of total within each group)

	CHINESE (n = 105)	FILIPINO (n = 52)	INDIAN (n = 100)	JAPANESE (n = 25)	KOREAN (n = 100)	VIETNAMESE (n = 25)	TOTAL (N = 407)
Median age at immigration	51.0	57.0	50.0	40.0	57.0	62.0	54.0
Percent not born in the U.S.	100.0	100.0	100.0	100.0	100.0	100.0	100.0
MAIN REASONS FOR COMING TO THE U.S.							
Political instability	11.0	8.0	1.0	4.0	2.0	28.0	9.0
Family reunion	66.0	58.0	53.0	40.0	85.0	28.0	62.0
Study	0.0	2.0	7.0	4.0	2.0	0.0	4.0
Employment	19.0	25.0	48.0	48.0	7.0	0.0	25.0
Feeling of Homesickness	60.0	45.0	31.0	72.0	17.0	38.0	38.0
CURRENT IMMIGRATION STATUS							
U.S. citizen	67.0	60.0	19.0	32.0	54.0	8.0	46.0
Permanent resident	33.0	33.0	54.0	64.0	36.0	88.0	44.0
Visa	0.0	0.0	11.0	0.0	2.0	0.0	3.0
Refused/don't know	0.0	8.0	16.0	12.0	8.0	2.0	7.0
ENGLISH PROFICIENCY (SPEAKING)****							
Not at all	70.2	2.0	28.0	0.0	42.0	59.1	39.1
Not too well	22.1	9.8	26.0	40.0	47.0	40.9	29.9
Somewhat	5.8	39.2	28.0	36.0	10.0	0.0	18.2
Very well	1.9	49.0	18.0	24.0	1.0	0.0	12.9
ENGLISH PROFICIENCY (READING)****							
Not at all	78.1	1.9	32.0	0.0	47.0	72.0	44.2
Not too well	15.2	9.6	23.0	40.0	36.0	28.0	23.8
Somewhat	4.8	36.5	25.0	36.0	13.0	0.0	17.4
Very well	1.9	51.9	20.0	24.0	4.0	0.0	14.5

(continued)

TABLE 2.4 (continued)

	CHINESE (n=105)	FILIPINO (n=52)	INDIAN (n=100)	JAPANESE (n=25)	KOREAN (n=100)	VIETNAMESE (n=25)	TOTAL (N=407)
ENGLISH PROFICIENCY (WRITING)**							
Not at all	82.9	1.9	32.0	0.0	45.0	75.0	45.1
Not too well	9.5	9.6	23.0	40.0	38.0	20.8	22.4
Somewhat	5.7	38.5	27.0	36.0	13.0	4.2	18.7
Very well	1.9	50.0	18.0	24.0	4.0	0.0	13.8
No One in Household Speaks English Well	38.0	2.0	4.0	8.0	29.0	68.0	23.0
HOUSEHOLD INCOME**							
<$6,000	36.0	48.4	24.5	0.0	30.2	48.0	30.9
$6,000–$10,000	34.7	16.1	20.2	13.0	51.2	52.0	30.2
>$10,000	29.3	35.5	55.3	87.0	18.6	0.0	38.8
Median household income (in $1,000/year)	6–8.5	<6	10–12.5	15–25	6–8.5	<6	6–8.5
Financially can't really get by	17.0	18.0	13.0	8.0	2.0	24.0	13.0
Social Security	29.1	51.3	52.9	77.8	66.9	0	48.0
SSI	36.2	27.4	8.3	12.2	64.1	79.4	36.7
Food stamps*****	30.5	21.2	28.2	12.0	42.7	84.0	34.0
Medicare A****	86.7	53.3	16.1	32.0	54.2	37.5	51.2
Medicare B****	87.5	60.8	43.9	87.5	66.3	47.1	66.1
Medicaid****	58.3	37.2	24.4	9.5	38.1	91.3	40.9
Private insurance*	8.1	15.8	21.4	25.0	4.2	6.3	13.7

Note: Chi-square statistics were used.

* p < .05.

**** p < .0001.

among the Chinese and Indians (31% and 28%, respectively), and relatively low among the Filipinos and Japanese (21% and 12%, respectively) (Mui et al. 2006).

DISCUSSION

The findings in this chapter are essential to understanding the complex backgrounds and communal needs of Chinese, Filipino, Indian, Japanese, Korean, and Vietnamese elders. The findings confirm the sociodemographic heterogeneity among American Asian immigrant elderly groups. Results are consistent with research done with small, localized samples among different Asian elderly communities (e.g., Mui 1996b, 1998, 2001; Mui and Shibusawa 2003). Study findings show that Asian immigrant elders differ in ethnicity, immigration history, English proficiency, educational attainment, and economic security. Given the diversity among the major Asian ethnic groups, practitioners working with Asian American immigrants in ethnic enclave communities and in the general population can better serve their clients by developing an understanding of the multifaceted nature of the immigration experience of these Asian Americans.

The findings also support the literature that found Vietnamese elders likely to be recent immigrants, with Chinese and Japanese elders having reported longer length of stays in the United States (Tran 1993). The factors that contributed to individuals' decisions to leave their country of origin, as well as their migration experience and their experiences since arrival in the United States, have all been found to have been influenced by the time in history when the immigration occurred. Such knowledge will enable social work and service professionals to capture the contextual aspects of the clients' experience and assess the impact of their experience on their personal functioning and social relationships. Variance in the length of time since they immigrated may also influence Asian elders' level of language acculturation, assimilation, and knowledge of the U.S. social welfare system and aging services (Mui 1998, 2001; Shibusawa and Mui 2001).

The reasons that these elders immigrated to the United States varied, as indicated by the data. The majority came to reunite with their families. However, more than one third of the Asian elders expressed homesickness and the wish to return to their home country if they had a choice. The expressed desire to go back to the home country may indicate poor adaptation, linguistic isolation, or a poor family relationship. Losing a sense of place or culture can be very difficult psychologically for immigrant elders, especially if they do not adjust well with their immigrant lives in the United States (Mui 1996b, 1998, 2001). Service providers need to be informed about and culturally sensitive to these issues when working with Asian immigrant elders and intergenerational families. This finding demonstrates that health care professionals and social workers should advocate for the need for culturally competent services in programs where they are lacking. Culturally responsive services have also been shown to improve service access among Asian Americans (Mui and Kang 2006; Sue et al. 1991).

Both the AAENYC study sample data in this chapter and its comparison to the U.S Census 2000 data and the New York City Census data reveal that the Asian immigrant elderly is not a homogenous group. As members of unique national origin groups, America's Asian immigrant elders have diverse cultural norms, social behaviors, immigration experiences, and other life experiences. To lump them into a large singular category is a mistake from both a clinical practice and policy perspective. Service providers would be well advised to recognize and acknowledge these variations both in planning and implementing intervention programs for the sample Asian American elderly groups in this study and the elderly Asian American community as a whole. With such recognition and acknowledgment, it is further hoped that Asian elders can be guaranteed what they deserve: culturally sensitive, high-quality, and timely interventions.

3

HEALTH STATUS AND HEALTH-RELATED
QUALITY-OF-LIFE INDICATORS

THERE IS NO QUESTION that a positive healthy condition is critical for older people to remain independent and continue to contribute to their families and communities. Health prevention, health maintenance, and health promotion programs are extremely important for older persons to have better health status. And of note, health prevention is much cheaper than intervention, both economically and emotionally (Mui and Kang 2006). The World Health Organization (WHO) has been leading the global initiatives in the promotion of good health and physical well-being among all ages, especially elders, for the last two decades (WHO 2004).

HEALTH STATUS AND HEALTH PROMOTION:
A GLOBAL PERSPECTIVE

WHO defines health as a state of complete physical, mental, and social well-being, not just the absence of disease and infirmity. To reach old age in good health and well-being requires individual effort throughout life and a flourishing environment in which such effort can succeed. The responsibility of individuals is to maintain a healthy lifestyle; the responsibility of government and the local community is to create a supportive environment that enables the advancement of health and well-being into old age (WHO 2005). From both humanitarian and economic perspectives, it is necessary to provide older persons with the same access to preventive, curative care and rehabilitation as younger people (United Nations 2007).

The cornerstone for such healthy aging among a globally diverse population of elders is equal access to health promotion programs that include disease prevention throughout life (United Nations 2007). Pertinent to such access is the design of health care and of health care services to meet their specific life stages and cultural needs. A life course perspective involves recognizing that health promotion and disease prevention activities need to focus on maintaining independence, preventing and delaying disease and disability, and improving older people's quality of life. One of the primary objectives of health programs at WHO is to do more prevention work in order to delay the onset of chronic illness and disability among older people (WHO 2005). A major goal in elder care for the twenty-first century is to make sure that the years added to life are quality years.

Chronic diseases place a heavy health and economic burden on elders as the potential for long-term suffering is increased. Although advanced aging is more likely to come with suffering through chronic illness and disability, poor health is not an inevitable consequence of aging (Center for Disease Control and Prevention [CDC] 2004). Much of the illness, disability, and death associated with chronic diseases can be avoided through preventive measures. Internationally WHO understands the need to focus on health prevention for elderly people, and since the 2002 Second World Assembly on Aging, WHO has launched a series of complementary projects focusing on the provision of integrated care in both developed and developing countries; these projects aim to be available, accessible, comprehensive, efficient, and culturally responsive to the aging population (WHO 2005).

In 2003 the *World Health Survey* collected information in seventy-one countries on population health status and health services coverage, including data on older age groups. This information has contributed immensely to an improved global understanding of the determinants of health and causes of morbidity at older ages. The objectives of WHO's project are to formulate integrated health care systems and create a database to support countries modifying policies toward integrated health and social care systems that better serve older populations (WHO 2005). National policies within the United States have had difficulty keeping up with this international movement of collecting meaningful data on the social and health indicators of minority elderly groups, especially Asian American elders.

HEALTH DISPARITIES AND HEALTH-RELATED QUALITY OF LIFE AMONG ASIAN AMERICANS

Two decades ago the U.S. government responded to this need through the national project "Healthy People 2010," whose mission is to improve the health of all people in their own communities through national and local initiatives. However, these efforts offer neither aging- nor ethnic-specific programs. Although a major goal of Healthy People 2010 is to eliminate health disparities, the programs have not systematically collected reliable and representative health data on aging minority populations. For example, in *Older Americans 2004*, published by the Federal Interagency Forum on Aging-Related Statistics (2004), out of the thirty-seven indicators of well-being, only four (ethnic and racial composition, educational attainment, living arrangements, and leading causes of death) were provided with comparative data on Asian American elders. The available demographic and health statistics on Asian Americans are usually of limited value because such research has categorized Asian Americans into one broad group, ignoring the enormous diversity that exists. Lack of basic data about aging Asian populations may be the result of language barriers that prevent them from participating in survey research (Federal Interagency Forum on Aging-Related Statistics 2004).

In 2004 the CDC reported that Asian Americans are disproportionately affected by many health disparities (President's Advisory Commission on Asian Americans and Pacific Islanders 2003). Inequalities in income and education underlie many health disparities for everyone in the United States, but Asian American elderly and other minority groups that generally suffer the worst health status also have the highest poverty rates and the least education. These disparities in income and education levels are statistically linked with differences in health insurance coverage, access to medical care, affordability of better housing and quality neighborhoods, and the opportunity to engage in health-promoting behaviors (U.S. Department of Health and Human Services [USDHHS] 2005). Even more important, Asian Americans of all ages have been struggling with cultural and linguistic barriers that may discourage or prevent them from accessing available health care services. As shown in chapter 2, Asian Americans are less likely to be proficient in English and have more difficulties understanding the U.S. health care system than white Americans. In addition, because of differences in cultural approaches to health care, Asian Americans may not perceive the value or necessity of obtaining care from Western medicine. This behavior may contribute to the diagnosis of diseases only in the later stages, leading to untreatable conditions (President's Advisory Commission on Asian Americans and Pacific Islanders 2003).

These cultural differences also contribute to Asian Americans' experiencing health disparities in the areas of prevention and intervention (President's Advisory Commission on Asian Americans and Pacific Islanders 2003) For example, only 2–3 percent of adult cancer patients participate in cancer clinical trials, with elderly, racial, and ethnic minorities even less likely to participate (National Cancer Institute [NCI] 2000). Cancer is one of the leading causes of death for Asian Americans in the United States (President's Advisory Commission on Asian Americans and Pacific Islanders 2003). Because Asian American women have the lowest cancer screening rates and so are usually diagnosed at a later stage of the disease compared to other racial and ethnic groups, cancer is the leading cause of death of Asian American women (President's Advisory Commission on Asian Americans and Pacific Islanders 2003). Hepatitis B is one of the largest health threats for Asians, accounting for more than half the deaths of Asian Americans. They are three to thirteen times more likely than Caucasians to die from liver cancer caused by hepatitis B. The risk of Chinese Americans dying from liver cancer is six times higher than that of Caucasians; for Korean Americans, the risk is eight times higher; and for Vietnamese Americans, it is thirteen times higher (President's Advisory Commission on Asian Americans and Pacific Islanders 2003).

Asian women have a high risk of contracting osteoporosis. The average calcium intake among Asian women has been observed to be half that of women in Western population groups. Asian Americans also have a higher prevalence of tuberculosis (TB) than all other racial and ethnic groups (President's Advisory Commission on Asian Americans and Pacific Islanders 2003). In terms of morbidity and mortality of Asian American elders, the three leading causes of death are heart disease, cancer, and cerebrovascular diseases. Irrespective of sex, race, or Hispanic origin, heart disease and cancer are the top two leading causes of death among all people age sixty-five and over. In 2001, for example, diabetes was the fifth-leading cause of death among African American men but the sixth among Caucasian and Asian men. Some older Asian American women have difficulty understanding illnesses involving the female reproductive organs and are therefore less likely to accept mammograms and Pap tests (Lum 1995).

Conventionally, the health outcomes of a population are measured in terms of etiology and pathogenesis. In recent years, however, health researchers have begun to realize that health status should not be assessed only by medical indicators. Health-related quality-of-life outcome measurement has emerged as the new reflection of modern medicine, as viewed from biopsychosocial perspectives (Tseng, Lu, and Gandek 2003). Recent clinical and health research has expanded the framework of health outcomes beyond the classical measures of mortality and morbidity by adding psychosocial functioning indicators (ibid.). The result is an increasing need for the development of standards to measure health outcomes in terms of health-related quality-of-life indicators.

Global assessment of quality of life includes all dimensions of life, including physical health, mental health, social support, access to health services, and coping resources. Health-related quality of life reflects a personal sense of physical and mental health and the ability to cope with environmental factors. Over the past twenty years, health researchers have established common, standardized, health-related quality-of-life measures through the *SF-36 Health Survey* (described in more detail below in the "Measures" section); these measures are considered reliable for use among different cultural or ethnic groups. Since the U.S. general population norms on SF-36 scales have been established, cross-study comparisons have become possible. In the literature, a handful of local studies using nonprobability sampling have examined the health status of Chinese and Japanese American elderly using the SF-36 Health Survey to measure health-related quality-of-life outcomes (Harada et al. 1998; Ren and Chang 1998). Results in the Los Angeles study of Japanese American elders showed that they reported better physical and mental health than the standard general U.S. age norms (Harada et al. 1998). Data from the Boston study of Chinese American elders found that their Chinese sample perceived similar or better physical health than their U.S. age peers but reported worse mental health than the U.S. age norms (Ren and Chang 1998).

CONCEPTUAL FRAMEWORK: SOCIOCULTURAL PERSPECTIVE

In understanding health-related quality-of-life outcomes among Asian American elders in the AAENYC study, cultural influences were examined, from a sociocultural perspective, focusing on perceived life stresses and cultural ways of coping. Social work literature suggests that health behaviors, symptom expression, pain tolerance, and perception of illness may be shaped by cultural values, beliefs, and norms governing interpretation, meaning, and valuation of the discomforting experience (Mui and Kang 2006). Based on the health belief model, health behavior in terms of readiness to seek help and motivation for self-care are determined by the following: perceived susceptibility to a medical condition, perceived severity of illness, perceived benefits of seeking help, and perceived barriers to receiving health services (Rosenstock, Strecher, and Becker 1988). The way in which Asian American elders view and understand illness and medical conditions affects their ways of coping and their health-seeking behavior. The way they perceive the efficacy of services (perceived benefits) as well as tangible and psychological costs of receiving services (perceived barriers) also influences their desire to use health services.

Culturally, Asian American elders may feel that seeking medical treatment from Western medicine costs more than the potential benefits received. For example, elderly Asians, most of whom do not speak English, may find it difficult to establish a rapport with health care providers. Communicating symptoms or discomfort with doctors through an interpreter, if they even have one, can be frustrating. Because of their unpleasant experience with migration and acculturation throughout their lives, elderly Asians may not trust the mainstream health care system. Cultural beliefs about illness may prevent them from seeking help because, in their culture, illness is often perceived as bad luck and hospitalization is considered to be a sign of impending death (Kemp 1999–2004). To avoid a bad fate, Asian American elders may find ways to discontinue treatment once having started it, without verbalizing their reasons for doing so. Sometimes, rather than informing doctors about side effects a certain medication may be causing, they may simply terminate treatment to avoid taking the medication.

Elderly Asians may also prefer ethnic health practices that include herbs or acupuncture. Research suggests that Chinese patients, needing to be culturally connected to their doctors, tend to seek Chinese medical care before availing themselves of Western medical services (Liu and Yu 1985), which, of course, delays medical treatment. Other cultural beliefs may also affect the health outcomes of Asian elders. Some believe, for example, that certain procedures such as drawing blood for testing or being X-rayed will do them more harm than good and damage the wholeness of their being (Mui 1996a, 2001). Apparently, for Asian American elders, health seeking has more disadvantages than benefits. These cultural beliefs and health practices may significantly influence their health-related quality-of-life outcomes.

MEASURES

DEPENDENT VARIABLE

The measure of the dependent variable was the SF-36 Health Survey, a standardized multidimensional instrument that evaluates health outcomes. The SF-36 consists of ratings on overall quality of life for eight physical and mental health subscales that are widely used in health surveys as quality-of-life constructs affected by disease and treatment (Ware 1995). Each of the eight subscales is transformed from raw scores into percentage scores with a range from 0 (poor health/functioning) to 100 (excellent health/functioning). The U.S. norms on the SF-36 were estimated and established from the data based on the National Survey of Functional Health Status, a cross-sectional survey done in 1990 (Ware 1993). The total sample ($n = 2,474$) was used to establish norms for the SF-36 eight subscales for different age groups, gender groups, and patient groups with different medical conditions (Ware 1993, 1995). Utilization of the SF-36 allows for comparison of the Asian American elderly respondents' data with these established national norms for the same measures. The SF-36 was designed for use in clinical practice and research, health policy evaluations, and general population surveys.

The eight aspects of physical and mental health assessed by the SF-36 are (1) physical functioning limitation; (2) physical limitation: limitations in usual role activities because of physical health problems; (3) bodily pain; (4) general health perceptions; (5) vitality; (6) social functioning: limitations in social activities because of physical or emotional problems; (7) role limitations: limitations in usual role activities because of emotional problems; and (8) mental health. The attributes contained in this thirty-six-item multidimensional scale are shown in table 3.2. The chosen health concepts represent the most frequently measured constructs in widely used health surveys (Ware 1995; Ware, Kosinski, and Dewey 2000). The questionnaire items selected also represent multiple operational indicators of health, including behavioral function and dysfunction, distress and well-being, objective reports and subjective ratings, and both favorable and unfavorable self-evaluations of general health status (Ware, Kosinski, and Dewey 2000). These national norms were used to compare Asian groups in order to obtain information about how the Asian American elders in the sample fare. The SF-36 has been translated and validated in Chinese and Japanese, although the instrument was originally developed for Western populations (Harada et al. 1998; Ren and Chang 1998). These validation studies indicate that the SF-36 has satisfactory psychometric properties after translation in terms of linguistic acceptability and conceptual equivalence.

PREDICTOR VARIABLES

Based on the sociocultural perspective, the predictor variables in this chapter include measures for perceived life stresses (language difficulty, number of medical conditions, depressive symptoms, number of stressful life events, and perceived generational gap), coping resources (in terms of religiosity, children in proximity, and assistance from children), and sociodemographic factors (gender; age; marital status; living arrangements; length of stay in the United States; having Medicare A and B, Medicaid, and private health insurance). Language difficulty (i.e., poor English proficiency) is conceptualized as a life stress because it represents a source of stress for the Asian American elders who struggle with this barrier daily. Respondents rated their ability to speak, read, and write English from "not well at all" (0) to "very well" (3). These responses were measured individually and then tallied to create a composite measure of overall language proficiency (range 0–9).

Depression was measured by the 30-item Geriatric Depression Scale (GDS; Yesavage et al. 1983). These items consisted of symptoms similar to DSM-IV criteria, such as depressed mood, feelings of hopelessness and worthlessness, diminished interest in activities, poor concentration, and/or indecisiveness (Mui, Burnette, and Chen 2003). Literature suggests that the GDS is a reliable measure of depression for Asian American elderly groups and that it has shown adequate reliability (Mui et al. 2003). The number of stressful life events variable was a composite score of a list of up to six stressful life events experienced by the respondent in the preceding three years. Examples of these events included major losses in life such as death of spouse/family member/good friend, serious illness/injury, having been robbed or had home burglarized, children having moved out, and relocation. The perceived generation-gap variable was a global measure evaluated by asking elders to assess how their view regarding family solidarity, adult children's elder care responsibility, older parents' approval of children's marriage and divorce differed from that of their children on a 4-point scale (not at all different = 0 to different in a very important way = 3).

Measures of coping resource variables were the elder's religiosity, number of children living within a two-hour drive, and the amount of instrumental, financial, and emotional assistance received from children. Religiosity was assessed in terms of respondents' perception about the level of importance of religion in their lives on a 4-point scale (not at all important=0 to very important=3). As controls, sociodemographic variables were used, including gender; age (young-old, 65–74, and old-old, 75 and older); living arrangements (living alone vs. living with others); length of stay in the United States; having Medicare Part A, Medicare Part B, private health insurance, and Medicaid. Since the income measure had a lot of missing data, Medicaid coverage was used as a proxy measure of the elder's financial status. Even though Medicaid entitlement may not be a precise measure of economic resources, it utilizes means testing and income based on federal poverty guidelines as eligibility requirements.

RESULTS

Sociodemographic profiles among the six Asian American subgroups in the study were presented in chapter 2, tables 2.3 and 2.4. Here we highlight the sample demographic characteristics (not presented in table form in this chapter) before discussing the health and health-related quality-of-life outcome variables. Variations based on national origin were found in many demographic and insurance variables. For example, among the whole sample, 44 percent were men, 19 percent lived alone, and 49 percent were married. Those in the Filipino and Indian groups were less likely to live alone (only 4% and 3%, respectively) than were those in the other groups. Compared to other groups, Japanese and Korean elders were less likely to be married (40% and 29%, respectively). The ages of the sample ranged from 65 to 96 (M = 72.4 years, SD = 6.2), with the Vietnamese group significantly younger than those in the other groups (M = 68.8 years). The average length of stay in the United States for the total Asian American elderly sample was 20.8 years (SD = 13.2, range = 1–72 years), with the Vietnamese group reporting the shortest U.S. residence (7 years only). About 41 percent (n = 167) of the total sample received Medicaid.

In terms of stress and coping resources, the Vietnamese elders, compared to the other groups, reported significantly poorer health, more medical conditions, a greater perceived generational gap between themselves and their adult children, and poorer English proficiency. On the other hand, they had more children living in proximity and, compared to the other groups, considered religion to be more important in their lives. They were also more likely than their counterparts to receive Medicaid (91%).

SELF-REPORTED MEDICAL CONDITIONS AND
PERCEIVED HEALTH STATUS

Table 3.1 shows the self-reported prevalence of selected chronic medical conditions among Asian American elders. Since there are no specific national health statistics on Asian American elders, the prevalence of selected chronic conditions was compared to the available health statistics on the total U.S. population aged sixty-five and older from the CDC (2004). When compared to the total U.S. aging population for prevalence of the same medical conditions, the Asian American elders reported higher rates of two disabling chronic conditions: arthritis (43.2% vs. 35.9%) and diabetes (17.5% vs. 15.2%). On the other hand, they reported a lower rate of hypertension (41.6% vs. 49.2%), heart failure (12.1% vs. 20.4%), stroke (3.3% vs. 8.6%), and cancer (2.8% vs. 19.9%). The burden of chronic medical conditions such as heart disease, cancer, stroke, hypertension, diabetes, and arthritis varied widely by Asian ethnicity. For example, 21 percent of Chinese elders had heart disease compared to 14.6 percent of Filipino elders and 14.3 percent of Vietnamese elders. And 62 percent of Vietnamese elders, 54 percent of Filipino elders, 50 percent of Korean elders, and 44.7 percent of Chinese elders suffered from arthritis compared to 35.9 percent of the total senior population in the nation. Findings showed that the average number of medical conditions also varied by national origin groups. Chinese elders reported the highest average number of medical conditions (3.4), followed by Vietnamese (3.2), Indian (2.9), Korean (2.5), and Filipino (2.2). The Japanese elders reported the lowest average number of medical problems (1.8).

As far as perceived health status is concerned. Asian American elders as a group were more likely to report fair or poor health status (54.3%) than the total U.S. aging population (26.6%). Findings also showed wide variation by country of origin in perceived health status. Compared to other national origin groups, Indian American elders reported the best health (73%), stating that they had "good" to "excellent" health. On the contrary, Vietnamese elders reported the poorest health among the six subgroups, with only 8 percent reporting "good" to "excellent" health.

The SF-36 Health Survey items and subscale information is presented in table 3.2. In order to examine the reliability of SF-36 for use with the six Asian American elderly groups in our study, reliability coefficients of the eight subscales were calculated (see the first column in table 3.2). Results indicated that these health-related quality-of-life outcome subscale measures have

TABLE 3.1 Self-Reported Medical Conditions and Self-Rated Health by Asian National Origin Groups

SELF-REPORTED MEDICAL CONDITIONS (%)[a]	CHINESE (n = 105)	FILIPINO (n = 52)	INDIAN (n = 100)	JAPANESE (n = 25)	KOREAN (n = 100)	VIETNAMESE (n = 25)	TOTAL (n = 25)	NATIONAL RATES
Heart failure*	21.4	14.6	7.0	4.2	8.0	14.3	12.1	20.4
Cancer	5.9	2.1	3.0	0.0	1.0	0.0	2.8	19.9
Stroke	6.7	4.1	3.0	4.2	0.0	0.0	3.3	8.6
Hypertension**	45.6	36.7	40.0	4.2	50.0	42.9	41.6	49.2
Diabetes	14.4	18.0	25.0	12.5	13.1	21.7	17.5	15.2
Arthritis**	44.7	54.9	29.0	25.0	50.0	61.9	43.2	35.9
High cholesterol	33.7	24.0	23.0	12.5	31.0	38.1	28.1	
Cataracts****	44.1	19.2	22.0	4.2	18.2	45.0	26.5	
Stomach ulcers	17.1	13.0	20.0	16.7	11.2	23.8	16.2	
Anemia	16.7	6.5	14.0	8.3	20.0	9.5	14.8	
Emphysema/chronic bronchitis***	18.1	4.3	25.0	4.2	9.2	0.0	14.1	
Osteoporosis****	25.5	8.9	1.0	4.2	16.2	10.0	12.8	
Kidney disease	12.4	2.1	13.0	16.7	9.1	27.3	11.6	
Glaucoma	8.7	8.5	17.0	4.2	5.0	10.0	9.6	
Prostate problems*	20.5	25.0	28.3	27.3	0.0	0.0	19.6	

(continued)

TABLE 3.1 (continued)

SELF-REPORTED MEDICAL CONDITIONS (%)[a]	CHINESE (n = 105)	FILIPINO (n = 52)	INDIAN (n = 100)	JAPANESE (n = 25)	KOREAN (n = 100)	VIETNAMESE (n = 25)	TOTAL (n = 25)	NATIONAL RATES
Gall bladder problems**	5.8	6.5	12.0	20.8	1.0	14.3	7.7	
Thyroid/other gland problems	4.2	6.5	7.1	20.8	3.1	4.8	6.0	
Liver disease	1.9	0.0	6.0	0.0	5.1	10.0	3.8	
	M(SD)	M(SD)	M(SD)	M(SD)	M(SD)	M(SD)	M(SD)	
No. of medical conditions[b]	3.4(2.6)[c]	2.2(1.9)[f]	2.9(1.7)[d]	1.8(.99)[g]	2.5(1.5)[e]	3.2(2.4)[c]	2.8(2.0)	
Self-rated health (%)[a] ****								
Poor/Fair	65.7	40.4	27.0	36.0	72.0	92.0	54.2	26.6
Good	21.0	44.2	37.0	44.0	21.0	4.0	28.3	35.3
Very good/Excellent	13.3	15.4	36.0	20.0	7.0	4.0	17.5	38.1

Source: CDC, National Center for Health Statistics, National Health Interview Survey, 2000–2001.
[a] Chi-square statistics were used.
[b] ANOVA statistics with Tukey's post hoc multiple comparisons were used to test the differences between means.
Means with the different letters are significantly different at less than the .05 level in the same variable.
* p<.05;
** p<.01.
*** p<.001.
**** p<.0001.

TABLE 3.2 The SF-36 Health-Related Quality-of-Life Outcome Measures

SCALE	SF-36 ITEM CONTENT[a]	SCORING RANGE
Physical functioning (alpha = .93)	Vigorous activities, such as running, lifting heavy objects, participating in strenuous sports	1–3
	Moderate activities, such as moving a table, pushing a vacuum cleaner, bowling, or playing golf	1–3
	Lifting or carrying groceries	1–3
	Climbing several flights of stairs	1–3
	Climbing one flight of stairs	1–3
	Bending, kneeling, or stooping	1–3
	Walking more than a mile	1–3
	Walking several blocks	1–3
	Walking one block	1–3
	Bathing or dressing yourself	1–3
Physical limitations (cut down on work for physical reasons) (alpha = .93)	Cut down the amount of time you spent on work or other activities	1–2
	Accomplished less than you would like	1–2
	Were limited in kind of work or other activities	1–2
	Had difficulty performing the work or other activities (for example, it took extra effort)	1–2
Bodily pain (alpha = .90)	Intensity of bodily pain	1–6
	Extent pain interfered with normal work	1–6
General health (alpha = .77)	Is your health: excellent, very good, good, fair, or poor?	1–5
	I seem to get sick a little easier than other people	1–5
	I am as healthy as anybody I know	1–5
	I expect my health to get worse	1–5
	My health is excellent	1–5
Vitality (alpha = .65)	Feel full of pep	1–6
	Have a lot of energy	1–6
	Feel worn out	1–6
	Feel tired	1–6

(continued)

TABLE 3.2 (*continued*)

SCALE	SF-36 ITEM CONTENT[a]	SCORING RANGE
Social functioning (alpha = .83)	Extent of health problems interferes with normal social activities	1–6
	Frequency of health problems interferes with social activities	1–6
Emotional limitations (cut down work due to emotional reasons) (alpha = .92)	Cut down the amount of time spent on work or other activities	1–2
	Accomplished less than I would like	1–2
	Didn't do work or other activities as carefully as usual	1–2
Mental health (alpha = .75)	Have been a very nervous person	1–6
	Felt so down in the dumps that nothing could cheer me up	1–6
	Felt calm and peaceful	1–6
	Felt downhearted and blue	1–6
	Have been a happy person	1–6

Note: Item scores were recoded when necessary so that a higher score indicates better health.
Source: (a) Ware, Kosinski, and Dewey 2000.

adequate reliability for use among the Asian American elderly sample, with alphas ranging from .65 to .93.

Table 3.3 presents data based on national origin groups across the eight scales in the SF-36. Findings suggest wide group variations. On all eight scales in the SF-36, Filipino American elders reported the highest scores, indicating the best quality of life and functioning, and Vietnamese American elders reported the lowest scores, indicating the poorest health status. Further comparisons showed that Vietnamese elders had scores that were worse than the U.S. age norms on all counts (not shown in the table). Filipino elders' scores were similar to the U.S. age norms but the reported scores were better in physical limitations, emotional limitations, and bodily pain (not shown in the table). Results showed that Filipino American elders tend to be more resilient than the U.S. older population as a whole.

TABLE 3.3 SF-36 Health Profiles: Asian American Elderly Within-Group Comparisons (mean)

Scale item	CHINESE (n=105)	FILIPINO (n=52)	INDIAN (n=100)	JAPANESE (n=25)	KOREAN (n=100)	VIETNAMESE (n=25)	TOTAL (N=407)
Physical functioning	55.0[a]	68.1[b]	57.3[a]	61.8[a]	42.5[c]	**36.2[d]**	53.3
Physical limitations	42.4[a]	80.8[b]	71.1[c]	76.0[d]	65.4[e]	**32.0[f]**	61.3
Bodily pain	68.1[a]	83.8[b]	68.8[a]	70.8[c]	73.6[c]	**42.1[d]**	70.1
General health	49.7[a]	57.7[b]	52.5[a]	49.5[a]	43.3[c]	**33.2[d]**	48.7
Vitality	49.4[a]	62.0[b]	58.1[c]	52.2[a]	46.6[a]	**40.7[d]**	51.9
Social functioning	51.3[a]	78.6[b]	58.6[c]	60.0[c]	64.0[d]	**46.9[a]**	59.8
Emotional limitations	47.6[a]	90.4[b]	75.8[c]	76.0[d]	85.2[e]	**48.0[a]**	70.8
Mental health	58.3[a]	78.4[b]	63.5[c]	57.8[a]	76.9[d]	**54.9[a]**	66.3

Note: ANOVA statistics with Tukey's post hoc multiple comparisons were used to test the differences between group means. Means with the different letters are significantly different at less than the .05 level in the same scale.
Scale means in bold were significantly lower than other Asian groups.
Scale means in italic were significantly higher than other Asian groups.

FACTORS ASSOCIATED WITH SF-36 HEALTH-RELATED QUALITY-OF-LIFE INDICATORS

Table 3.4 presents results of the regression analyses of the eight SF-36 health-related quality-of-life domains. These eight models contain data for the entire sample. When considering the health-related quality-of-life outcomes, predictors in all eight models were statistically significant ($p<$ .0001). The R-squares, ranging from .25 to .51, tell the most about predicting the respondent's general health ($R^2 = .51$) and the least about predicting the respondent's mental health ($R^2 = .25$). The data pointing to predictors most significant across the health outcomes were depressive symptoms and English-language difficulty (seven outcomes each); having assistance from children (four outcomes); having Medicare Part A coverage, stressful life events, and a number of medical conditions (three outcomes each); having Medicaid as well as children living in proximity (two outcomes each); gender, marital status, and religiosity (one outcome each). These findings demonstrate the importance of language proficiency in predicting variance in seven of eight SF-36 health outcomes. Only physical functioning was not predicted by language proficiency.

DISCUSSION

ETHNIC DIFFERENCES IN HEALTH-RELATED QUALITY-OF-LIFE OUTCOMES

Overall, evidence from our findings suggests that there are significant variations based on national origin in health-related quality-of-life outcome assessment. Group differences in these health indicators observed in this chapter reinforce the importance of service providers being very careful not to assess Asian American elderly as a single group. Findings (not shown in the table) indicated that Asian American elders were at greater risk of poor health outcomes and worse off than the U.S. norms in most health outcomes; they also showed resilience. Those Asian American elders reported better scores in the physical limitations scale demonstrates that they were unlikely to slow down even though they had physical health problems (Mui et al. 2007). This cohort of Asian American elders consisted of U.S. immigrants born in the 1920s and 1930s. As discussed in chapter 1, they were more likely to have experienced

TABLE 3.4 Health-Related Quality-of-Life Subscales Regression Models

INDEPENDENT VARIABLES	PHYSICAL FUNCTIONING b(SE)	PHYSICAL LIMITATIONS b(SE)	BODILY PAIN b(SE)	GENERAL HEALTH b(SE)	VITALITY b(SE)	SOCIAL FUNCTIONING b(SE)	EMOTIONAL LIMITATIONS b(SE)	MENTAL HEALTH b(SE)
SOCIODEMOGRAPHICS								
Gender (male=1)	9.54(4.04)[a]							
Age (young-old=1)								9.87(3.72)[b]
Marital status (married=1)								
Living alone (yes=1)								
Length of stay in the U.S. (1–72)								
Medicare Part A (yes=1)	9.93 (3.98)[a]				6.02(2.55)[a]		6.10(5.64)[b]	
Medicare Part B (yes=1)								
Medicaid coverage (yes=1)			9.02(3.11)[b]	4.19(1.89)[a]				
Private health insurance (yes=1)								
COPING RESOURCES								
Religiosity (0–3)				-3.03(.97)[b]				
Children live within two hours (0–10)		-5.87(1.82)[b]					-3.77(1.71)[a]	
Assistance from children (0–8)		2.11(1.03)[a]		1.23(.34)[c]	1.58(.43)[c]			-1.59(.46)[c]
LIFE STRESSES								
Perceived generation gap (0–3)	2.64(1.23)[a]			1.24(.62)[a]				-4.07(1.67)[b]
Stressful life events (0–6)	-4.61(1.11)[d]			-2.12(.56)[c]	-1.49(.71)[a]			2.20(.81)b
Medical conditions (0–12)	-1.06(.29)[c]	-2.67(.43)[d]	-1.76(.24)[d]	-1.15(.15)[d]	-1.41(.18)[d]	-2.37(.27)[d]	-2.53(.41)d	
Depressive symptoms (0–30)		-7.88(2.71)[b]	-3.59(1.49)	-2.31(.91)[a]	-2.32(1.15)[a]	-6.04(1.67)[c]	-9.10(2.54)[c]	-4.54(1.23)[c]
Language difficulty (0–9)								
R² Total	.40[d]	.33[d]	.40[d]	.51[d]	.44[d]	.43[d]	.34[d]	.25[d]
Adjusted R² Total	.35[d]	.28[d]	.35[d]	.47[d]	.40[d]	.38[d]	.29[d]	.20[d]

Notes: Depressive symptoms (GDS score) was not included in the "Mental Health" model.

[a] $p < .05$.
[b] $p < .01$.
[c] $p < .001$.
[d] $p < .0001$.

trauma and hardships as a result of civil or world wars or both in the course of their lives. These data confirm the Asian cultural virtues that value persever-ance and endurance in difficult life situations (Mui 2001; Mui and Kang 2006), and this group is a model of resilience. This finding also lends support to Asian elders' strong sense of family obligation. Within the Asian family context, elders are guardians of the family, and family needs take priority over all else, even individual concerns (Browne and Broderick 1994). Therefore, Asian elders may be unwilling to use a health problem as a reason to neglect family obligations such as being caretakers of grandchildren at home. In some cases, elders may be the only available caregivers, and they may have no choice but to continue their family caretaking responsibilities regardless of illness. These findings imply that it is important for social workers and other health care providers to be culturally informed and sensitive while working with Asian American elderly patients who are carrying familial burdens.

Group differences in perceived health status and self-reported medical conditions are difficult to compare, as there may be variations in perception and reporting patterns within the national origin groups. A common phe-nomenon among Asian elderly immigrants is their unwillingness to seek fur-ther treatment for ailments because of obstacles they encounter in the health care system. For example, among the three leading causes of mortality (heart disease, cancer, and stroke), Asian American elders as a group admitted to significantly lower rates of having these illnesses than the general older popu-lation (CDC 2004). However, it is unclear whether Asian American elders underreported their disease conditions or were uninformed about their medi-cal conditions due to their unwillingness to seek medical services. We will discuss medical service utilization in chapter 7.

Based on the findings from the regression analysis, interventions designed to improve Asian American elders' health-related quality of life need to pay attention to the risk factors of these health outcomes. Among the demo-graphic variables, older Asian women were at greater risk of poor physical functioning than older Asian men while old-old Asians reported poorer men-tal health than young-old Asians. Gender and age differences observed are consistent with other research in this area (Tseng, Lu, and Gandek 2003). Physical and mental health programs should be designed to target older Asian women, often primary caregivers at their own health expense, and old-old Asians of both genders, often unwilling to be a burden to family by admitting mental and physical health problems, to improve their physical and psycho-logical functioning.

CORRELATES OF HEALTH-RELATED QUALITY-OF-LIFE OUTCOMES

Multivariate findings indicate that health promotion and health maintenance programs designed to improve Asian American elders' health-related quality of life need to address the following issues: Medicare and Medicaid coverage, religiosity, availability of children in proximity, and assistance from children. Not surprisingly, having health insurance coverage, children living nearby, and religious support may improve Asian elders' quality of life. Findings illuminate the importance of insurance coverage (Medicare and Medicaid) as a predictor of better health outcomes (Underwood and Adler 2005).

In terms of coping resources, receiving more assistance from children had a negative impact on elders' mental health outcome. However, having children in proximity, available to perform interdependent duties, often has a positive effect. This finding confirms the notion that "it is easier to give than to receive" (Liang, Krause, and Bennett 2001). Culturally, Asian elders view themselves as family decision makers and the guardians of family (Browne and Broderick 1994). When elders perceive that they receive more assistance from children than they can give, they can feel a deep sense of loss, especially the loss of face and of authority. Being dependent is not a good feeling because Asian elders may rely on their children not only physically but also financially and linguistically. However, interdependent caregiving is crucial to family roles and survival, as long as honorable duties are performed by the appropriate generation. So, although Asian elders view financial dependence on the younger generation as a failure, they expect the younger generation to help them navigate the new cultural and linguistics system of their home in the United States and to be supportive as they continue to lead the family, preserving respect. Social workers who serve Asian multigenerational families should be trained to understand Asian cultural familial values and family dynamics.

Regarding the impact of life stresses on quality-of-life outcomes, data indicate that perceived generational gap, stressful life events, medical conditions, depressive symptoms, and language difficulty are major concerns of Asian American elders. It is notable that elders' perception of a generation gap affects only their mental health outcome and not the other dimensions of health-related quality of life. Asian elders seem to hold family agreement and conformity in high regard and expect family harmony (Browne and Broderick 1994; Mui and Kang 2006). Within the family context, elders' perception about value differences between generations may reflect their discontent with the next family generation, who often do not conform to Confucian values of filial piety in the same way that the elders do (Browne and Broderick 1994). In reality, they may worry that children will not be available to help them in the same way that they helped the generations that preceded them when the need arose. In working with Asian families, social workers need to understand the value conflicts and to provide families with culturally meaningful intervention to improve elders' psychological well-being. Besides the generation gap factor, Asian elders' physical functioning, general health, and mental health are associated with increasingly stressful life events and more self-reported medical conditions. The association between poor health outcomes and stressful events and medical conditions are well documented (Liu and Yu 1985; Mui 2001; Mui and Kang 2006; Pang et al. 2003).

Among the five significant life stress factors, the depressive symptoms variable explained significant variance in all health-related quality-of-life outcomes except the mental health model (the depression variable was not included in this regression analysis). The relationship between depression and poor health-related quality-of-life outcomes is extremely complex but consistent with previous work (Falcon and Tucker 2000; Mills and Henretta 2001; Mui 1996b). Basically, depression may prevent Asian elders from accessing health services and medications, causing further psychological distress. Coping with a depressive condition, medical conditions, and stressful life events creates an extremely daunting experience when approaching health services. And coupled with the fact that most of these Asian American elders do not have English-language skills, they are disabled when negotiating with the U.S. health care system.

LANGUAGE BARRIERS AND POOR HEALTH-RELATED QUALITY-OF-LIFE OUTCOMES

One of the most important findings in this chapter is the strong association between language difficulty and all poor health-related quality-of-life outcomes, with the exception of physical functioning. This finding underlies the importance of training culturally competent health care providers to deal with language barriers and of providing language programs for linguistically isolated Asian American elders. Not only the data in this study but also previous expert literature suggests that language barriers among non–English-speaking patients pose many issues related to accessing health care and to the quality of that care (USDHHS 2005).

For Asian American elders, linguistic difficulty discourages them from seeking Western health services when needed, especially as they are not able to report their symptoms or syndromes accurately before and after treatment or medication. From the elder's perspective, the risk of being in a situation where critical treatment is handled inappropriately and creates a poor outcome is terrifying. Communication and effective use of language are critical not only for proper treatment but also for building doctor-patient rapport. This inability of providers and patients to communicate meaningfully compromises the therapeutic and understanding relationship between the two parties (Woloshin et al. 1995). But language is not the only barrier to an effective relationship. Language is one of many sociocultural factors associated with the quality of communication between health care professional and patients. Background differences such as social class, income, education, occupation, social network, race, ethnicity, nationality, and cultural background can also influence the quality of patient-provider communication. Additionally, the cultural meaning associated with certain body language may be different in different cultures. For example, Asian American elders would appear to be modest and agreeable by nodding to the health care providers, but they may not have any intention of following the prescribed treatment and medication (Underwood and Adler 2005). Being understood and respected is a source of comfort to patients as well as a necessity for proper treatment.

Culturally, communication barriers are critical in Asian American elders not seeking Western medical care; they want to avoid embarrassment over their inability to communicate and thereby maintain pride in being able to handle their own affairs (Mui 1996a, 2001; Mui et al. 2007). Furthermore, when a physician cannot understand the nature of a patient's complaints because of linguistic or cultural differences, serious clinical consequences may ensue if these differences result in a less medically compliant patient (Woloshin et al. 1995).

These findings support the health belief model that associates common barriers that immigrants face with reduced health-seeking behaviors. Our data show the strong predictive power of language barriers in predicting poor health outcomes. There is growing evidence in the literature that minorities, including Asian Americans, suffer from poor health because of the increasing disparity caused by language and cultural barriers (Damron-Rodriguez, Wallace, and Kington 1994; U.S. Department of Health and Human Services, Office of Minority Health 2003; Woloshin et al. 1995).

Documented demographic forecasts point to increased linguistic and cultural heterogeneity among the American elderly patient population (CDC

2004; U.S. Department of Health and Human Services, Office of Minority Health 2003). The health care system and health care professionals have the compassionate burden to become culturally sensitive to and competent to serve these increasingly prevalent groups, which are important segments of American society. Since 2006 the Joint Commission on Accreditation of Health Care Organizations has required hospitals and other health care organizations to become aware of each patient's language and communication needs to assure that assistance can be provided to them (AHA *News Now* 2005). It is essential that programs are designed to support linguistically isolated elderly Asians and other immigrant elders to ensure that they receive equal access to quality health prevention, health promotion, and health maintenance services.

4

INDICATORS OF PSYCHOLOGICAL WELL-BEING

Depression and Life Satisfaction

PSYCHOLOGICAL WELL-BEING is referred to in the literature as subjective well-being (Mui, Choi, and Monk 1998). In recent years psychological well-being has been used as a key indicator in research on successful aging. Elders are considered to be aging well when they have the strengths and capacities to undertake various tasks and cope with life stresses (Ryff 1999). Highlighting strengths and ability leads to an understanding of the way elders remain resilient in the face of physical, psychological, and social changes as they age. It is evident that the definition and factors associated with psychological well-being may vary from one culture to another, as the perception of psychological well-being is shaped and determined by cultural values and beliefs. From a life course perspective, aging is a time of self-reflection, search for a sense of meaningfulness, and life review (Mui and Kang 2006). Psychological well-being is the process of evaluating all aspects of life, known as "cognitive appraisal" (Diener and Diener 1995). A person's evaluative reaction to his or her life can be conceptualized in terms of life satisfaction (cognitive evaluations) or depression (negative affect or emotional reaction) (Diener and Diener 1995).

Ingersoll-Dayton and colleagues (2004) studied Asian Thai elders and found that psychological well-being is multidimensional and that the perception of well-being is determined by cultural values. Their observations suggest that a sense of well-being among this group of elders depends on their sense of harmony and interconnectedness with other people (Ingersoll-Dayton et al. 2004). Asians value family and community relationship even at the expense of individual needs more so than white Americans do (Oyserman, Coon, and Kemmelmeier 2002). White Americans sometimes view social relationships as less important in the process of achieving personal goals (Fiske et al. 1998).

Asian individuals are expected to evaluate themselves based on their contributions to the community (Fiske et al. 1998). For most Asians, having harmonious relationships with others is a vital source of well-being.

In this chapter we examine depression and life satisfaction as indicators of psychological well-being. Research shows that it is important to examine both positive and negative indicators of psychological well-being, as these two components have different correlates (Diwan, Jonnalagadda, and Balaswamy 2004). This exploration of psychological well-being from the perspective of Asian American elders contributes to our understanding of risk and resilience from a cross-cultural perspective. Clinically speaking, knowledge about risk or protective factors is also critical in planning interventions that influence both negative affect (depression) and positive affect (life satisfaction) in Asian American elders (Diwan et al. 2004).

ASIAN AMERICAN ELDERS: RISK FOR DEPRESSION AND SUICIDE

Evidence in the literature suggests that depression may occur more frequently in Asian American elders than white Americans because they have limited resources to cope with physical, financial, linguistic, and emotional challenges associated with adapting and acculturating to American life (Mui and Kang 2006). Epidemiological studies in the United States have documented the prevalence of depressive symptoms in noninstitutionalized elderly samples, using various assessment tools and scales. Depending on the established cut-off points and assessment tools, estimates of the prevalence rates of major depression varied widely. Using *Diagnostic and Statistical Manual of Mental Disorders*, 4th ed. (*DSM IV*)–based criteria for major depression, the one-year prevalence rate is estimated to be 5 percent or less among elderly populations living in the community (Mui, Burnette, and Chen 2001). Depressive symptoms are more prevalent than major depression in this population, with about 15–20 percent of noninstitutionalized elders admitting to having them (Gallo and Lebowitz 1999). Based on the Geriatric Depression Scale (GDS), the prevalence of depressive symptoms among elders living in the community ranged from 12–50 percent (Haller et al. 1996; Mui 1996c, 2001; Shibusawa and Mui 2001). However, at least one report indicates that these data for Asian American elders and other ethnic elderly populations were underestimated as a result of both the low cultural relevance of standardized depression measures and possible underreporting (Mui et al. 2001). Along with physical, cognitive, and functional impairment, factors contributing to underestimation may include differences in acculturation, perception, interpretation, expression, and tolerance of symptoms. The fact is that regardless of severity, depression is *not* a normal part of aging, and it requires psychiatric evaluation and treatment. But because depression often co-occurs with other serious illnesses such as heart disease, stroke, diabetes, cancer, and Parkinson's disease (Horwarth 1992), and because many older adults face these illnesses as well as various social and economic difficulties, health care providers sometimes assume that depression is a normal reaction to these problems (Gottlieb 1991; Mui et al. 2001).

Depression is one of a number of risk factors associated with suicide in older populations, and it is also a widely underrecognized and undertreated medical illness (Conwell and Brent 1995). About a quarter of all late-life suicides are the result of depression (AARP 1997; Mui et al. 2001). Older Americans are disproportionately more likely to attempt suicide than the rest of the U.S. population; although comprising only 13 percent of the population, individuals sixty-five and older accounted for 18 percent of all suicide deaths in 2000. The highest rates were among white men eighty-five and older: 59 deaths per 100,000 persons in 2000, more than five times the national U.S. rate of 10.6 per 100,000 (Centers for Disease Control and Prevention, National Center for Injury Prevention and Control, Office of Statistics and Programming 2006). Asian Americans in psychiatric distress are more likely to commit suicide than similarly situated Americans of other racial and ethnic groups (Bartels et al. 2002). National data show that Asian women sixty-five and older have the highest suicide rate in the country compared to all other populations in that age group (Asian American Health Initiatives 2005).

Literature also suggests that Asian American elders underutilize mental health services compared to all other racial/ethnic groups in the United States (Mui 2001; Mui and Domanski 1999; U.S. Department of Health and Human Services, Public Health Service, Office of the Surgeon General [US-DHHS] 2001). Arguably the elders' underutilization may be attributed to the cultural convention among Asian elderly groups that they may not be willing to accept Western-style mental health intervention. This is compounded by the known challenges in delivering mental health services to needy individuals in the Asian American community, which arise from the scarcity of culturally sensitive services, social stigma, and differing cultural interpretations of mental illness. Although some small, culturally specific outreach mental health programs are found around the nation, Asian American elders continually avoid using mental health services until their needs reach crisis proportions (Mui 2001; Mui and Kang 2006; Snowden and Cheung 1990). The service delivery system is also culturally and linguistically inaccessible to Asian American elders (Mui et al. 2007). When accessing health services, Asians are less likely than white Americans to have their psychiatric distress recognized, even in cases where there are ethnic and language matches between primary care physicians and patients (Bartels et al. 2002). As stated in the Surgeon General's Report, "Current mental health practices and delivery systems have not been designed to meet the needs of ethno cultural minorities; poor understanding of the interplay of cultural, financial, organizational, and diagnostic factors contributed to inappropriate service utilization, individual suffering, and deep social and economic cost" (USDHHS 2001). Therefore, one of the national goals in the Healthy 2010 is to reduce health disparity across racial and ethnic groups (USDHHS 2001).

FACTORS ASSOCIATED WITH DEPRESSION

Studies on depressive symptoms among ethnic elders indicate that female gender, self-rated poor health, living alone, and having a poor quality of social support are risk factors for greater depression (Krause 2004; Mui and Kang 2006). A preponderance of other studies of white and other ethnic elders have shown that older women are more depressed than elderly men (Diwan et al. 2004; Mui et al. 2001). Other researchers have found that social support was associated with less depression because it can mediate the impact of stress on the elders (Husaini et al. 1990; Krause 2004). Furthermore, it was not the size of the support network but the perceived satisfaction with social support that was associated with less depression (Borden, 1991; Mui and Kang 2006). There is also evidence of cultural and ethnic differences in family support. Several reports indicate that Hispanic elders consistently have higher levels of support from their children compared to black or white elders (Markides and Mindel 1987; Mui 1993), which implies that some differences in family support between ethnic groups were attributable to culture, socioeconomic status, and immigration patterns.

Recent research examining correlates of depression among ethnic elders paid special attention to family support and its impact on the elders' psychological well-being. Evidence shows that elders with fewer family contacts and a smaller social network have higher levels of depression (Hovey 2000; Stokes et al. 2001). Other research found that Asian American and other ethnic elders prefer assistance from their family members (Mui 1996b, 2001). Data confirm that Asian American elders receive a considerable amount of emotional and instrumental support from adult children and that the quality of their family relationship is a protective factor that mitigates depression (Mui 1996b, 2001; Mui and Kang 2006). Culturally, Asian American elders expect their families to assist them in their old age and to treat them with respect. What is obvious from these studies is the cultural expectation factor in family support among elderly Asian Americans, an expectation that highlights the difference of Asian American elders from other ethnic groups. Within the Asian community, variations are seen in the level of support exchange and reciprocity between generations. Although the level of social support and reciprocity is relatively high within the community, Asian American elders reported high levels of depression when they perceived less support from their young generations (Mui and Kang 2006).

Other research on ethnic elders examined the relationship between the process of acculturation and their psychological well-being. Acculturation—a process by which an ethnic group adopts the beliefs and practices of the mainstream culture (Mills and Henretta 2001)—is usually measured by length of stay in the United States and English proficiency. The process is multidimensional and includes physical, psychological, financial, spiritual, social, language, and family adjustment; it can be highly stressful for Asian American elders, especially those with fewer resources (income, education, English proficiency) to adapt to their life situation in America (Black, Markides, and Miller 1998; Casado and Leung 2001). Pressures to acculturate may be offset where the maintenance of one's traditional cultural values or ethnic identity as an American is a resource for coping with life's stresses. Research findings on the impact of acculturation on psychological well-being are mixed. Studies indicate that the lower the level of acculturation, the greater the level of depression among Hispanic elders (Falcon and Tucker 2000; Gonzalez, Haan, and Hinton 2001; Hovey 2000). Studies on Asian American elderly samples found a similar relationship between less acculturation and high levels of depression (Stokes et al. 2001). Other correlates of depression among different ethnic groups include poor health, life stresses, financial strain, dependency on children, social isolation, and lack of social support (Gonzalez et al. 2001, Hovey 2000). Depression among Asian American elders may be owing to historical traumatic events (e.g., wars, combat experiences, the loss of loved

ones, or the loss of a sense of culture place), migration stress, adaptation difficulties, poverty, illness, and weakening family support (Gelfand and Yee
1991; Mui and Kang 2006; Ngo et al. 2001; Pang 1998).

CORRELATES OF LIFE SATISFACTION

Life satisfaction has been defined as an individual's cognitive evaluation of
his or her life, as determined by the fit between life goals and actual outcomes, and thus involves a total assessment of goals and outcomes of the elder's entire life course (Krause 2004; Litwin 2005). Studies have confirmed
that correlates of life satisfaction among elderly from diverse backgrounds are
emotional and instrumental support from friends and family (Bisconti and
Bergeman 1999), relationships with others (Cheng and Chan 2006), relationship harmony (Leung, Moneta, and McBride-Chang 2005), and increased
social support (Litwin 2005).

A greater sense of life satisfaction has been associated with self-worth, living longer, higher levels of education, males, self-esteem, financial status, religiosity, higher levels of physical functioning, and better health (Leung et al.
2005; Bisconti and Bergeman 1999).

Researchers also point out that individuals' cognitive evaluation of their
lives is influenced by their cultural beliefs and values learned through socialization in their culture (Krause 2004; Triandis et al. 1993). When studying life satisfaction, we need to account for the impact of culture and value
perspectives on the perception of life satisfaction. Some culture-related
studies have focused on the individualism and collectivism aspects of cultures (Schaller, Parker, and Garcia 1998). Research has shown that people
from individualistic cultures tend to give first priority to the goals of individuals to the extent that they put family and community needs second. In
contrast, people raised in Asian cultures seem to focus on collective values
and tend to give priority to the goals of the family and community, share
both successes and failures with others, and have close relationships with
members of their ethnic community (Triandis et al. 1993). In the American
culture, individual happiness and satisfaction are considered very important
in one's life, and people are socialized to attend primarily to their own needs
and satisfaction. In contrast, Asian American elders are socialized to fit into
the community, and their life satisfaction is related to fulfilling their responsibilities to their family and community (Triandis et al. 1993). Culturally

speaking, factors associated with life satisfaction among Asian American elders may include more family and relationship variables than among their non-Asian counterparts.

The literature confirms this cultural explanation of life satisfaction. For example, Diwan and his colleagues (2004) found that the cultural correlates of greater life satisfaction among their Indian American elderly sample are comfort with one's cultural identity and satisfying relationships with friends. Another study of a nationwide sample of 1,518 older Americans found that life satisfaction is associated with marriage, emotional support, and fewer lifetime traumas (Ingersoll-Dayton et al. 2004; Krause 2004). Life satisfaction research also found that ethnic elders with stronger social ties have a higher level of life satisfaction than those who did not have strong ties (Bisconti and Bergeman 1999; Cheng and Chan 2006; Krause 2004). These studies suggest that the greater the social support, the greater the life satisfaction among elderly people. Based on Krause's work (2004), life satisfaction is an important indicator of psychological well-being, as it is based on continuing life evaluation throughout life and reflects contentment with life in general. Life evaluation may become especially meaningful in later life, as that is a time for deep self-reflection, a time when elders learn to accept what they have become and the accomplishments and struggles they have experienced. Apart from demographic and health variables, the overall findings indicate that both intrapersonal variables (self-esteem, self-worth, religiosity) and interpersonal variables (harmony in relationships, social support, social ties, emotional support) are important in promoting greater life satisfaction among elders.

UNDERSTANDING PSYCHOLOGICAL WELL-BEING: THE SOCIOCULTURAL FRAMEWORK

In this chapter we used a sociocultural framework to examine the effects of culture, particularly the roles of life stress and cultural coping resources in predicting depression and life satisfaction among the Asian American elders in the study. The sociocultural perspective of both depression and life satisfaction could provide a framework for understanding how the social and cultural features of specific cultures define perceptions and emotional responses. The conceptual model used in this chapter expands the stress and coping model usually found in the literature by examining the role of culture norms and cultural values in explaining psychological well-being.

In analyzing the risk and protective factors for depression and life satisfaction of Asian American elders, this chapter points to the cultural variations in the expression and interpretation of depression as well as life satisfaction (Ingersoll-Dayton et al. 2004; Krause 2004). Expression and interpretation of psychological well-being may be determined by Asian collectivist values that determine harmonious relationships and family interconnectedness (Ingersoll-Dayton et al. 2004). These values prize reciprocity, family, and community over the individual's preferences. Individuals view the self as interdependent, and they evaluate themselves based on their contributions to the family (Fiske et al. 1998). In Asian communities, maintaining harmonious relationships with others is a vital source of well-being, and the ability to adapt one's own interests to those of family groups or institutions is highly valued (Fiske et al. 1998; Mui 2001; Mui and Kang 2006).

Therefore, we examine the role of culture in predicting elders' depression and life satisfaction, with special attention to their cultural resources in terms of *harmony variables* (belief in family values, perceived cultural gap, satisfaction with family, religiosity) and *interconnectedness variables* (children living nearby, assistance from children, assistance to children). Research data point to the role of social support and family support as factors protecting against depression and fostering greater life satisfaction among Asian American elders (Diwan et al. 2004; Ingersoll-Dayton et al. 2004). In addition, the lack of harmony factor, in terms of dissatisfaction with family, has been found to be a risk factor for more depression and less life satisfaction (Mui and Kang 2006). Life stresses were also examined, because Asian American elders' emotional reactions and cognitive evaluation of their lives may be affected by their unique social circumstances (e.g., migration experience, language difficulty, historical traumatic experience, recent stressful life events, and health challenges).

MEASURES

The Geriatric Depression Scale (GDS) was used to assess the negative affect of psychological well-being (Yesavage et al. 1983). The scale includes of a list of symptoms similar to those in the *DSM-IV* criteria, such as depressed mood, feelings of hopelessness and worthlessness, diminished interest in activities, poor concentration, and/or indecisiveness (Mui et al. 2001). The assessment of depression in an elderly population is more difficult than in a younger population because elders have a higher prevalence of somatic complaints, genuine physical problems, and medication use. A strength of the GDS is that it has no somatic items that can introduce age bias and thus inflate total scores among the elderly population (Kessler et al. 1992). This GDS lists positive and negative statements that respondents either agree or disagree with by checking a box (Mui 1996a; Yesavage et al. 1983). The scores for the respondents are sorted into three group distribution ranges: a normal range of depressed feelings (score of 0–10), a mildly depressed range (11–20), and a moderately to severely depressed range (21–30). Based on the literature, the classification of depressed is based on the established cut-off point of a total GDS score greater than 11 (Yesavage et al. 1983). The scale has high reliability and validity (test-retest reliability of .85; internal consistency of .94), and the literature suggests that it can reliably measure depression in Asian American elderly groups (Mui 1996c; Mui et al. 2003). The computed alpha coefficients of the GDS for different groups in this chapter ranged from .85 to .92, indicating that the reliability is more than adequate.

Life satisfaction, on the other hand, was assessed by a single-item global measure. Respondents were asked to respond to the question: "All things considered, on a four-point scale how satisfied are you with life in general these days, with 1 meaning very dissatisfied and 4 meaning satisfied?" The literature indicates that a single-item measure has been used widely to assess satisfaction with life as a whole (Krause 2004).

Other independent variables that were measured in the multiple regression models were the cultural coping resources of Asian American elders conceptualized in terms of *harmony variables* (*intrapersonal and interpersonal*) and a *family interconnectedness* variable. Harmony variables included the endorsement of family values, the perceived generation gap, satisfaction with family, and religiosity. The *family values endorsement* variable was a composite score (alpha coefficient = .80) of twelve family value items that measured the degree to which elders endorsed these items. The twelve family value questions measured elders' cultural beliefs regarding extended family, nuclear family, elder care, marriage, divorce, gender roles, and family living arrangements. Elders stated their beliefs on a four-point scale (not at all important = 0 to very important = 3) so that a high score indicated that the elder was attached more to that family value. The *perceived generation gap* was a global measure evaluated by asking elders to assess how their view regarding these family values differed from that of their children on a four-point scale (not at all different = 0 to different in a very important way = 3). Satisfaction with family was a single-item measure that evaluated the quality of the relationship between generations by asking elders to respond, on a four-point scale, to the question, "How satisfied are you with your relationship with your family at the present time?" (very dissatisfied = 1 to very satisfied = 4). Religiosity was assessed by respondents' perception of the level of importance of religion in their lives on a four-point scale (not at all important = 0 to very important = 3).

Family interconnectedness variables included children in proximity, assistance from children, and assistance to children. Children in proximity was assessed by the number of children living within a two-hour drive. Assistance from children and assistance to children were assessed by determining how much instrumental, financial, and emotional assistance was received from and given to children.

Life stresses were operationally defined by language proficiency, perceived health, the number of medical conditions, and the number of stressful life events. Language proficiency was determined by respondents' ability to read, write, and speak English. Each item was assessed on a four-point scale (not at all = 0 to very well = 3). In the analyses reported in this chapter, language proficiency was seen as a life stress because it is involved in elders' daily struggles with the mainstream culture through their interaction with service systems. Perceived health was assessed on a five-point scale, with a low score indicating poor health. The number of self-reported medical conditions included chronic conditions such as heart disease, cancer, stroke, diabetes, and arthritis. The *stressful life events* variable was a composite score of up to six stressful life events experienced by the respondent in the preceding three years. Examples of these events included major losses in life such as the death of a spouse, family member, or good friend; serious illness or injury; robbery or home burglary; children having moved out; and relocation.

Sociodemographic variables were considered when cultural coping resources and life stress factors were assessed. These variables included gender, living arrangements, marital status, age, length of stay in the United States, and Medicaid. Because the income measure had considerable missing data, Medicaid coverage was used as a proxy measure for elders' financial status. Even though Medicaid may not be a precise measure of economic resources, it uses means testing and income related to federal poverty guidelines as eligibility requirements.

RESULTS

DESCRIPTIVE STATISTICS

Table 4.1 shows the GDS mean scores (mean = 10.1; SD = 7.0) for the total sample and for each ethnic group. About 40 percent of the total sample scored 11 or higher, indicating possible depressive symptomatology. There were differences based on national origin in terms of depression experienced by members of the six groups. Japanese respondents reported significantly higher levels of depression than the other groups (mean = 15.0; SD = 7.7), followed by Vietnamese respondents (mean = 12.4; SD = 5.7), Chinese (mean = 11.4; SD = 7.7), and Indian (mean = 11.1; SD = 6.8). Korean and Filipino respondents reported significantly lower levels of depressive symptoms (mean = 7.8; SD = 5.8 and mean = 6.2; SD = 5.0, respectively). The incidence rate of depression (not shown in the table) for the total sample was 40 percent, and subgroup variations are as follows: the Japanese group was the highest (76%), followed by the Vietnamese (64%), the Indian (50%), the Chinese (45.7%), the Korean (24%), and the Filipino (15.4%). These findings all exceed the 15–20 percent prevalence rates of depressive symptoms or syndromes among community-dwelling elders (Gallo and Lebowitz 1999). Regarding life satisfaction, the distribution of scores indicated that the Filipinos were most satisfied with their lives (mean = 3.4; SD = 0.6), followed by the Vietnamese (mean = 3.2; SD = 0.6). Regarding life satisfaction distribution (not shown in the table), the majority (80%) of respondents were either satisfied or very satisfied with their lives. When examining the life satisfaction distribution by groups, there were wide variations within groups. Filipino (94%), Japanese (92%), and Vietnamese (92%) elders were more satisfied with their lives than Chinese (68%), Indian (62%), and Korean (77%) elders. Correlation coefficients between the depression score and life satisfaction score were calculated for the whole sample and by groups. Although the two measures of psychological well-being shared considerable variance (r = -.58, p = .0001), they represented two different constructs in minds of the Asian American elders.

FACTORS ASSOCIATED WITH DEPRESSION AND LIFE SATISFACTION

Table 4.2 presents results of the multiple regression models on depression and life satisfaction. The whole sample was used to do the modeling analyses, because subgroup sizes were too small for meaningful comparison in multivariate

TABLE 4.1 Descriptive Statistics of Variables in Regression Models by Asian National Origin Groups

	CHINESE (n=105)	FILIPINO (n=52)	INDIAN (n=100)	JAPANESE (n=25)	KOREAN (n=100)	VIETNAMESE (n=25)	TOTAL (n=407)
				Mean(SD)			
Dependent variables							
GDS (0–30)	11.4(7.7)[a]	6.2(5.0)[b]	11.1(6.8)[a]	15.0(7.7)[c]	7.8(5.8)[d]	12.4(13.0)[e]	10.1(7.0)
Life satisfaction (1–4)[e]	2.9(0.9)[a]	3.4(0.6)[b]	3.0(0.7)[a]	3.0(0.5)[a]	2.9(0.7)[a]	3.2(0.6)[c]	3.01(0.73)
Sociodemographics							
Gender (male=1)	0.44(0.50)[a]	0.33(0.47)[a]	0.62(0.49)[b]	.48(0.51)[a]	0.26(0.44)[a]	0.64(0.49)[b]	0.44(0.50)
Living arrangement (alone=1)	0.32(0.47)[a]	0.04(0.19)[b]	0.03(0.17)[b]	.28(0.46)[a]	0.25(0.44)[a]	0.24(0.44)[a]	0.19(0.39)
Marital status (married=1)	0.53(0.50)[a]	0.52(0.50)[a]	0.62(0.49)[a]	.40(0.50)[b]	0.29(.46)[b]	0.68(0.48)[a]	0.49(0.50)
Age (65–96 yr)	75.1(7.1)[a]	73.2(6.6)[a]	70.3(4.2)[b]	70.9(4.7)[b]	72.3(6.1)[b]	68.8(3.5)[c]	72.4(6.2)
Medicaid coverage (yes=1)	0.58(0.50)[a]	0.37(0.49)[a]	0.24(0.43)[b]	0.10(.30)[c]	0.38(.49)[a]	0.91(0.29)[d]	0.41(0.49)
Length of stay in the United States (1–72 yr)	26.2(14.8)[a]	18.9(14.6)[b]	21.2(12.7)[b]	30.8(10.1)[c]	16.3(8.1)[b]	7.0(3.0)[d]	20.8(13.2)
Cultural coping resources							
HARMONY (INTRAPERSONAL AND INTERPERSONAL)							
Family values endorsement (0–36)	25.9(6.1)[a]	28.8(5.3)[b]	26.1(4.0)[a]	25.0(3.0)[a]	24.9(5.0)[a]	34.1(3.1)[c]	26.4(5.4)
Perceived generation gap (0–3)	1.89(0.68)[a]	1.70(0.78)[a]	2.01(0.47)[b]	2.05(0.38)[b]	1.76(0.87)[a]	2.14(0.83)[c]	1.89(0.71)
Satisfaction with family (1–4)	3.15(0.73)[a]	3.55(0.54)[b]	3.17(0.64)[a]	3.00(0.51)[c]	3.41(0.72)[b]	3.24(0.83)[a]	3.27(0.69)
Religiosity (0–3)[e]	1.60(1.19)[a]	2.90(0.36)[b]	2.30(.72)[c]	2.36(.57)[c]	2.49(0.97)[c]	3.00(0.0)[b]	2.30(0.98)
FAMILY INTERCONNECTEDNESS							
Children in proximity (0–10)	2.38(1.82)[a]	1.84(1.51)[b]	1.71(1.27)[b]	1.23(0.97)[c]	1.85(1.53)[b]	2.63(1.95)[a]	1.97(1.58)
Assistance from children (0–8)	3.74(2.41)[a]	4.56(2.68)[a]	6.60(1.67)[b]	5.95(2.13)[b]	3.31(2.42)[c]	3.44(2.89)[c]	4.57(2.65)
Assistance to children (0–6)	1.42(1.68)[a]	3.05(1.99)[b]	4.40(1.57)[c]	3.59(1.76)[d]	1.29(1.68)[a]	2.29(1.99)[e]	2.55(2.14)

LIFE STRESSES

Language proficiency (0–9)[e]	0.96(1.86)[a]	7.06(2.24)[b]	4.00(3.22)[c]	5.52(2.40)[c]	2.20(2.25)[d]	0.92(1.38)[a]	3.06(3.15)
Perceived health (1–5)[e]	2.41(1.25)[a]	2.91(1.12)[a]	3.32(1.11)[b]	3.02(1.05)[a]	2.02(1.13)[c]	1.75(0.82)[d]	2.60(1.25)
No. of medical conditions (0–12)	3.35(2.65)[a]	2.23(1.93)[b]	2.85(1.73)[a]	1.80(1.00)[c]	2.50(1.48)[b]	3.17(2.43)[a]	2.77(2.04)
No. of stressful life events (0–6)	1.78(1.49)[a]	1.71(1.18)[a]	2.63(1.47)[b]	1.88(1.27)[a]	0.90(1.14)[c]	1.36(1.47)[d]	1.74(1.48)

Note: ANOVA statistics with Tukey's post hoc multiple comparisons were used to test the differences between means.

[a, b, c, d] Means with the different letters are significantly different at less than the .05 level in the same variable.

[e] High scores indicate favorable ratings.

testing. The depression model was significant statistically ($R^2 = .53$; $p < .0001$) with poor perceived health having the strongest effect (beta = -.46), followed by dissatisfaction with family (beta = -.25), more stressful life events (beta = .23), more assistance from adult children (beta = .15), fewer children living nearby (beta = -.14), perceived wider cultural gap (beta = .13), longer length of stay in the United States (beta = .12), and lower level of religiosity (beta = -.10). In the life satisfaction model, five protective factors were significant in predicting a greater sense of life satisfaction among Asian American elders ($R^2 = .36$; $p < .0001$). Significant correlates include better perceived health (beta = -.38), satisfaction with family (beta = .34), greater religiosity (beta = .17), living alone (beta = .12), and perceived smaller cultural gap between generations (beta = -.10). It is notable that living alone was not a risk factor for depression but had a beneficial impact on life satisfaction. Respondents who lived alone were more likely to be satisfied with their lives than those who lived with others. In terms of coping resources, the number of children living nearby and assistance from children were not factors fostering life satisfaction but instead resulted in increased levels of depression. Further, the *stressful life events* variable was a risk factor for depression but had no effect on the life satisfaction score. Findings clearly indicated that coping and stress factors had different effects on both the positive and negative aspects of psychological well-being. The common risk factors for increased depression and decreased life satisfaction were less religiosity, poorer perceived health, an apparently wider cultural gap between generations, and dissatisfaction with family. When the pair-wise respective regression coefficients of these four variables were compared (t-test), results showed that the effects of these four variables were significantly stronger in predicting an increased depression score than reduced life satisfaction.

DISCUSSION

THE SOURCES OF PSYCHOLOGICAL WELL-BEING

The findings reported in this chapter add to research on indicators of psychological well-being among Asian American elders by including measures of both positive and negative affect. The results of the study show that 40 percent of the sample were considered to be at least mildly depressed, based on the GDS normative cut-off point. The data suggest that the negative affect in terms of depression among these elders was extensive. Compared to other

TABLE 4.2 Depression and Life Satisfaction Regression Models

VARIABLES	DEPRESSION		LIFE SATISFACTION	
	b(SE)	Beta	b(SE)	Beta
Sociodemographics				
Gender (male=1)	.46(.73)	.03	.06(.08)	.04
Living arrangement (alone=1)	1.12(.97)	.06	.21(.11)*	.12*
Marital status (married=1)	−.14(.74)	−.01	.05(.08)	.04
Age (65–96 yr)	−1.03(.71)	−.07	−.08(.08)	−.06
Medicaid coverage (yes=1)	.12(.67)	.01	.02(.08)	.02
Length of stay in the United States (1–72 yr)	.07(.03)*	.12*	.00(.00)	.09
Cultural coping resources				
HARMONY (INTRAPERSONAL AND INTERPERSONAL)				
Family values endorsement (0–36)	.09(.06)	.07	.01(.01)	.05
Perceived generation gap (0–3)	1.00(.45)**	.13**	−.07(.05)*	−.10*
Satisfaction with family (1–4)	1.69(.51)****	.25****	.28(.06)****	.34****
Religiosity (0–3)[e]	−.44(.35)*	−.10*	.09(.04)**	.17**
FAMILY INTERCONNECTEDNESS				
Children in proximity (0–10)	−.55(.19)**	−.14**	.02(.02)	.04
Assistance from children (0–8)	.41(.13)**	.15**	.01(.01)	.05
Assistance to children (0–6)	.13(.20)	.05	.04(.02)*	.14*
LIFE STRESSES				
Language proficiency (0–9)[e]	.00(.12)	.00	.01(.01)	.03
Perceived health (1–5)[e]	−77(.12)****	−.46****	.05(.01)****	.38****
No. of medical conditions (0–12)	.22(.17)	.06	.00(.02)	.01
No. of stressful life events (0–6)	1.05(.22)****	.23****	.04(.03)	.09
R^2 Total	.53****		.36****	
Adjusted R^2 Total	**.50****		**.32****	

* $p < .05$.
** $p < .01$.
*** $p < .001$.
**** $p < .0001$.
[e] High scores indicate favorable ratings.

studies in the literature, the rates and incidence of depression in these six groups of Asian American elders were much higher (40%) than observed in most other community ethnic elderly samples (15–20%; Ferraro, Brian, and Iwona 1997; Hazuda et al. 1998; Shibusawa and Mui 2001; Woo et al. 1994). Depression is a treatable disease but it is likely to be undetected or misdiagnosed in ethnic minority elders because of cultural barriers (Bartels et al. 2002; Mui 2001).

Our data suggest that there is substantial variation in the perception of depression and life satisfaction among the national origin groups. Relatively speaking, the cognitive appraisal and emotional reaction of the Filipino American group to their lives are more positive than those of other groups. Compared to the other groups, they seem to have adjusted better to their life in the United States, reporting lower levels of depression and higher levels of life satisfaction. This is not surprising, as they reported higher scores than the other subgroups on all health-related quality-of-life measures and had a higher level of English proficiency. Of the six subgroups, Filipino American elders had the most human capital in terms of health and language resources. However, the Japanese, Vietnamese, Chinese, and Indian American elders were more vulnerable and at greater risk of depression because, according to previous research, their depression rates were much higher than those of other elderly populations (Hazuda et al. 1998; Mui 1996b, 2001; Mui et al. 2003). Regarding the life satisfaction score, the majority of the sample (80%) reported that they were either satisfied or very satisfied with their lives. The positive affect data reflect a resilient picture of Asian American elders, with only one-fifth of the sample reporting dissatisfaction with their lives. Data suggest that, as a group, Asian American elders are more comfortable reporting positive than negative affect. The mean score of life satisfaction among Vietnamese American elders ranked second after that of Filipino American elders. It is noteworthy that the Vietnamese elders also ranked second in their depression scores. The other four subgroups of Asian elders reported mean scores in life satisfaction that were a bit lower than those of the Filipino and Vietnamese elders.

Our findings suggest that Asian American elders may have mixed feelings about their lives. On the one hand, they may be satisfied with their lives because they have immigrated to the United States and may consider legal residence in the U.S. to be an accomplishment (Mui 2001). On the other hand, they still have to deal with the reality of growing old in a foreign land, coping with age-related losses, managing acculturation stress, having financial difficulties, encountering a language barrier, and dealing with other life stresses every day. Being a person of color and an immigrant, coping with daily struggles (such as microaggression, prejudice, racial discrimination, or racial oppression) are extremely difficult emotionally. In the process of cultural adaptation, Asian American elders who feel the loss of homeland or of cultural connection with the community may experience migration grief and depression (Casado and Leung 2001; Mui and Kang 2006).

Comparing the two models, more variance was explained by depression than life satisfaction, suggesting that the model may better fit the negative rather than the positive effect of psychological well-being. There are eight predictors in the depression model alone, five in the life satisfaction model, and four that are common to both. The latter are the generation gap, dissatisfaction with family, high levels of religiosity, and poor perceived health. These four variables, however, were found to be better predictors of depression than of life satisfaction, as indicated by the magnitude of the un-standardized regression coefficient. Interventions targeting these four areas would reduce depression and improve life satisfaction in this elderly population.

INTERPERSONAL AND INTRAPERSONAL HARMONY FACTORS AND PSYCHOLOGICAL WELL-BEING

As predicted, the harmony variable, as measured by dissatisfaction with family, is associated with increased depression and reduced life satisfaction. This relationship is consistent with research among Asian elders (Cheng and Chan 2006; Hovey 2000; Lee et al. 1996; Litwin 2005; Mui 1998, 2001). This predictor of interpersonal harmony, which explains both the positive and negative aspects of psychological well-being, made sense culturally and suggests that these elders fervently need harmonious relationships with the younger generation (Litwin 2005; Mui and Kang 2006). The possible explanations may have to do with cultural expectations as well as survival. Asian elders need to depend on a good relationship with their adult children as an important resource to help them deal with life stresses. Family work to promote better intergenerational relationships is critical for the psychological well-being of Asian American elders.

The perceived generation gap, another measure of interpersonal harmony, was found to trouble Asian American elders, affecting their symptoms of depression and their life satisfaction, confirming other studies in the literature (Mui and Kang 2006; Tran et al. 1996). This finding may reflect generational differences between elders and their adult children in cultural beliefs and values regarding elder care, gender roles, care of grandchildren, lifestyle choices, divorce, and even living arrangements. The perceived generation gap may also be a proxy measure of a troubled relationship or value conflict between the generations. Asian American elders may worry that their adult children will develop different elder care values and then no longer care for them. When Asian elders perceived a wider gap between themselves and their children, they were more depressed and less satisfied with their lives. These findings point to the need to develop interventions that help Asian American elders deal more effectively with intergenerational communication, value differences, and issues of elder care expectations.

Religiosity is a measure of intrapersonal harmony that is associated with greater life satisfaction and less depression. The link between religiosity and psychological well-being noted here is consistent with the literature (Ai et al. 1998; Hovey 2000). Asian American elders were considered to be more spiritual when they said that religion was very important to them. Asian elders may find inner harmony more easily if they feel a sense of spiritual meaning in their struggles and their lives. Religious resources may provide faith, courage, strength, patience, and purpose in coping with life and adversity (Mui and Kang 2006). Faith coming from intrapersonal harmony with the higher being might help elders accept life losses. Besides internal peace, religion also brings social and emotional support from the faith community (Ai et al. 1998).

THE FAMILY INTERCONNECTEDNESS PREDICTOR AND PSYCHOLOGICAL WELL-BEING

Children living nearby is an important measure of family interconnectedness that protects against depression. The association between depression and social isolation, as a result of fewer children living in proximity, is consistent with research in the United States and Asia (Chi and Chou 2001; Krause and Goldenhar 1992; Lee et al. 1996). Culturally, Asian parents may expect their adult children to live close by, as they need their children's assistance as English interpreters and helpers in a crisis (Mui and Kang 2006). Having fewer children available may reduce their sense of security and increase their anxiety and depression.

Regarding the variable of family interconnectedness, receiving more assistance from children risked greater depression but had no effect on life satisfaction. This is consistent with a national study which also found that receiving benefits as a care recipient was associated with increased psychological distress (Liang, Krause, and Bennett 2001). The findings of that study support the general notion that it is easier to give than to receive. It is possible that caregiving relationships took away the elderly parents' sense of power, authority, and status in the family. Intervention programs must be sensitive to the negative impact of the caregiving relationship on Asian American elders. Although these elders seem to expect family interconnectedness in terms of physical closeness and filial assistance, the assistance from children actually costs these elders their pride and dignity and becomes a risk factor for depression. In contrast, elders' giving assistance to children is psychologically beneficial, as it has a significant positive impact on life satisfaction. By assisting children and grandchildren, Asian American elders may gain self-worth and improve their psychological well-being (Caprara and Steca 2005; Fry 2001). Service providers must understand the Asian American elders' sources of psychological well-being and provide culturally meaningful intervention to support intergenerational exchange and interconnectedness.

LIFE STRESS, LIVING ARRANGEMENT, AND PSYCHOLOGICAL WELL-BEING

The risk factor for both increased depression and less satisfaction with life is poorer perceived health. The association between poorer perceived health and depressive symptoms and life satisfaction is consistent with the literature (Mui 2001; Mui and Kang 2006; Litwin 2005). Comorbidity between health and depression may be recursive; depressive symptoms can be reactions to medication taken for physical illness; and poorer perceived health can bring on stress that only increases depression, especially in linguistically challenged Asian American elders. As discussed in chapter 3, language barriers are sources of poor health outcomes. Asian American elders who experience health problems may feel powerless and helpless because of their dependence. Coping with physical losses and the loss of status and authority can reduce Asian elders' sense of satisfaction in life and increase their depression. Culturally sensitive intervention through individual and group therapy may be effective in helping Asian American elders and their families cope with illnesses.

The only unique protective factor in greater life satisfaction is living alone, which has not been developed in the literature. This is the most significant finding, because the cultural belief that Asian American elders prefer to live with children is not supported by our data. Our data suggest, instead, that Asian American elders who live alone feel more satisfied with their lives than those who live with their families. One possible explanation is that the Asian American elders who live alone may feel a new sense of autonomy and perceived self-worth. Research data indicate that self-worth is associated with global life satisfaction (Caprara and Steca 2005; Fry 2001; Leung et al. 2005).

In the depression model, which is inconsistent with the literature, the longer Asian Americans remain in the United States, the greater their risk of increased depression (Black et al. 1998; Mills and Henretta 2001; Stokes et al. 2001). A possible cultural explanation for this is that the longer elders live in the United States, the more likely they are to have American-born children and grandchildren. From the previous discussion regarding the generation gap, it appears that value differences could explain why Asian American elders may have more problems with American-born children than with those born in their country of origin (Casado and Leung 2001).

The data reported in this chapter provide important empirical information for service providers working with Asian American elders and their families. When designing programs directed at increasing the life satisfaction of Asian American elders and reducing their depression, providers should pay special attention to their clients' length of residence in the United States, their English proficiency, religiosity, proximity of adult children, intergenerational exchange, perceived health, experience of stressful life events, perception of the generational gap, and satisfaction with family. Consideration of these variables is essential to the design of programs and interventions that are culturally appropriate for Asian American elders and their families.

5

TRADITIONAL AND CURRENT EXPECTATIONS OF
FAMILY RELATIONSHIPS

AS NOTED IN CHAPTER 1, the majority of Asian Americans aged sixty-five and older was born outside the United States (U.S. Census Bureau 2000). Over 90 percent of Filipino, Indian, Korean, and Vietnamese elders and 86 percent of Chinese elders in the United States are foreign born (table 5.1). It is also notable that many elders from Asia immigrated after reaching late adulthood. Over 40 percent of Vietnamese and Indian elders and over 30 percent of Chinese, Filipino, and Korean elders living in the United States immigrated after the age of sixty (table 5.2). A large portion of the participants in the AAENYC survey also immigrated after the age of sixty (Chinese, 21%; Filipino, 20%; Indian, 43%; Korean, 30%; Vietnamese, 44%, respectively). Over 40 percent of elders in the AAENYC survey are linguistically isolated because of poor English proficiency, an indication that many continue to live within the

TABLE 5.1 Percentage of Asian Elders (65+)
in the United States Who Are Foreign Born

NATIONALITY	PERCENTAGE
Vietnamese	97.4
Indian	95.7
Korean	93.8
Filipino	91.5
Chinese	86.7
Japanese	28.0

Source: Data from U.S. Census 2000.

confines of their families and ethnic communities. As a result, the Asian American community has a large number of elders who do not participate in mainstream U.S. society.

Late life immigration is culturally, socially, and economically driven. Many move to the United States to help their adult children with household chores, including child care, and others move because they have no sources of support in their home country. The cultural norm of co-residence with adult children is also a strong motivating factor for immigrating late in life. A core cultural value that dictates relationships in Asian families is filial obligation. In traditional Asian families, adult children are expected to live with their parents and care for them when they become frail.

This chapter examines the characteristics of traditional Asian families and the extent to which immigrant elders endorse these traditional values. As pointed out in earlier chapters, Asian cultures are diverse and to discuss traditional Asian families as if they represented a single prototype would be misleading. Traditional values and norms regarding families differ according to social class, geographical location within nations, historical political backgrounds, and migration patterns within the Asia Pacific region. Discussed in this chapter are the core characteristics that subsume such regional and social class variations.

TABLE 5.2 Age of Asian American Elders (65+) at Immigration

NATIONALITY	AFTER 40	AFTER 60
Vietnamese	89.9%	43.6%
Indian	79.1	43.0
Chinese	69.7	34.9
Filipino	65.0	34.7
Korean	67.9	30.2
Japanese	19.2	5.2

Source: Data from U.S. Census 2000.

CHARACTERISTICS OF TRADITIONAL ASIAN FAMILIES

FAMILY ORGANIZATION

There are two types of family systems in Asia: the patrilineal/patrilocal system and the bilateral system (Mason 1992). The former, based on a patriarchal ideology, is found in East Asia (China, Japan, Korea, and northern Vietnam) and in the northern part of South Asia (Bangladesh, northern India, Nepal, and Pakistan). The more egalitarian bilateral system is found in South-East Asia (Thailand, Indonesia, Philippines, and southern Vietnam) and in the southern areas of South Asia (southern India and Sri Lanka).

Patrilineal/patrilocal families are hierarchical in structure, and men have all the authority and decision-making powers. Men also have permanent membership in their natal families, and the family lineage is succeeded through them. The women are considered outsiders, having moved from their natal families into their husband's family at the time of marriage (Chung 1992; Koyano 1989; Min 1998). Men also have greater independence, personal autonomy, and educational opportunities compared to women, who occupy a marginalized position within the family and have little power. Because men are accorded more privilege, the preference for sons is stronger in patrilineal/patrilocal families than in bilateral families.

Family values and norms espoused by Confucianism is a prime example of a patriarchal ideology embedded in a patrilineal family system. According to Confucianism, human relationships can be categorized into five relationships (father-son, ruler-minister, husband-wife, older-younger siblings, and friend-friend), with specific rules pertaining to each. First, parent-child relationships are privileged over marital relationships. Among the five relationships, the father-son relationship is paramount; the father is expected to treat the son with care and kindness, and the son is expected to treat the father with honor, obedience, devotion, and respect (Ho 1994b; Ng 1998; Sung 1995). The Rule of Three Obediences dictates that women must first obey their fathers, then their husbands after marriage, and lastly their sons when widowed (Lim 1997).

In bilateral family systems both men and women have equal membership in their natal families, and emphasis is placed on the conjugal relationship rather than on cross-generational parent-child relationships. Whereas women move in with their husband's family in patrilineal/patrilocal systems, married couples in bilateral systems start their own families. Couples live near extended families or reside with the woman's parents rather than the man's parents (Mason 1992). Families in southern states of India such as Kerala are matriarchal where family lineage is succeeded through women (Mullatti 1995). Nonhierarchical kin networks play an important role in bilateral family systems. For example, in many Filipino families, extended family members such as second and third cousins are considered a core part of the family (Root 2005). Emotional rather than authoritarian connections between family members are also emphasized, as illustrated by the close mother-daughter connections in Indonesia and Thailand (Mason 1992). Gender roles in bilateral family systems are more egalitarian than those in patrilineal families, as seen in Indonesia (Piercy et al. 2005) Women in Filipino families command more respect than do women in East Asian and northern South Asian families (Root 2005). At the same time, researchers observe that *machismo* is an important part of the male culture because of the Spanish influence (Yap 1986).

FAMILY AND SELFHOOD

Regardless of family structure, the goals and needs of the family take precedence over the desires of individual members in traditional Asian families. Individuals are identified in terms of family membership and are expected to sacrifice their desires for the sake of the family (Agbayani-Siewert 1994; E. Lee and Mock 2005a). Clear differences exist in early childhood socialization between traditional Asian cultures and contemporary European American culture. European Americans are encouraged from a young age to develop a sense of self that is independent from others. Although there may be gender differences, children who grow up in Euro-American culture, on the whole, are taught to assert themselves and to value self-determination. Asians, on the other hand, are taught to suppress their wishes in the interest of the family and group, and to mold themselves according to the demands of the environment (Ho 1994a; Shibusawa 2001). Children in traditional Asian cultures are taught to respect the family hierarchy and the authority of grandparents, parents, and eldest sons. This respect for the family is also exhibited through doing well in school and society to honor for the sake of their family (Chao 1995).

In Indian families, emphasis is placed on family bonds. Value is placed on family collectivism and on loyalty and obedience to the family (Kakar 1978).

In India, over 80 percent of the population is Hindu and the notions of self and family are strongly influenced by Hinduism (Pillari 2005). The individual self is defined as an extension of the cosmic absolute and viewed as being part of a collective whole (Pettys and Balgopal 1998). The Indian self-identity is also defined by the family (Segal, 1991). Indian families place value on the extended family and discourage autonomy (Jambunathan and Counselman 2002). Studies indicate that Indian immigrants in Western countries continue to base their lifestyles on traditional values and expectations many years after immigration. They remain relatively collectivistic in orientation, emphasizing the extended family, traditional gender roles, obedience to elders, and group interdependence.

Filipino culture emphasizes loyalty and solidarity with family and kin groups. Individual interests or desires are sacrificed for the good of the family, and cooperation among family members is stressed over individualism (Agbayani-Siewert 1994). An individual's problems creates a loss of face for his or her family, suggesting that parents did not do their jobs, and there is a sense of shame (*hiya*) when individuals fail to meet an expected goal or do things that meet disapproval from their families (Agbayani-Siewert 1994). Filipino families also emphasize mutual support and the importance of belonging to the family (Wolf 1997). The sense of self is highly identified with family in Filipino culture (Tompar-Tiu and Sustento-Seneriches 1995). In addition, value is placed on "smooth relationships," and conflicts between people are minimized (Agbayani-Siewert 1994). People are discouraged from displaying anger or aggression, and are expected to behave in a passive, cooperative manner (Agbayani-Siewert 1994).

Traditional Chinese, Korean, Japanese, and Vietnamese cultures are heavily influenced by Confucianism, which dictates the position and roles of individuals within families. The sense of self is defined and expressed in relationship to others within a hierarchically structured family context. Expectations are placed on individuals to maintain social order and harmony by honoring the requirements and responsibilities of their family roles (Bond and Hwang 1986). Family roles are rigidly prescribed, and children are expected to obey and respect their parents and women are expected to submit to male members of their family (Kim and Choi 1994). Since individuals are defined by their family affiliation, any wrong doing on the part of an individual is considered to bring shame on their families. It is important, however, to note diversity within nation states that have been influenced by Confucianism. For example, in Japan, the extent to which Confucian norms dictated family ideologies differed according to social class. Confucianism was more entrenched among ruling class families than merchant class or agricultural families.

IMPORTANCE OF ANCESTORS

In Asian cultures, the spirits of ancestors and deceased family members are believed to dwell at the heart of the family and to guide the behavior of each of its members (Yee, Huang, and Lew 1998). In traditional and contemporary Indian cultures, adult children have a moral obligation not only to care for older parents, but also to continue nurturing them as ancestors after their deaths (Savishinský 2004). In Hinduism, the term *dharma*, which is translated as "duty" in English, incorporates both the prescribed roles of family members across the life cycle as well as loyalty to family, especially to children and aging parents. In Buddhist cultures, upon death, family members are considered to become spirits that protect their families. This belief is also reinforced by Confucian norms that institutionalized ancestor worship (Park and Cho 1995). Chinese show respect to their ancestors by honoring their deeds and memories and make offerings to assure that their spirits will protect them. In Korea, ancestors are thought to remain dependent on their children, and performing ritualized services to honor their spirits are considered as part of their filial obligations (Janelli and Janelli 1982). Vietnamese families also honor their ancestors by celebrating the anniversary of the death of a loved one and making offerings during important rituals marking life transitions, such as starting a new business.

FILIAL OBLIGATIONS TO ELDER CARE

Taking care of parents in old age is understood as a major part of carrying out filial obligations in Asian cultures. Until recently, placing elders in nursing homes was not viewed as an option in Asian countries. In fact, placing one's parents in a nursing home is still considered unacceptable in India (Pillari 2005). In Hinduism, fulfilling one's duty in this life means a release from the cycle of deaths and rebirths (*karma*) (Pettys and Balgopal 1998). Elders in India do not save for their old age, but depend on their children, especially sons, to provide for them (Gupta 2000). The cultural meaning of caregiving for the elderly is expressed as *seva*, or service to the elderly parents, and is understood as a form of reciprocation for the parents having given birth to the children and provided them with care when they were young (Vatuk 1990). In Filipino culture, children are indebted to parents for having given them birth, and life is considered an unsolicited gift that can never be repaid. In Chinese, Korean, Japanese and Vietnamese cultures caring for one's parents in old age is part of the Confucian norms.

CONCEPTUAL FRAMEWORK: ACCULTURATION

Acculturation affects Asian families in the United States in three main areas: (1) living arrangements, (2) status of elders in the family, and (3) availability of elder care. When immigrant families achieve financial stability after moving to the United States, family structure tends to change from extended three-generational units to nuclear units (adult parents and children) (E. Lee and Mock 2005). Families with older adults who are recent immigrants tend to live in multigenerational households, as the older generation has less facility with the English language and fewer financial resources. In newly arrived immigrant families, both men and women have to work, and the older generation provides help with housework and caring for the grandchildren. Acculturation often results in shifts in power between generations, and the discrepancy between traditional roles and new cultural demands is problematic for many older immigrants (Gelfand 1989). Younger generations often become more proficient in English and have difficulty communicating with older generations (Ou and McAdoo 1993). For the elders, their grandchildren's lack of fluency in their native language and strong identification with their host culture is perceived as a loss (Detzner 1996; Pettys and Balgopal 1998; Treas and Mazumdar 2004; Yee 1992).

As with other immigrant groups, Asian immigrant children compare images of parents in the host culture as a measuring stick to evaluate their own parents and grandparents. In contrast to Western families, many traditional Asian families do not physically express affection or demonstrate it openly in other ways. Asian immigrant parents also tend to stress academic achievement and family obligation (Dugsin 2001; Wu 2001). As a result of these cultural differences, Asian immigrant children who grow up watching European American families end up feeling a lack of affection from their parents and grandparents, which can result in increased distance between Asian elders and their grandchildren.

Research indicates that traditional values of family obligation have been transmitted to younger generations in Asian immigrant families. For example, a study of Chinese and Filipino adolescents in Northern California demonstrates that they have a strong sense of family obligation and tend to seek advice from their parents and siblings (Fuligini, Tseng, and Lam 1999). Overall, Asian adolescents in the study, compared to their white counterparts, had stronger cultural values and greater expectations about their duty to assist, respond, and support families. At the same time, a recent study of Korean and Vietnamese college students indicates that children of immigrants tend to idealize the "normal American family." The students' image of the American family is one where parents (1) are democratic; (2) respect the autonomy and individual well-being of their children; (3) encourage emotional expressiveness; (4) are intimate and emotionally nurturing; and (5) are supportive, understanding, and forgiving of their children (Pyke 2000). These students viewed their own families in a negative light compared to their idealized image of the American family. They saw their own parents as (1) having high expectations for duty and responsibility; (2) emphasizing the importance of family over the individual; (3) being overly strict; and (4) being emotionally distant. As their children and grandchildren acculturate into mainstream U.S. society, many older Asian immigrants face the need to find a balance between holding on to the traditional cultural values of their homeland and adapting to the family norms of U.S. society.

Immigration also decreases the availability for elder care in the family. In most newly arrived immigrant families, men and women both need to compete in the labor market to make ends meet, which results in fewer family members able to provide care for elders in the home. In working-class immigrant families, employment, though often low-wage, is more available to immigrant women than to men (Espiritu 1997). Women have more opportunities in the garment and microelectronic industries (Espiritu 1997). In families that operate small businesses such as grocery stores, women work with their husbands to reduce labor costs (Min 1998). Among Filipinos, it is usually the women, as is the case with health care professionals, who sponsor their families to immigrate to the United States (Espiritu 1997).

MEASURES

The Traditional Family Values Endorsement Scale elicits the extent to which elders uphold traditional cultural values. The scale consists of twelve statements designed to examine the elders' cultural beliefs regarding extended family, nuclear family, elder care responsibilities, marriage, divorce, gender roles, and family living arrangements. Elders indicated the level of importance of each statement on a 4-point scale (not at all important=0 to very important=3). High scores indicated a strong endorsement of traditional Asian cultural beliefs about families.

The twelve statements were the following:

1. Knowing family ancestry and lineage (i.e., tracing the family tree)
2. Knowing one's extended family and having close relationships with them
3. Remembering family ancestors who have died and honoring them on anniversaries and special occasions
4. Acknowledging the eldest son as an authority figure in the absence of the father
5. Children respecting and obeying their parents
6. Children living with their parents
7. Elders being able to rely on their children for support
8. Parents being entitled to receive care from their children in return for the sacrifices they have made for their children
9. Meeting family obligations for elder care
10. Families, and not the government, caring for elders
11. Obtaining parental approval for a marriage partner
12. Adult children not letting their family down by divorcing

Factor analysis was conducted to extract components of these attitudinal variables. The three components extracted were (1) importance of ancestors and extended family: 3 items, $\alpha = .84$; (2) parental authority: 4 items, $\alpha = .80$; and (3) filial responsibility: 5 items, $\alpha = .86$.

The following variables were then included to examine the factors associated with the attitudinal components:

Acculturation was measured by the length of stay in the United States and by English proficiency, which is a composite score (0–9) of the respondents' ability to read, write, and speak English (each item was assessed on a 4-point scale: not at all =0 to very well=3).

Family relationship was measured by satisfaction with family, which is a single-item measure that evaluates the quality of the relationship between generations by asking elders to respond to the question, "How satisfied are you with your relationship with your family at the present time?"

Perceived generation gap is a global measure that asked elders to assess the degree to which their opinions about beliefs and expectations about family differ from those of their adult children, on a 4-point scale (not at all important = 0 to very important = 3).

Assistance from children was assessed by counting the number of times that children provided instrumental, financial, and emotional assistance.

Religiosity was measured by respondents' perception of the level of importance of religion in their lives on a 4-point scale (not at all important = 0 to very important = 3).

Self-rated health was assessed on a 5-point scale, with the lowest score indicating poor health (excellent = 1 to poor = 5).

Unmet needs were measured by asking respondents whether they could have used much more help the past year with tasks of daily living such as shopping, housecleaning, cooking, and transportation. The responses were assessed on a 4-point scale (could have used a lot more help = 1 to received all the help needed = 4).

Backup help availability was measured on a 4-point scale by asking respondents whether there were people on whom they could count for help (most of the time = 1 to not at all = 4); and whether they have a confidant or someone they feel close to (yes/no).

Willingness to seek help was assessed by asking the participants whether they discussed problems with others (yes/no).

RESULTS

The percentages of elders, according to national origin groups, endorsing traditional cultural values are shown in table 5.3, and endorsement according to gender and age (young-old, old-old) is presented in table 5.4.

IMPORTANCE OF ANCESTORS AND EXTENDED FAMILY

The majority of respondents except for Chinese elders agreed that knowing one's ancestors and family history was important. There were no differences based on gender or age. The same group felt that having close relationships

TABLE 5.3 Percentages of Asian American Elders (65+) Endorsing Family Values as Important, by Asian National Origin Groups

	CHINESE	FILIPINO	INDIAN	JAPANESE	KOREAN	VIETNAMESE
Importance of ancestors/extended family [3 items (0-9), α=.84] (mean)	**5.59**[a]	**8.38**[b]	**6.73**[c]	**7.25**[c]	**6.82**[c]	**8.92**[c]
Know your family ancestry and history****	61.2	94.2	92.0	96.0	81.8	100
Have close relationship with extended family****	56.9	98.0	98.0	96.0	83.8	100
Remember dead family members on the anniversaries of their deaths or on special occasions****	71.0	98.1	92.0	92.0	67.7	100
Parental authority [4 items (0-12), α=.80] (mean)	**8.73**[a]	**10.13**[b]	**7.67**[c]	**6.63**[d]	**9.92**[b]	**11.16**[e]
Adult son should be the decision maker in the absence of the father****	66.3	80.4	46.5	40.0	90.9	100
Children are obliged to obey/respect parents****	89.2	96.1	91.0	92.0	93.0	100
Adult children should get their parents' approval when they select their mates****	70.7	71.1	68.0	44.0	84.7	92.0
Adult children should not let their family down by divorcing****	76.0	90.4	88.0	44.0	96.0	92.0
Filial responsibility [5 items (0-15), α=.86] (mean)	**11.11**[a]	**10.27**[a]	**11.66**[a]	**10.63**[a]	**8.21**[b]	**14.16**[c]
Your children live with you****	69.7	66.7	96.0	88.0	50.5	92.0
You can rely on your children for support****	83.2	63.5	96.0	96.0	37.5	100
Parents are entitled to return from children****	80.4	59.8	84.0	72.0	45.3	100
Elder care should be shared by family****	85.1	76.5	96.0	96.0	65.3	100
Family should not let government take care of elders in any circumstances****	78.9	78.4	93.9	96.0	58.2	100

(continued)

TABLE 5.3 *continued*

	CHINESE	FILIPINO	INDIAN	JAPANESE	KOREAN	VIETNAMESE
Perceived generation gap****						
All in all, how much do you think your opinions about these family values differ from those of your children?						
Not at all	3.0	8.5	0.0	0.0	7.1	0.0
Only in small ways	20.2	23.4	10.4	4.6	31.5	27.3
In some ways	61.6	57.5	78.1	86.3	39.8	31.8
In very important ways	15.2	10.6	11.5	9.1	21.4	40.9

Note: Percentages were tested using Chi-square statistics.

ANOVA statistics with Tukey's post hoc multiple comparisons were used to test the differences between means.

[a,b,c,d,e] Means with the different letters are significantly different at less than the .05 level in the same variable.

****** $p < .0001$.

TABLE 5.4 Percentage of Endorsement of Family Values by Gender and Age

	GENDER		AGE	
	Male	Female	Young-old	Old-old
Importance of extended family				
Know your family ancestry and history	78.6	85.0	85.3	75.8
Have close relationship with extended family	82.7	85.3	89.7*	72.6*
Remember dead family members on the anniversary of their death or on special occasions	81.5	83.3	85.6*	74.6*
Parental authority				
Adult son should be the decision maker in the absence of the father	63.8	74.5	66.9	75.6
Children are obliged to obey/respect parents	91.6	93.0	93.7	89.2
Adult children should get their parents' approval when they select their mates	71.5	74.5	74.4	70.1
Adult children should not let their family down by divorcing	83.8	88.6	86.2	82.0
Filial responsibility				
Your children live with you	83.0*	66.7*	76.9	67.2
You can rely on your children for support	86.4*	65.5*	76.3	71.3
Parents are entitled to return from their children	80.0*	64.6*	71.4	71.3
Elder care should be shared by family	89.4*	78.7*	84.1	82.3
Family should not let government take care of elders in any circumstances	84.5	75.8	81.7	75.4
Perceived generational gap				
All in all, how much do you think your opinions about these family values differ from those of your children?				
Not at all	3.0	4.2	3.1	4.8
Only in small ways	17.7	22.8	20.0	21.8
In some ways	65.1	54.9	60.0	58.1
In very important ways	14.2	18.1	16.9	15.3

Note: Chi-square statistics were used.
* $p < .05$

with extended family was important. Here there were no gender differences, but there were differences based on age. Having close relationships with extended family was more important to the young-old than the old-old. A larger number of Filipino, Indian, Japanese, and Vietnamese than that of Korean and Chinese elders felt it was very important to know and remember ancestors. No gender differences were noted, but remembering ancestors was more important to the young-old than the old-old.

ROLE OF THE OLDEST SON AND FILIAL OBLIGATION

More Filipino, Korean, and Vietnamese elders felt that, in the absence of the father, the eldest son, rather than the mother, should make important decisions about the family. Among all the elders, 65 percent believed that this tradition was either somewhat or very important. The Japanese and Indian elders were the most apt to feel that this was not important, and the Chinese elders were almost evenly distributed in their opinions across all three rankings (very important, 29.7%; somewhat, 36.6%; not at all, 33.7%). Most elders felt that it was important for children to obey and respect their parents; no gender or age differences were observed here. Ethnic differences emerged regarding the belief that adult children should obtain parents' approval when selecting a marriage partner. Whereas only 44 percent of Japanese elders believed this was important, the majority of other ethnic elders believed that it was. Likewise, only 44 percent of Japanese elders believed that adult children should not disappoint their family by divorcing, and the majority felt otherwise. Overall, Vietnamese, Filipino, and Korean elders most highly endorsed parental authority.

FILIAL RESPONSIBILITY

A large majority of Vietnamese, Indian, and Japanese elders believed that their adult children should live with them, a belief endorsed by only half the Korean elders (50.5%). Similarly, only 37.5 percent of Korean elders felt that they could rely on their children for support or that parents were entitled to receive returns from their children for the sacrifices they had made for them. Indian (83.5%), Japanese (96.0%), and Chinese (96.0%) elders believed that they could rely on their children for support. Only two-thirds of the Filipino elders (63.5%) believed that they could rely on their children. All Vietnamese (100%) and most Indian (96%), Japanese (96%), and Chinese (85.1%) elders felt that elder care should be shared by the family. They also believed that the family should not allow the government to take care of its elders (100%, 93.9%, and 96%, respectively). Less than 60 percent of Korean elders believed that government should not be involved in caring for elders.

Women and men had differences regarding filial responsibilities. More men endorsed all the items. The greatest difference between women and men was the belief that it is important to be able to rely on their children for support. Whereas 86 percent of men endorsed this belief, only 66 percent of women felt it was important.

Gender, family relationships, health, and help seeking were associated with a belief in filial responsibility and the expectation that one's children would provide elder care ($R^2 = .32$; $p < .01$). That expectation was preeminent among males, among those satisfied with their family, those receiving help from adult children, those with unmet needs, and those lacking backup help.

GENERATION GAP

Overall, a large number of elders reported experiencing the generation gap with their children in some important ways (Chinese, 6.8%; Filipino, 68.1%; Indian, 88.6%; Japanese, 95.1%; Korean, 61.2%; and Vietnamese, 72.7%). The group with the highest percentage reporting this was the Vietnamese (40.9%), followed by the Koreans (21.4%).

FACTORS ASSOCIATED WITH TRADITIONAL CULTURAL VALUES AND EXPECTATIONS TOWARD FAMILY

Multiple regression analyses were conducted to examine the effects of the demographic and sociocultural variables on each of the attitudinal factors. Each of the three attitudinal factors was regressed with sociodemographic variables, acculturation, family relationships, health and help seeking, and religiosity. The sociodemographic variables included gender, age, financial status (using Medicaid as a proxy of income), and living arrangements. Table 5.5 presents the results of the multiple regression models on (1) the importance of extended family, (2) parental authority, and (3) filial responsibility/expectation for elder care. Only respondents who had children were included in the analysis ($n = 378$).

IMPORTANCE OF EXTENDED FAMILY AND KNOWING ABOUT ANCESTORS

Gender, age, acculturation, satisfaction with children, and religiosity were associated with belief in the importance of extended family and ancestors ($R^2 = .24$; $p < .001$). Being female, being young, having resided in the United States for a shorter period, poor English proficiency, dissatisfaction with one's family, and a higher level of religiosity were associated with a belief in the importance of extended family and knowing about one's ancestors.

PARENTAL AUTHORITY

Gender, financial status, family relationships, health, help seeking, and religiosity were associated with a belief in parental authority ($R^2 = .38$; $p < .0001$). Being female, the need for financial assistance, dissatisfaction with one's family, poor health, fewer unmet needs, a lack of confidence, and a higher level of religiosity were all associated with a belief in parental authority.

DISCUSSION

Because of the small sample size of the Filipino, Japanese, and Vietnamese elder groups, generalizing the findings of these sample groups to the larger national origin groups is not possible. Certain findings, however, do warrant discussion. For example, it is notable that a large majority of only the Chinese did not believe that extended family was important or knowing about one's ancestors. This is surprising, given the emphasis that traditional Chinese culture places on ancestor worship. The survey results may be associated with the fact that Confucian philosophy and other religions were banned during the Cultural Revolution in China (E. Lee and Mock 2005). Filipino and Vietnamese elders had the highest endorsement rates regarding the importance of parental authority, and the Japanese elders had the lowest. Japanese elders in our study were the most acculturated, which may explain their low endorsement of the importance of parental authority. Overall, the Vietnamese elders had the highest endorsement regarding filial responsibilities, and Korean elders had the lowest. Many Korean elders also reported experiencing the generation gap with their adult children. Our findings concur with previous research, which indicates that Korean elders have low expectations regarding their adult children (Kauh 1997).

Few differences in attitude were found based on age (i.e., between the young-old and the old-old groups). The one exception was the belief regarding ancestors and extended family. The young-old endorsed these values more frequently, possibly because these immigrants had arrived in the U.S. more recently and so had stronger feelings about their ancestors in their own daily lives as well as about their relationships with their extended family in their home country.

It is noteworthy that gender differences were apparent only regarding beliefs concerning filial responsibility. More men than women endorsed the

TABLE 5.5 Regression Models of Traditional Family Values on Asian Elders Who Had Children

INDEPENDENT VARIABLE	IMPORTANCE OF EXTENDED FAMILY b(SE)	PARENTAL AUTHORITY b(SE)	FILIAL RESPONSIBILITY b(SE)
Sociodemographics			
Gender (male=1)	−.50(.25)*	−.55(.28)*	.92(.39)
Age (65–96)	−.05(02)*		
Medicaid (yes=1; proxy of income)		.60(.27)*	
Living alone (yes=1)			
Acculturation			
Length of stay in the U.S. (1-72)	−.03(.01)*		
English proficiency (0-9)	−.12(.05)**		
Family relationship			
Satisfaction with children (1-4)	−.50(.17)***	−.48(.19)*	.78(.27)**
Receiving help from children (0-8)			.36(.09)****
Giving help to children (0-8)			
Perceived generational gap (0-3)			
Caring for grandchildren (yes=1)			
Health and help seeking			
Self-rated health (1-5)		−.36(.11)**	
Unmet needs (0-3)		−.26(.13)*	.57(.18)**
Backup help availability (0-3)			−.74(.19)***
Willingness to seek help (yes=1)			
Having confidant (yes=1)		−1.49(.31)***	
Religiosity (0-3)	.38(.13)**	.37(.14)**	
R2 Total	.24**	.38****	.32**
Adjusted R2 Total	.19****	.34****	.27**

Note: High scores indicate favorable ratings except for unmet needs and a perceived generation gap.
* $p<.05$.
** $p<.01$.
*** $p<.001$.
**** $p<.0001$.

values of filial obligation and believed that parents should live with their adult children and that parents should be able to rely on their children for support, and that elder care should be provided by the family. The fact that filial responsibilities usually rest on women's shoulders may account for these gender differences. Because women generally are the ones who care for older parents, especially when living in the same household, they may feel burdened by this traditional expectation. As a result, they may not be as inclined as men to believe in the importance of filial responsibility.

The findings of the multivariate analyses suggest that elderly women are more likely than men to believe in the importance of the extended family and honoring the memory of ancestors, possibly because it is the women who usually make sure that the rituals for honoring ancestors are maintained even though the actual rituals may be carried out by men. Women also tend to maintain contacts with extended family members, whereas men do not. Elders who are less acculturated are also more likely than those who are acculturated to place importance on honoring ancestors and the extended family. Acculturation, however, is not associated with beliefs regarding the importance of parental authority or filial responsibility. The importance of the extended family and honoring ancestors may be more abstract than parental authority and filial responsibility, which are based on concrete interactive experiences between respondents and their children. Apparently acculturation does not affect the expectations that elders have toward their adult children. At the same time, elders who are less satisfied with their children are more likely to endorse the importance of ancestors and extended family than those who are satisfied with their children. The dissatisfaction of elders toward their children may stem from the fact that their children do not adhere to their parents' belief about the importance of ancestors and extended family. Religiosity is also associated with beliefs in the importance of extended family and honoring ancestors. This is not surprising, since Buddhism and Hinduism view ancestors as spiritual entities that protect the family.

Elders who believe in the importance of parental authority are likely to be women, to be in financial need, dissatisfied with family relationships, in poor health, have fewer unmet needs, lack confidence, and value religion compared to their counterparts who do not hold this belief. Elders in financial need and in poor health may receive financial assistance and care from their adult children, which may reinforce their belief in the importance of parental authority. The same may be true for elders whose needs are met. Elders may feel that their children meet their needs out of respect for parental authority. On the other hand, elders with more unmet needs may lose their own sense of parental authority and therefore lose any belief in parental authority that they may have had. Elders who are dissatisfied with their family relationships may think that their lives would be better if they had more authority over their children. Adult children of elders who have high expectations of them may keep more distance from their parents, which in turn may lead to dissatisfaction among these elders. Those who believe in parental authority may not be as likely to have their children as confidants, because asserting their authority may preclude their need to confide in their children. That women are more likely to believe in parental authority may be the result of their socialization. As mentioned previously, in patrilineal/patrilocal families, men have more authority than women. Since men are usually the head of the family, women in their roles as mothers may believe that they need to teach their children to respect their fathers.

Men are more likely than women to believe in the importance of filial responsibilities. That women are less likely to endorse the importance of filial responsibility may be owing to their experiences of having struggled with elder care as daughters-in-law, resulting in their wish not to impose the same burden on their children. Elders who believe in the importance of filial responsibility are more likely to be satisfied with their children. From a Western perspective, this association may seem counterintuitive. In a study with primarily non-Hispanic, white American elders, Lee and colleagues (1994) reported that expectations of filial responsibility were associated with aid given to children but not with aid received from children. The researchers argued that expectations for filial responsibility may lead elders to be dissatisfied with their adult children because their expectations toward filial responsibilities are not fulfilled (Lee, Netzer, and Coward 1994). Asian elders, on the other hand, may feel satisfaction that they succeeded in inculcating their children with the values of filial responsibility. This reasoning can be applied to the positive association with receiving help from children. On the other hand, elders who have more unmet needs and who do not have backup help also are more likely to believe in filial responsibility. These elders may believe that their needs would be better met if their children provided more care for them.

In sum, this chapter examined traditional values and beliefs regarding the family. It is often assumed that Asian elders steadfastly hold on to traditional norms about the family, and that they expect their children to fulfill their obligations and responsibilities. Most research analyzes traditional beliefs about the family as if it were one-dimensional. Our findings indicate that there are three different components to these traditional beliefs and that the endorsement of these beliefs differs by national origin groups, age, gender, and level of acculturation. When working with Asian elders who struggle with family conflicts, it is important not only to assess the extent to which they hold on to traditional values about the family but also to understand the specific aspects of the values they consider important.

6

INFORMAL SUPPORT AND INTERGENERATIONAL RELATIONSHIPS

THE PREVIOUS CHAPTER DISCUSSED the norms and structure of traditional families, presented the extent to which elders endorsed these values, and examined the factors associated with these beliefs. This chapter examines the elders' social and family relationships by assessing their social support network and intergenerational exchanges.

SOCIAL SUPPORT AND ELDERS

The two major components of social relationships are their structure and function. The structural aspect, or social networks, is conceptualized as the existence or the number of relationships (Berkman 1985). The size of social networks is important, especially for older adults, because support is more likely to be available at any given time when there is a larger number of people in one's network. Social networks also promote social integration by providing elders with a place to socialize, retain group membership, and maintain social roles. Elders with small social networks are vulnerable, as the inevitable loss of loved ones diminishes the availability of support (Angel, Angel, and Henderson 1997). Asians who immigrate in mid-life and in later life are likely to have smaller social networks than people who "age in place," because immigration often results in loss of social support networks. The size of an elder's family is important, for it indicates the potential number of people that can provide support. For example, older adults without children or who only have one child are significantly more likely to be living alone compared to elders who have more children (Soldo, Wolf, and Agree 1990).

Social support refers to the quality and utilitarian aspects of the relationships. Social support contributes to elders' well-being through personal interactions that mitigate the negative effects of daily stressors (Antonucci 1990). Social support is also associated with health outcomes in older adults. Having supportive family and friends can lower the risks of decline in overall function and diseases such as cancer (Berkman 1995). In addition to providing access to information about health and health care services, social support networks promote the physical well-being of elders by encouraging healthy behaviors and rendering tangible aid (Thoits 1995). The quality of social support is usually assessed subjectively and determined by an elder's perception of the relationship (Angel, Angel, and Henderson 1997). In fact, perceived support has been found to have stronger buffering effects against stressful life events than the objective amount of support available (Wethington and Kessler 1986). The most common measures used to assess social support networks of elders include (1) density, (2) size, (3) homogeneity, (4) number of interactions exchanged within the dyad, (5) reciprocity or symmetry of exchanges, (6) geographical proximity, and (7) nature of the relationship (Antonucci 1990).

Most studies on social support among Asian elders focus on their relationship with their adult children. Little information is available about the relationships elders have with their siblings, extended family members, and neighbors. The few available studies indicate that smaller social networks are associated with higher rates of depression among Asian American elders (Lee, Crittenden, and Yu 1996). For older immigrants who have small social networks, adult children are often the only source of support. The need to rely on adult children is especially pronounced among elders with limited finances. Elders who immigrate late in life tend to be less financially stable, to lack health insurance, and to be under- or unemployed compared to native-born elders or those who immigrate earlier in life (Angel et al. 1999; Wilmoth 2004). Not surprisingly, immigrant elders have higher rates of living with their extended family compared to native-born elders and younger immigrants (Burr and Mutchler 1993).

CONCEPTUAL FRAMEWORK: SOCIAL EXCHANGE AND INTERGENERATIONAL SOLIDARITY

This chapter is guided by the framework of social exchange and intergenerational solidarity. Social exchange theory analyzes how people provide support to one another from a cost-benefit model of human interaction. Originally taken from economic theory and the theory of operant conditioning, social exchange theory sets forth a set of propositions regarding social behavior (Emerson 1972). The utility theory of economics stipulates that humans try to obtain maximum benefits in exchanges, and the theory of operant conditioning purports that humans seek positive reinforcement in their relationships. Social exchange theory contends that people, when given alternatives in social interaction, will chose activities that bring material or psychological rewards or both of higher value than their costs.

The notion of applying economic theory to human behavior has been criticized on the grounds that it "dehumanizes" people, characterizing them as passive actors responding only to reward/cost contingencies; nevertheless, the theory has been effective in testing and exploring relationships between elders and their surroundings. Two main gerontological theories based on social exchange are disengagement and modernization. Disengagement theory is based on the notion that elders become disengaged from social interactions as they age, as they have fewer resources such as income and physical strength that they can exchange with others (Dowd 1975). According to this theory, elders remove themselves from unbalanced relationships where they receive more than they give. Modernization theory contends that older adults in traditional societies enjoy a higher status, because their resources are valued more than in industrialized societies (Cowgill and Holmes 1972). This theory has been used to explain why elders in Asia enjoy a higher status than their counterparts in Western nations (Palmore and Maeda 1985). Social exchange theory also posits that elders lose authority in their families when they can no longer provide for their family (Brackbill and Kitch 1991). At the same time, some researchers have challenged the universal assumption that elders receive more than they give. A prime example is grandparents who assume primary responsibility for their grandchildren.

Intergenerational relationships between older parents and adult children are based on a lifelong pattern of family experiences and exchange (Bengtson and Roberts 1991). The solidarity or cohesiveness of the relationship between elders and their adult children can be examined from the following six dimensions:

1. *Structure*: the geographic distance that constrains or enhances interaction between family members
2. *Association*: the frequency of contact and activities shared by family members

3. *Affect*: the feelings of emotional closeness between family members
4. *Consensus*: the agreement among family members about values and lifestyles
5. *Function*: the exchange of instrumental support between family members
6. *Norms*: obligations that family members feel toward one another

Studies of adult children who care for older parents indicate that adult daughters are motivated to provide support because of affectional ties, whereas adult sons are motivated by obligation (norms) and frequency of contact (association) (Silverstein, Parrott, and Bengtson 1995). Strong filial obligations are also associated with providing instrumental support to older parents but not emotional support (Silverstein and Litwak 1993). As discussed in chapter 5, filial obligation is a primary characteristic of traditional Asian families. In India, caring for one's parents (*seva*) is a way for adult children to reciprocate having been born and raised by them. In China, Korea, Japan, and Vietnam, the Confucian values of filial piety are the foundation of intergenerational relationships (Le 1997; Sung 1998). Filial piety, like *seva*, is based on the belief that children must reciprocate for the care they received from their parents (Sung 1998).

ASIAN AMERICAN ELDERS AND INTERGENERATIONAL RELATIONSHIPS

We do not know the extent to which Asian immigrants adhered to traditional family norms while in their home country. Industrialization and urbanization are bringing about profound changes in family relationships in Asian countries, and so we cannot assume that changes that occur in Asian immigrant families are solely the result of acculturation. For example, the number of multigenerational families has been steadily decreasing in countries such as Japan and Korea. Encountering and adjusting to new values and norms set forth by the younger generation is a common task during mid- and late adulthood in most countries. Moving to the United States, however, can intensify the challenges families face in negotiating the balance between continuities and discontinuities. Common changes that occur in Asian families as a result of moving to the United States include (1) fewer multigenerational family structures and more nuclear families, (2) erosion of the patriarchal family structure, (3) an increase in bilateral family structures, (4) equal importance placed on sons and daughters, (5) fewer arranged marriages, (6) women joining the labor market, and (7) children leaving home at college age (Lee and Mock 2005).

A greater number of older Asian immigrants live with extended families compared to white elders (Wilmoth 2001). Although the assumption is that living with adult children is a cultural preference (Koh and Bell 1987), there are a number of reasons for co-residence including health, disability, socioeconomic status, number of children, and availability of services (Wilmoth 2001; Yee, Huang, and Lew 1998). Immigration and welfare policies also influence co-residence by dictating the extent to which families are responsible for immigrant elders. Current immigration policies mandate that those who are sponsoring family members must provide evidence that they can support the immigrants financially until the latter become citizens (Wilmoth 2004). Recent changes in federal policies have also made it more difficult for elders to rely on government resources. The Personal Responsibility and Work Opportunity Reconciliation Act of 1996, known as the Welfare Reform Act, exclude legal immigrants who arrived after August 1996 from receiving means-tested benefits including Supplemental Security Income (SSI), Medicaid, and food stamps for five years following their arrival (Lim and Resko 2002).

Studies suggest that acculturation encourages elders to live separately from their adult children (Ishii-Kuntz 1997; Lan 2002; Wong, Yoo, and Stewart 2006; Yoo and Sung 1997). Some research indicates that elders move out of their children's homes not out of choice but because of conflicts with their children. Problems with daughters-in-law are often presented as a main source of conflict. Other studies indicate that elders prefer to live on their own. Among Korean Americans, the rate of co-residence decreased from 75 percent in 1980 to 57 percent in 1990 (Yoo and Sung 1997). Financial resources are a major factor contributing to Asian elders living on their own. A study of Asian immigrants, based on 1990 Census data, indicates that immigrants with higher incomes are significantly less likely to live with extended family (Wilmoth, DeJong, and Himes 1997). The availability of low-cost senior housing and SSI benefits enable immigrant elders with limited financial resources to live independently (Yoo and Sung 1997).

The availability of resources within ethnic communities also influences living arrangements of Asian elders. Elders whose children live in the suburbs may prefer to live in senior housing located in the center of ethnic communities where they have access to senior programs and community-based social services (Shibusawa, Lubben, and Kitano 2001). Participation in senior programs promotes social integration, and services such as congregate enhance elders' ability to live independently without relying on their children.

In Western societies, elders dread having to depend on their adult children because of the value they place on independence and autonomy (Hockey and James 1993). In Western cultures, independence and dependence are polar opposites, and relationships are viewed from a strict either/or perspective. In discussing dependency among elders, Hockey and James (1993) note that dependency is acceptable in Western society only if it is limited to a certain time period. When it persists beyond a culturally arbitrated period, the individual is seen as a burden.

Studies among elders in the United States suggest that the most important factor underlying self-esteem among the elderly is not the care they receive from families but independence, or lack thereof, in economic, physical, social, or emotional spheres (Stoller 1985). In a society where the main thrust is to be self-reliant, elderly who are unable to cope on their own are thought to suffer from embarrassment, shame, a sense of failure, or all three.

In traditional Asian societies, dependency is viewed from the perspective of interdependence, in which mutual dependence is emphasized. In traditional patriarchal families, men relinquish their authority as head of the family to their eldest sons when no longer able to act as the head of the household. However, interdependence between the older fathers and adult children are maintained because of the status accorded the elders as possessing a wealth of knowledge that can be imparted to the younger generation. For example, age sixty is celebrated as an important milestone in many Asian countries, including China, Korea, Japan, and Vietnam. The twelve-year animal zodiac cycle has five elements, and age sixty, which marks the completion of the entire cycle, is viewed as a time to return to the astrological combination of one's birth (Doi 1991). In Japan, the traditional custom for celebrating one's sixtieth birthday is to don a red baby cap and vest, symbolizing the return to babyhood. Under the traditional patrilineal family structure, it was customary for a man to retire as the head of the household at age sixty and pass control of the family on to his eldest son. It is said that his wife passed on the *oshamoji* (rice paddle) to the eldest son's wife, symbolizing the transfer of household responsibilities to the daughter-in-law.

Once retired as head of the household, the elderly couple continued to provide important supplementary labor by babysitting, doing chores, and helping with the family enterprise. Although the elderly disengaged from responsibility, their situation differed from the Western notion of "disengagement" in that the elderly couple retained the status as the "elders" of the family.

MEASURES

We examined the informal social support network of Asian American elders and factors associated with intergenerational exchange: giving help to children and receiving help from them. *Structural and associational solidarity* were measured by single-item indicators of family size: (1) number of children living in the United States, (2) number of children living outside the United States, (3) number of children living within two hours' driving distance, (4) frequency of face-to-face and phone contact with children, (6) number of siblings living in New York City, (7) number of relatives other than children and siblings, (8) number of relatives with regular contact, and (9) number of helpful neighbors. *Affectional solidarity* was measured by the desire to see children more frequently, and *functional solidarity* was examined by asking the elders about (1) the kind of assistance they provided to their children, (2) the kind of assistance they received from them, and (3) whether they provided care for their grandchildren. The responses to these questions were dichotomous (yes/no). *Normative solidarity* was measured by asking about a *perceived generation gap*, a global measure that asks elders to assess the degree to which their opinions about beliefs and expectations about family differs from those of their adult children (4-point scale: not at all important = 0 to very important = 3). To assess the need for support, we asked information in two areas: (1) availability of backup support, and (2) unmet needs. *Availability of backup support* was assessed by asking elders how often someone they could count was there to help when extra assistance was needed with tasks of daily living (TDLs) such as shopping, housecleaning, cooking, and transportation. The elders were asked to respond to a 4-point Likert-like scale (most of the time = 1 to not at all = 4). *Unmet needs* were measured by asking respondents whether they could have used a lot more help with the TDLs cited above during the past year. The responses were assessed on a 4-point scale (could have used a lot more help = 1 to received all the help needed = 4). *Acculturation* was measured by the length of stay in the United States and by English proficiency, which is a composite score (0–9) of the respondents' ability to read, write, and speak English (each item was assessed on a 4-point scale: not at all = 0 to very well = 3). *Religiosity* was assessed by respondents' perception of the level of importance of religion in their lives on a 4-point scale (not at all important = 0 to very important = 3). *Self-rated health* was assessed on a 5-point scale, with the lowest score indicating poor health (excellent = 1 to poor = 5).

RESULTS

SOCIAL NETWORK AND SUPPORT

FAMILY COMPOSITION Table 6.1 presents the structural aspects of social support among our respondents. The majority of the elders had at least 1 child living in the United States (*n* = 359; 88%). On average, the elders had 2.6 children living in the United States and 1.2 children living elsewhere. Vietnamese elders reported the largest number of children living in the United States (mean = 3.2) followed by Chinese (mean = 3), and Filipino, Indian, and Korean elders (mean = 2.3, 2.4, and 2.4, respectively). The Japanese elders had the fewest children living in the U.S. (mean = 2). Filipino and Indian elders reported the largest number of children living outside the United States (mean = 1.8 and 1.7, respectively). The average number of children living within a two-hour drive of their parents was between 1 and 2.

CONTACT WITH CHILDREN Close to 40 percent of the respondents saw their children every day, and 22.7 percent saw them at least once a week. The Indian respondents were the most likely to report seeing their children every day or weekly (84%), followed by Chinese (61.9%), Korean (57%), Japanese (50%), Vietnamese (48%), and Filipino (44.3%). Over 29 percent of all respondents spoke on the phone with their children daily.

SIBLINGS, RELATIVES, AND NEIGHBORS There were no significant differences among the ethnic groups, with all reporting, on average, less than one sibling living in the New York City area. There were significant differences in the number of other relatives in their social network. The Chinese (mean = 2.3) and Indian (mean = 2.1) elders had the most other relatives in their social network, and the Vietnamese (mean = 0.3) elders had the fewest. Although Indian and Chinese elders reported having, on average, at least one relative with whom they were close, the average number for other national groups was less than one. There was a wider range in the average number of helpful neighbors (0.9 to 3.1). Japanese and Indian elders reported the highest number of helpful neighbors (mean = 3.2 and 3.1, respectively), and Chinese elders reported having an average of less than one helpful neighbor.

ASSISTANCE TO CHILDREN As seen in table 6.2, Asian elders reported assisting their children in six different areas: 56.2 percent did so when someone was ill; 44.7 percent kept house for them; 41.4 percent shopped or ran errands for them; 60.7 percent gave advice on running a home or bringing up a child (grandchild); 34.7 percent fixed things around their house; and 22.4 percent assisted them financially. Overall, a larger portion of Indian, Japanese, Filipino, and Vietnamese elders provided assistance to their children. Indian elders (71.4%) were the most likely and Chinese elders the least likely (24.4%) to assist their children with housekeeping. Indian elders were the most likely (78%) and Korean elders (7%) the least likely to fix things around their children's houses. Japanese elders (47.6%) and Indian elders (46.2%) were the most likely and Vietnamese and Korean elders (both 5.6%) the least likely to assist their children financially. Indian and Japanese elders (64%) were the most likely and Korean elders (21%) the least likely to run errands for their children. Conversely, Korean elders (66.3%) were the most likely and Indian elders (8.8%) the least likely to give their children advice about housekeeping or child rearing. Indian elders (89%) were the most likely and Korean elders (32.6%) the least likely to help their children when someone was ill. Close to 30 percent of all elders reported that they helped care for their grandchildren. Indian elders (60.5%) were the most likely and Japanese elders (6.3%) the least likely to provide care for their grandchildren on a regular basis.

ASSISTANCE FROM CHILDREN More elders reported receiving assistance from their children than giving it to them. More than half the respondents reported receiving assistance from their children in six out of the eight activities: 84.1 percent of the elders received help from their children when they were ill, 70.4 percent received help with shopping or running errands, 62.4

TABLE 6.1 Social Support Network: Comparison by Asian National Origin Groups

	CHINESE (n=105)	FILIPINO (n=52)	INDIAN (n=100)	JAPANESE (n=25)	KOREAN (n=100)	VIETNAMESE (n=25)	TOTAL (N=407)
	MEAN	MEAN	MEAN	MEAN	MEAN	MEAN	MEAN
Average number of children in the U.S.	3.0[a]	2.3[b]	2.4[c]	2.0[d]	2.4[e]	3.2[a]	2.6
Average number of children outside the U.S.	.6[a]	1.8[b]	1.7[c]	.1[a]	1.1[d]	1.4[e]	1.2
Average number of children living within two hours[a]**	2.2[a]	1.4[b]	1.6[c]	1.0[d]	1.5[e]	2.0[a]	1.7
	%	%	%	%	%	%	%
Face-to-face contact with children****							
Never to less than several times a year	7.6	23.1	9.0	12.5	26.0	24.0	15.8
Once a year or less	3.8	21.2	1.0	.0	3.0	8.0	5.2
Several times a year	15.2	5.8	5.0	16.7	8.0	16.0	9.9
Every month to every day	11.4	5.8	1.0	20.8	6.0	4.0	6.9
Every week	31.4	7.7	12.0	25.0	33.0	16.0	22.7
Every day	30.5	36.6	72.0	25.0	24.0	32.0	39.7
Phone contact with children****							
Never	11.4	32.7	10.0	12.5	15.0	32.0	16.0
Once a year or less	1.0	.0	4.0	.0	1.0	.0	1.5
Several times a year	15.2	3.9	14.0	.0	1.0	16.0	9.1
Every month	7.6	11.5	20.0	4.2	8.0	12.0	11.3
Every week	46.7	23.1	30.0	54.2	27.0	12.0	33.0
Every day	18.1	28.9	22.0	29.2	48.0	28.0	29.1

TABLE 6.1 (continued)

	CHINESE (n = 105)	FILIPINO (n = 52)	INDIAN (n = 100)	JAPANESE (n = 25)	KOREAN (n = 100)	VIETNAMESE (n = 25)	TOTAL (N = 407)
Desired amount of contact with children ****							
Don't see my children	6.7	23.1	9.0	12.5	14.0	32.0	13.1
Would like to see less often	1.0	.0	.0	.0	.0	8.0	.7
Would like to see as much as now	41.0	28.9	22.0	20.8	67.0	36.0	39.7
Would like to see more often	51.4	48.1	69.0	66.7	19.0	24.0	46.6
	Mean	Mean	Mean	Mean	Mean	Mean	Mean
Siblings, Relatives, and Neighbors							
No. of siblings in the same area	2.3[a]	.9[b]	2.1[a]	1.0[a]	1.0[c]	.3[d]	1.5
No. of other relatives besides children/siblings	1.3[a]	.6[b]	1.5[a]	.8[a]	.4[c]	.2[d]	.9
No. of close relatives							
No. of helpful neighbor	.9[a]	2.2[b]	3.1[c]	3.2[d]	1.4[a]	2.3[e]	1.9

Note: Percentages were tested using Chi-square statistics.
ANOVA statistics with Tukey's post hoc multiple comparisons were used to test the differences between means.
[a,b,c,d,e] Means with the different letters are significantly different at less than the .05 level in the same variable.
**** $p < .0001$.

percent were helped with transportation, 58 percent had children who fixed things around the house, 57.3 percent were given advice on money matters, 51.3 percent received financial assistance, 47.4 percent had children who kept or cleaned their home, and 43.3 percent had their meals prepared by their children.

CONFIDANT The majority of respondents (68.9%) identified one or more individuals to whom they felt close and with whom they could share confidences. All elders reported having, on average, two people (2.2) as confidants and close to two neighbors (1.9) who were helpful. Indian and Japanese elders reported the highest average number of confidants and helpful neighbors (each mean≥3), and Chinese elders reported the lowest number (mean = 0.9).

EXCHANGE HELP WITH NEIGHBORS Close to 44 percent of the elders reported that there was "a lot" of mutual support between them and their neighbors. Another 36 percent reported exchanging help with neighbors in emergencies. About 21 percent reported that they did not exchange help with their neighbors. The extent to which the elders engaged in mutual support differed according to nationality. The majority of Japanese (79.2%) and Indian (70.7%) elders reported exchanging "a lot" of help with their neighbors, whereas none of the Vietnamese elders (0%) reported engaging in "a lot" of mutual help with their neighbors. The Vietnamese elders (88.9%) were the most likely to report that mutual support with neighbors was limited to emergencies. Close to 74 percent of Chinese elders reported that they did not engage in any reciprocal assistance with their neighbors.

BACKUP HELP Elders were also asked if the extra help they needed had been available during the past year. Nearly a third of the respondents (28.6%) reported that such assistance was available "most of the time." Of all the elders, 34 percent reported that extra help was available "some of the time," and 23.2 percent reported that they occasionally had extra help. Another 14.3 percent reported having no extra help available. Close to half the Vietnamese elders (48%) reported having "no help," and close to half (also 48%) reported "only occasionally" having help. Half the Korean elders reported "no help" (24%) or "only occasionally" having help (30%). Among Chinese elders, only

TABLE 6.2 Support Exchanges: Comparison by Asian National Origin Groups

	CHINESE (N=105)	FILIPINO (N=52)	INDIAN (N=100)	JAPANESE (N=25)	KOREAN (N=100)	VIETNAMESE (N=25)	TOTAL (N=407)
Assistance to children (%)							
Help when someone is ill****	34.1	60.5	89.0	81.0	32.6	72.2	56.2
Give advice****	44.8	69.8	91.2	81.0	33.7	72.2	60.7
Shop or run errands****	24.7	56.8	63.7	61.9	21.4	44.4	41.4
Help children with money****	12.1	23.8	46.2	47.6	5.6	5.6	22.4
Fix things around child's house****	11.5	41.9	78.0	42.9	7.0	33.3	34.7
Keep house for child****	24.4	59.5	71.4	33.3	29.9	61.1	44.7
Assistance from children (%)							
Help when you are ill****	84.3	81.8	97.8	95.2	69.3	77.8	84.1
Give advice****	34.1	48.9	84.6	95.2	51.1	38.9	57.3
Shop or run errands****	72.0	68.9	92.2	76.2	50.0	50.0	70.4
Fix things around house****	58.3	60.5	87.9	81.0	16.5	55.6	58.0
Keep or clean house****	32.6	61.4	75.8	61.9	24.1	33.3	47.4
Prepare meals, but not keep house****	31.0	50.0	68.1	66.7	22.0	25.0	43.1
Help out with money****	48.5	44.4	72.5	38.1	46.0	16.7	51.3
Provide transportation****	53.5	46.7	85.2	71.4	56.8	50.5	62.4
Grandparenting[b]** (%)**	**25.7**	**25.0**	**49.0**	**0**	**22.0**	**24.0**	**28.8**
Being a primary caregiver of grandchildren**	55.0	30.0	13.6	0	72.7	50.0	45.0
Have a confidant****	36.9	76.0	92.9	95.8	66.3	77.3	68.9
No. of confidants (mean)****	.9	2.2	3.7	3.0	2.0	2.2	2.2

Exchange help with neighbor** (%)**

Not at all	74.2	40.4	21.0	12.5	62.0	36.0	47.8
Only in an emergency	16.2	42.3	14.0	12.5	24.0	64.0	23.7
A lot	9.5	17.3	65.0	75.0	14.0	0	28.6

Backup help availability** (%)**

Not at all or only occasionally	18.1	15.4	3.0	8.3	24.0	48.0	14.3
Only occasionally	32.4	13.5	8.0	12.5	30.0	48.0	23.2
Some of the time	28.6	17.3	60.0	62.5	23.0	4.0	34.0
Most of the time	21.0	53.9	29.0	16.7	33.0	.0	28.6

Unmet needs** (%)**

Have all help needed	21.0	51.9	17.0	16.7	56.0	8.0	31.5
Need a little or some more help	33.3	21.2	9.0	25.0	35.0	28.0	25.4
Need some more	27.6	17.3	56.0	25.0	3.0	32.0	27.3
Need a lot more help	18.1	9.6	18.0	33.3	6.0	32.0	15.8

Note: Chi-square statistics were used.

** $p < .01$.

**** $p < .0001$.

18.1 percent reported "no help," and 32.4 percent reported having help "only occasionally."

UNMET NEEDS Only 31.5 percent of respondents reported that they received all the help they needed. Close to 16 percent stated that they needed "a lot more help," and 27.3 percent needed "some more" help. This indicates a highly vulnerable population whose need for assistance could burden the familial sources of informal support discussed earlier.

FACTORS ASSOCIATED WITH INTERGENERATIONAL EXCHANGE

Regression models were used to examine factors associated with intergenerational exchange. Following the social exchange framework, assistance to and from children was regressed with sociodemographic variables, informal support and personal resources, and life stressors. Sociodemographic variables included gender, living arrangement, marital status, age, length of stay in the United States, and financial status. As discussed in previous chapters, receiving Medicaid was used as a proxy for financial status. Informal support included number of children, number of children living within two hours' driving distance, number of close relatives, caring for grandparents, availability of backup help, and unmet needs. Personal resources included English proficiency and religiosity. Life stressors included self-rated health, depressive symptoms, number of stressful events, and perceived generation gap. Receiving help from children was included in the regression for giving help to children, and vice versa. As in the preceding chapters, we did not enter national origin because subgroup sizes were too small for a meaningful comparison with multivariate testing.

Table 6.3 presents the results of the regression models on intergenerational exchange. Giving help to children was significantly associated with being younger, a shorter stay in the United States, providing care for grandchildren, English proficiency, self-rated health, higher number of stressful events, and receiving help from children. Living alone and being on Medicaid were negatively associated with giving help to children ($R^2 = .53$, $p < .0001$).

Receiving help from children was associated with having children living within a driving distance of two hours, number of close relatives, availability of backup help, having unmet needs, and giving help to children. Receiving help was negatively associated with the number of stressful events ($R^2 = .53$, $p < .0001$).

TABLE 6.3 Intergenerational Support Regression Models

INDEPENDENT VARIABLE	GIVING HELP TO CHILDREN b(SE)	RECEIVING HELP FROM CHILDREN b(SE)
Sociodemographics		
Gender (male=1)		
Living alone (yes=1)	−.68 (.25)**	−1.06(.39)**
Marital status (married=1)		
Age (young old=1)	.69 (.19)***	
Length of stay in the U.S. (1-72)	−.40(.21)*	
Medicaid (yes=1)	−.02(.01)*	
Intergenerational Solidarity		
No. of children		
No. of close relatives		.13 (.06)*
Children living within 2 hours (0-10)		.24 (.09)*
Receiving help from children (0-8)	.34 (.04)****	Not included in this regression
Giving help to children (0-8)	Not included in this regression	.59 (.07)****
Grandparenting (yes=1)	1.23 (.20)****	
Perceived generation gap (0-3)		
Personal Resources		
English proficiency (0-9)	.22(.09)*	
Religiosity (0-3)		
Backup help availability (0-3)		.53 (.12)****
Life Stresses		
Self-rated health (1-5)	.09 (.04)*	
Depressive symptoms (0-30)		
No. of stressful life events (0-6)	.13 (.06)*	−.22 (.08)**
Unmet needs (0-3)		−.47 (.11)****
R² Total	**.53******	**.47******
Adjusted R² Total	**.51******	**.44******

* $p<.05$.
* $p<.01$.
*** $p<.001$.
**** $p<.0001$.

DISCUSSION

SOCIAL NETWORK AND SOCIAL SUPPORT

The findings demonstrate that the majority of the elders in this study had a small social support network. On average, the elders also had regular contact with a small number of relatives other than their children. Filipino, Japanese, Korean, and Vietnamese elders reported an average of less than one close relative. Indian elders had the highest average of close relatives, but their average was also very low (1.5 relatives). Indian elders also had the highest average number of confidants (3.7), but the overall average number of confidants was 2.2. For Chinese elders, the average number of confidants was less than one. The average number of helpful neighbors was also low. Japanese and Indian elders reported having an average of at least three neighbors, and Chinese elders reported less than one.

Older adults generally have smaller social networks than do younger cohorts. Elders see members of their networks less frequently, have people in their networks who are less proximal, and have more family members in their networks (Antonucci and Akiyama 1987). The concentration of family members in the network may be the result of physical limitations that hinder elders from visiting friends (Cantor, Brennan, and Sainz 1994). Increasing need for support may also intensify interaction with family members (Antonucci and Akiyama 1987).

Despite the decrease in the size of the social network, studies on social support among elders suggest that they have a core social support network that is stable over time. According to the "social network convoy model" by Kahn and Antonucci (1980), older adults have a network of social relationships that moves with the person through life. Although this network may change in structure, it provides continuity in the exchange of support. In a national probability sample survey, Antonucci and Akiyama (1987) found that U.S. adults aged fifty-five and older have an average of nine members in their social support convoy. The number of people Asian elders report having in their social support network is much smaller than the number presented by Antonucchi and Akiyama (1987). That Asian American elders have small social networks may not only be because of their age but also because of their immigration experiences. As noted in chapter 3, the majority of Asian elders immigrated during mid-life, and a third did so after age sixty. The elders may have left their families in their home country, which would explain why so few have siblings living in the same geographical area. Immigration can also cause discontinuity in social relationships because of geographical distance. Elders may have lost their support system when they left their home country. Establishing new relationships in a new environment is difficult, especially when one is linguistically isolated. Elders who live in ethnic communities may be able to converse with others in their native language, but overseas ethnic communities cannot replicate the personal networks that were built over time in their home countries. It is difficult to establish relationships with people who do not share the same background or history. In light of the significant need for extra help with ADLs and unmet needs, the small size of the elders' social networks is of concern as they offer limited social capital.

The elders in this study reported having close contact with their children. Elders of all ethnic groups reported having an average of at least one child living within a two-hour drive. Of all the elders, 62 percent reported seeing and/or having phone contact with their children every day or at least once a week. These findings are consistent with other research that indicates close contact between Asian elders and their children (Kauh 1997). It is important to note, however, that despite frequent contact with their children, close to 47 percent reported that they would like to see their children more often. It is not possible from this study to examine whether this desire stems from their need for increased affective connection or for additional instrumental support. It does indicate that the elders experience a need for increased contact with their children.

Reciprocity in the provision of informal support was observed between the elders and their children, and between the elders and their neighbors. As one might expect, elders reported receiving more assistance than they provided. The amount of support elders provide to their children differs according to their nationality. Overall, Indian, Japanese, and Filipino elders provide the most support to their children, and Chinese and Korean elders provide the least. Despite the assistance from their children, most elders reported a need for additional support with ADLs and that such support was unavailable. These findings imply that the availability and accessibility of personal social service programs need to be expanded.

INTERGENERATIONAL EXCHANGE

Giving help to children is positively associated with age (young-old), providing care for grandchildren, English proficiency, receiving help from children (exchange), having more stressful life events, not living alone, and self-rated health. Elders who were younger, had greater English proficiency, did not live alone, had more life stressors, and were in good health were more likely than others to provide assistance to their children. Elders who lived in close proximity to their children, had more close relatives, had backup help available, had fewer stressful events, and had unmet needs were more likely than others to receive help from their children. The findings that elders who experienced fewer stressful events were more likely to receive help from their children and that those who report more stressful events were likely to give assistance to their families may seem counterintuitive. However, stressful events may have been experienced by the entire family, not just by the elder. Elders with families experiencing stressful events would end up providing more support, whereas elders whose families were not under stress would receive more help from them.

English proficiency and length of stay in the United States, which can be considered as proxies for acculturation, were associated with providing help to children but not with receiving help from them. In other words, being less acculturated does not necessarily indicate that elders receive more help from their children. It is important to note, however, that in addition to not being acculturated, elders who do not have many financial resources, who are older, and who are in poor health are less likely to be able to provide support to their children. This may lead to nonreciprocal exchanges, which over time may become problematic. Studies indicates that high levels of support from adult children can be related to a decrease in well-being (Silverstein, Chen, and Heller 1996).

As noted previously, exchange theory suggests that reciprocity in intergenerational exchange is essential to psychological well-being. Even in Asian populations, where interdependence is valued, extreme dependency or nonreciprocity can result in negative outcomes (Kim et al. 2000; Shibusawa 2001). For example, a study of intergenerational support among Korean families found that unequal exchanges in which elders need extensive support from their adult children can result in their feeling guilty for burdening their children (Kim and Kim 2003). It is important for service providers to be cognizant of the mental health status of elders who are not able to reciprocate the help they receive from their children.

Although the level of acculturation of Asian elders was not associated with receiving assistance from their children, other research on Asian elders indicates that length of stay in the United States is a factor in elders' living independently from their children. As noted in chapter 5, a study of Korean elders reported that, although 75 percent of Korean elders in the United States lived with their children in 1980, this figure decreased to 57 percent in 1990 (Yoo and Sung 1997). We do not know if the children's acculturation level influences their propensity to provide assistance to their older parents. In a study of intergenerational exchange of Chinese, Korean, and Japanese elders in the United States, Ishii-Kuntz (1997) reported that later-generation children (i.e., those who are more acculturated) showed a slightly lower degree of filial obligation. Future studies on intergenerational exchange will need to account for the acculturation level of both the elderly parents and their adult children.

Having unmet needs and having backup help available is also associated with receiving help. These findings indicate elders' sizable need for assistance with ADLs. Having backup help does not deter their children from assisting their parents. That more than half the elders reported needing some or a lot more help for their ADL activities is a source of concern. The inability of families to meet all their elders' needs can potentially have negative effects on the intergenerational relationship. Parents may become resentful or depressed for not getting the assistance they need from their children, or they may feel guilty for overburdening their children. The children, on the other hand, may feel overwhelmed by their parents' needs and feel guilty for not being able to provide more help, or resentful about the amount of help their parents require.

Caregiving relationships do not cause elder abuse (Anetzberger 2000); however, difficult caregiving relationships can intensify problematic relationships. Despite the increased awareness of elder abuse in mainstream society, the Asian American community has not been open about elder abuse that occurs in its midst. There is indication that elder abuse does take place in Asian families (Le 1997). For example, in California, the San Francisco Protective Services Agency noted that 10 percent of the cases of elder abuse reported as of March 2001 involved Asian Americans. The victims included people of Chinese, Southeast Asian, Japanese, and Korean origin (Manigbas 2002). According to Manigbas (2002), Self-Help for the Elderly, a nonprofit organization that serves the Chinese community in San Francisco, assists with sixty cases of abuse each year. It is important, therefore, for service providers to be aware of the possibility of abuse when working with elders who appear to have conflictual relationships with their adult children.

Formal services may fill the need for additional assistance among the elders. However, Asian families have low utilization rates of services from nonkin. A recent survey of family caregivers found that Asian Americans, of all ethnic groups, reported the lowest use of community-based support services such as meal delivery programs, adult day care, and home health care (National Alliance for Caregiving and the American Association of Retired Persons 1997). According to the survey, only 15 percent of Asian families used personal or nursing services, which is half the utilization rate of other ethnic groups. Furthermore, many Asian caregivers were not aware of available services. Thus education regarding geriatric services is very important for the

Asian American community. Families may also need assistance in connecting to these services.

It is notable that having more stressful events was associated with elders providing assistance to their children, which may indicate that elders were more involved with their families because the family as a whole was experiencing stressful events. Having fewer stressful events was also associated with receiving support from children. Again, families under less stress may be able to provide more assistance to older family members. It is therefore important to assess the context of family life and stressful events that families may be facing when examining their elders and the assistance they need. It is also important to note that, despite changes in family relationships prompted by acculturation, intergenerational exchange was not associated with a perceived generation gap. Although some research (Yoo and Sung 1997) indicates that Asian elders are not getting the help they need because of changing norms around filial obligation among their children, this was not the case in our study.

The findings of this chapter indicate that the majority of the elders are connected with their children through intergenerational exchange. At the same time, this connection may easily become vulnerable because so much rests on the shoulders of the adult children. Elders on the whole have small families with few other extended family members living nearby. Furthermore, although a group of elders engage in reciprocal support with their neighbors, others have no helpful interactions with neighbors. Despite the amount of help elders receive from their children, many still require assistance with ADLs. Clearly this points to the need for formal support services and indicates that elders are not receiving the services they need. The findings also point to the need for community education around formal services as well as the development of culturally appropriate geriatric care.

7

FORMAL SERVICE UTILIZATION

Community-Based, In-Home, and Health Services

AS WE CONTINUE TO EXAMINE the help-seeking behaviors of Asian American elders, it is important to remember that our sample had a higher level of physical and mental health needs than the general older U.S. population, as discussed in chapters 3 and 4. Recent government publications reviewing the effects of race, culture, and ethnicity on health status and service utilization found that the health care system underserved racial and ethnic minorities (U.S. Department of Health and Human Services [USDHHS] 2001). As a group, Asian American elders are much poorer than their white counterparts, but they are represented far less than their reported objective needs indicate (Mui and Kang 2006). Asian American elders are underserved by Administration on Aging programs, which are not means tested but are largely geared to low-income populations. For example, Medicaid payments for services for older persons in 2003 constituted 9 percent (4.4 million persons), and over 41 percent of the total Medicaid cost was paid for persons using nursing-home facilities or home-health services, which few Asian American elders use (Center for Medicare and Medicaid Services [CMS] 2005).

Upon entering the health care system, racial and ethnic minorities encounter a culturally biased system that may misdiagnose individuals based on racial and cultural characteristics (Chow, Jaffee, and Snowden 2003; Snowden 2003). It has been suggested that the development of culturally and linguistically competent physical and mental health services systems for racially and ethnically diverse populations would ameliorate health disparity (USDHHS 2001). Multiple barriers to minority elders', especially Asian Americans', service utilization have been identified, including language access issues, a fragmented health care system, lack of insurance, and a lack of knowledge of existing resources (Jang, Lee, and Woo 1998; Ma 1999; Mui and Kang 2006). Empirical data on health and social service utilization by Asian American elders are very limited, and patterns and reasons for persistent underutilization are poorly understood (Abe-Kim, Takeuchi, and Hwang 2002; Ngo-Metzger et al. 2003). In this chapter we conduct a systematic inquiry of differences among Asian elders based on national origin groups in their help-seeking decisions to use formal services (i.e., community-based, in-home, and health services [physician care, emergency room use, and hospital use]).

LITERATURE REVIEW ON FACTORS ASSOCIATED WITH FORMAL SERVICES UTILIZATION

ETHNICITY, CULTURE, AND FORMAL SERVICE USE

Research on social service utilization among elderly populations has examined community-based, in-home, and nursing home care. Consistent evidence has shown that ethnicity is associated with different patterns of service use. Data from the National Channeling Demonstration project indicated that white elders were more likely to use in-home and nursing home services than were minority elders (Mui and Burnette 1994). Asian, Hispanic, and African American elders were more likely to use informal care rather than formal in-home services compared to white elders (Borrayo et al. 2002, 2004; Burnette and Mui 1995; Moon, Lubben, and Villa 1998). This pattern of use may point either to the lack of access to formal services or the cultural preferences of minority elders.

Other research examined the impact of culture and found that higher levels of acculturation have been associated with increased use of physicians' services (Burnette and Mui 1999). Cultural contextual factors also impact the level of service use. Among the foreign-born, pre-immigration factors, such as the degree of choice in the decision to immigrate, influenced the use of services after immigration (Portes, Kyle, and Eaton 1992). Research has also suggested that members of ethnic groups who experienced social discrimination because of language barriers were less likely to use mental health services (Spencer and Chen 2004). National data has indicated that Asian Americans underutilize mental health services (USDHHS 2001). Further, Asian Americans are more likely to seek services from primary care physicians (Proctor et al. 1999) or emergency services (Phan 2000) rather than from mental health specialists. Barriers to mental health service utilization were associated with language difficulties, a sense of stigma, and a lack of knowledge about mental health care systems (Aroian, Wu, and Tran 2005). Underutilization of mental health care among Asian Americans may also result from their tendency to focus on physical problems rather than emotional distress (Nguyen and Anderson 2005).

FAMILY SUPPORT, HEALTH CARE NEEDS, AND FORMAL SERVICE USE

Social support has been documented as an important predictor of service utilization. Among ethnic minority elders, having family members was associated with increased community-based service use (Borrayo et al. 2004; Mui and Burnette 1994). Social support in terms of the number of children and frequency of contacts with them was positively associated with increased physician visits (Burnette and Mui 1999). Family members of ethnic elders usually functioned as their liaison with and linkage to formal services.

The need for services because of poor health was associated with increased in-home, community-based, or institutional services (Borrayo et al. 2002). Research also found that cognitive impairment and need for help with Activities of Daily Living (ADLs) and Instrumental Activities of Daily Living (IADLs) were associated with increased use of physician, in-home, and community-based services (Borrayo et al. 2004; Mui and Burnette 1994). Mental health issues was a risk factor for decreased service use among Asian elders. Research supported the tendency of Asian elders with fewer mental health issues to use more community services; poor affect was found to decrease the level of community-based service utilization (Mui and Kang 2006). Studies also found that elders who used in-home services were more likely to use community-based services than were their counterparts who did not use in-home services (Mui and Burnette 1994; Wallace, Campbell, and Lew-Ting 1994). This may reflect the work of care managers in the long-term care system that would provide information and linkage to other services in the service continuum (Burnette and Mui 1995; Mui and Burnette 1994).

BARRIERS TO FORMAL SERVICE USE

Research examining health service utilization included analyses of barriers and access to health service utilization in terms of physician use, emergency room use, and hospital use. Among studies examining barriers to the use of health services, persons of older age, female gender, and minority status were more likely than the comparison group to perceive barriers to access of health care (Fitzpatrick et al. 2004). A study on Chinese Americans found that those who had language difficulty and those who endorsed traditional Chinese remedies encountered more barriers to accessing the health care system than did those with higher levels of English ability or those who believed in the efficacy of Western medicine (Ma 1999). The internal capacity to trust and negotiate the Western health care system enabled Chinese Americans to overcome some barriers in accessing medical services.

Several researchers have focused on the issue of access to health care among Asian American groups in the United States. Those who were younger and more proficient in English were more willing to use Western medical services (Chung and Lin 1994). Asian elders who were married and were U.S. citizens were also more likely to access health service than were their single counterparts without citizenship (Jang et al. 1998; Jenkins et al. 1996). Poorer language proficiency was associated with lesser utilization of the health care system (Jang et al. 1998). Other research examined factors associated with physician visits. Asian Americans were found to use more outpatient services but fewer mental health services than other groups (Hu et al. 1993; Leong 1994). Additional studies have found Asian Americans less likely than members of other racial/ethnic groups to be hospitalized for treatment of psychiatric problems (Virnig et al. 2004). Variation within the Asian race has been reported—notably, that Southeast Asians were more likely to access health care than were people of other Asian ethnicities (Hu et al. 1993). These findings suggest that service utilization among different ethnic elderly groups may be owing to access barriers and cultural preference. Other contextual variables also affect elders' willingness to access services, for example, cultural sensitivity of a service delivery system and the availability of culturally effective services (Borrayo et al. 2002).

CONCEPTUAL FRAMEWORK: A HEALTH BEHAVIORAL MODEL

Research on formal service utilization typically employed the behavioral model of Andersen and his colleagues (Andersen 1995; Andersen and Newman 1973; Phillips et al. 1998). This model views service use as a function of three variables: *predisposing factors*, such as sociodemographic characteristics;

enabling factors, such as family and social resources that facilitate or impede service use; and *need*, determined by the health conditions for which services are sought. This behavioral model is the most widely accepted framework for studying health and the use of long-term care services among minority elderly populations (Burnette and Mui 1995, 1999; Mui and Burnette 1994), and therefore we have adapted it as the conceptual lens through which we explain the variables used in this chapter.

Mui and Burnette (1994) found that the relative impact of predisposing, enabling, and need factors varies by the type of service, need being the most influential on nondiscretionary services (i.e., hospital) and social, cultural, and economic factors more relevant to discretionary services. Hospital use is largely a function of provider and insurance variables and is the least discretionary service considered here. Home health care requires professional determination of eligibility and referral, and is thus partially discretionary (Mitchell and Krout 1998). Physician services are subject to individual and cultural definitions of need (Burnette and Mui 1995, 1999; Mui and Burnette 1994). On a continuum, physician services may be more discretionary compared to home health care, emergency room use, and hospitalization.

This chapter examines two questions: What proportion of the elderly Asian Americans in our sample used community-based, in-home, and health services (physician, emergency room, and hospital)? And what were the predisposing, enabling, and need factors associated with their use of each of these services? Because not all respondents used each of these services, the data analysis examined, instead, the *likelihood* of their using particular services. Because the utilization of nursing homes was extremely low (2.5%) in our Asian American elderly sample, this service was not analyzed.

MEASURES

The predictor measures used in the multivariate analysis of formal service use were determined based on the factor categories in the Andersen and Newman (1973) health behavioral model. The predisposing variables included sociode-mographic factors such as gender (male = 1), living alone (yes = 1), age (65–96 years old), and length of stay in the United States (range = 1–72 years). The marital status variable was not included in the multivariate models because of its high correlation with the "living alone" variable. Enabling factors included whether the elder were a participant in Medicare Part A, Medicare Part B, and Medicaid. These data were used because having health insurance coverage enabled service use. Because a lot of income data was missing in this survey, Medicaid coverage was used as a proxy measure of elders' financial status. Even though Medicaid may not be a precise measure of economic resources, it does use means testing and income related to federal poverty guidelines as eligibility requirements.

Other enabling measures were English proficiency, religiosity, social support (number of children living within a two-hour drive, and the amount of instrumental, financial, and emotional assistance received from children), satisfaction with doctor's care, and the elder's attitude toward nursing homes. English-language proficiency was a composite score (0–9) of Asian elderly respondents' ability to read, write, and speak English (each item was assessed on a 4-point scale: not at all = 0 to very well = 3). For the purpose of this analysis, English proficiency was conceptualized as an enabling factor because it represented elders' behavioral efforts to cope with the host culture. Religiosity was assessed in terms of respondents' perception of the importance of religion in their lives on a 4-point scale (not at all important = 0 to very important = 3). Satisfaction with doctor's care was a single-item measure evaluated by asking elders, "Are you satisfied with the treatment and attention you get from your doctor(s)?" on a 2-point scale (satisfied = 1 to not satisfied = 0). Attitude toward nursing home placement was assessed by asking elders, "In general, how do you feel about moving to a nursing home for long-term care?" on a 5-point scale (1 = strongly against to 5 = strongly in favor).

Need factors were operationally defined by five variables: perceived health, number of medical conditions, number of stressful life events, perceived generation gap, and mental health status. The life stressors variable was a composite score of a list of up to six stressful life events that the respondent experienced (yes = 1, no = 0) in the preceding three years. Examples of these events included major losses in life such as death of spouse/family member/good friend, serious illness/injury, having been robbed or had home burglarized, children having moved out, and relocation. The global measure was evaluated by asking elders to assess how their own view regarding family values differed from that of their children, on a 4-point scale (not at all different = 0 to different in a very important way = 3). The Geriatric Depression Scale (GDS) (score = 0–30) was used to measure elderly respondents' mental health status. The GDS measure consists of a thirty-item inventory of positive and negative statements with which respondents either agree (yes = 1) or disagree (no = 0). These responses are then summed up to create a composite measure (Mui and Kang 2006).

Dependent variables in the logistic regression models were five categories of formal service use reported by the Asian American elderly respondents. These included community-based service use (including all government services and community services listed in table 7.1); in-home service use (including home care and visiting nurse service); and health services (i.e., doctors' visit[s], emergency room visit[s]; and hospital admission). For physician and home care services, the actual volume of use (number of visits) was gathered. For emergency room or hospital use, the respondents were asked whether they had been a patient in an emergency room or hospital within the preceding twelve months. Since the volume of most of these services was highly skewed (see use percentages in table 7.1), the variables were coded dichotomously, with 1 indicating users of at least one service within each category and 0 denoting non-users. Logistic regression analyses were used to examine factors associated with the likelihood of an elderly respondent's being a user of each type of service.

RESULTS: DIFFERENTIAL USE OF FORMAL SERVICES

GOVERNMENT SERVICES

Table 7.1 presents the percentage of Asian American elders in each of the six Asian national origin groups who reported utilization of all types of formal services in the twelve months preceding the survey. Data indicated significant diversity in use among different groups for all other service categories. Services that were most used or approached by the Asian American elders with significant ethnic differences were government programs, that is, Social Security (41.6%) and Medicare (34.6%). The next service category used by the respondents was Medicaid (27.7%), with one-third or more of the Filipino, Korean, and Indian elders reporting that they had used this service. Among other public services, Vietnamese and Indian elders both reported the highest rates of usage of Immigration Services (about 30%). Indian elders seemed to have more encounters (16.3%) with the Police Department than other Asian subgroups in the survey.

TABLE 7.1 Utilization Rates of Formal Services by Asian American Elderly in the Twelve Months Prior to the Study Survey

	CHINESE (N=105)	FILIPINO (N=52)	INDIAN (N=100)	JAPANESE (N=25)	KOREAN (N=100)	VIETNAMESE (N=25)	TOTAL (N=407)
	%	%	%	%	%	%	%
Government services							
Social Security Office**	35.2	59.6	42.4	68.0	34.0	32.0	41.6
Medicare Office****	16.4	45.1	44.6	36.0	43.3	16.0	34.6
Medicaid Office****	13.6	34.7	43.5	12.0	33.3	8.0	27.7
Department for Aging**	6.7	16.0	7.6	20.0	2.0	4.0	7.6
Immigration Services****	5.7	13.7	29.4	0.0	3.0	29.2	12.6
Department of Social Services****	10.5	10.0	4.4	0.0	3.5	27.6	7.3
Police Department****	3.8	4.0	16.3	0.0	1.0	0.0	5.6
Housing Department**	1.9	0.0	4.4	0.0	12.0	0.0	4.5
Community-based services							
Senior center****	38.8	28.0	1.1	32.0	26.3	16.0	23.7
Minister/priest/monk services	18.3	20.0	21.5	8.0	24.2	20.0	20.2
Transportation services****	6.7	21.2	23.2	32.0	7.1	0.0	13.8
Legal services****	1.9	6.0	32.6	24.0	0.0	0.0	10.4
Citizenship classes****	5.7	4.0	2.2	0.0	14.1	32.0	8.1
English classes****	0.0	0.0	7.5	0.0	18.0	16.0	7.3
Social worker****	8.7	1.9	1.0	0.0	4.1	26.1	5.3
In-home services							
Home care services****	24.0	0.0	1.0	36.0	3.2	0.0	9.6
Visiting nurse services****	23.1	0.0	2.0	20.0	2.1	0.0	8.3
Institutional services							
Nursing home****	1.0	0.0	2.2	24.0	1.0	0.0	2.5

Note: Chi-square statistics were used.

** p<.01.

**** p<.0001.

COMMUNITY-BASED SERVICES

Data indicated that Asian elders enjoyed socialization and congregate meals in the Community Center. The Senior Center was the community-based service most reported, with 23.7 percent of the elderly respondents using this service. Specifically, Chinese elders used senior centers (38.8%) more than any other service, having the highest utilization rate among all the ethnic groups, followed by Japanese (32%), Filipino (28.0%), Korean (26.3%), and Vietnamese (16%) respondents. On the other hand, only 1.1 percent of Indian elders used the Senior Center. Regarding other community-based services, Korean (18%), Vietnamese (16%), and Indian (7.5%) elders attended English classes, whereas no other ethnic group reported doing so. Compared to other groups, a significantly higher percentage of Vietnamese elders (32%) attended citizenship classes than did their counterparts from other groups. Transportation services were very important to some Asian elderly groups, with Japanese (32%), Indians (23.2%), and Filipinos (21.2%) being the major consumers. By contrast, none of the Vietnamese elders reported using public transportation. More Indian (32.6%) and Japanese (24%) elders made use of legal services than other Asian ethnic groups in the sample. Finally, only a small proportion of Asian American elders used services provided by social workers (5.3%).

IN-HOME AND INSTITUTIONAL SERVICES

Very few Asian American elders reported using nursing home services (2.5%), and less than 10 percent reported using in-home services. The average use reported by all respondents for in-home and nursing home service is skewed by the use of these services by two ethnic groups: Chinese and Japanese elders. Chinese elders used more in-home services (home care services, 24%; and visiting nurse services, 23.1%) than institutional services. Japanese elders used more nursing home (24%) and home care services (36%) than did all other ethnic groups. Like the Chinese, they were also high users of visiting nurse services (20%). All other ethnic groups made no use (Filipinos and Vietnamese) or hardly any use (Indians) of in-home and nursing home services. These discrepancies may be the result of barriers different ethnic groups experience to service delivery systems such as accessibility, affordability, and acceptability in using in-home and institutionally based services.

UTILIZATION OF HEALTH SERVICES AND PERCEPTION ABOUT QUALITY

Asian American elders' use of physicians, emergency room services, and hospitals along with their perception of these services is presented in table 7.2. The results show that 81 percent of the whole sample of Asian elders had a regular doctor and 90 percent had actually seen a physician in the preceding year. Nevertheless, 14 percent of the Asian elders reported dissatisfaction with their doctor's service. Just over one-fourth of these elders delayed medical treatment for various reasons: the high cost of the doctor's visit (67%); the belief that the doctor could not help them (47%); preferred to wait for their routine appointment (34.9%); or preferred an alternative healer (21%). All except the Indian elders (48.5%) had a regular relationship with a doctor (84.6–96.0%) with Japanese elders reporting the highest rate. Of interest is that the elders with the lowest (Indian) and highest (Japanese elders) reports of regular physician care also reported significantly higher rates of dissatisfaction with their doctor's care than any other group (31.0% and 20.0%, respectively). Only the Vietnamese elders did not delay seeking medical treatment. Generally the reasons for delays included the cost, which applied to a large majority of Filipino, Indian, and Japanese elders, and the desire to wait, which was true of three-fourths of Indian elders and all Japanese elders.

Seventeen percent of all these Asian elders used hospitals and emergency room services. As noted in table 7.1, very few (2.5%) reported using a nursing home. Japanese elders had the highest percentage of utilization (24%), whereas only 2 percent of Indians and no one from other groups used nursing home services. It appears from the additional data gathered in this study that the low rate of nursing home use may be linked to negative attitudes toward nursing homes. A large proportion of these Asian elders (69.4%) were either strongly against (47%) or somewhat against (22.4%) nursing home use. In contrast, only 13.2 percent were strongly (5%) or somewhat (8.2) in favor of nursing home use. Vietnamese (92%), Filipino (74.5%), and Chinese elders (53.9%) voiced the strongest opposition to nursing home services. Even though Japanese elders had the highest usage rate, four out of five were against nursing home use. These findings are not surprising, given that intergenerational caregiving is intrinsic to many Asian cultures.

TABLE 7.2 Asian American Elders' Use of Medical Services in the Preceding Year and Perception about Services Received

	CHINESE (N = 105)	FILIPINO (N = 52)	INDIAN (N = 100)	JAPANESE (N = 25)	KOREAN (N = 100)	VIETNAMESE (N = 25)	TOTAL (N = 407)
	%	%	%	%	%	%	%
Had a regular doctor****	91.4	84.6	48.5	96.0	91.0	95.8	80.5
Had a doctor visit***	90.7	86.0	83.7	96.0	93.0	100.0	90.2
Had hospital use*	13.5	15.3	22.2	44.0	13.4	8.3	17.5
Had emergency room use*	14.4	15.4	17.5	44.0	14.1	16.7	17.2
Dissatisfied with doctor care***	10.2	2.0	31.0	20.0	9.5	0.0	13.9
Had delayed treatment****	22.1	10.0	57.0	20.8	14.4	0.0	26.0
Reasons for delayed treatment							
Doctors too costly***	33.3	66.7	81.8	80.0	25.0	0.0	67.1
Do not believe doctor can help**	40.0	33.3	47.3	60.0	100.0	0.0	47.1
Waited for routine appointment***	5.6	75.0	37.0	100.0	0.0	0.0	34.9
Prefer alternative healer****	24.5	9.6	14.0	12.0	35.4	4.0	20.7
Attitude toward nursing home**							
Strongly against it	53.9	74.5	30.0	28.0	36.4	92.0	47.0
Somewhat against it	11.8	7.8	46.0	52.0	13.1	8.0	22.4
Neither for nor against it	20.6	13.7	16.0	16.0	22.2	0.0	17.4
Somewhat in favor of it	7.8	2.0	5.0	4.0	18.2	0.0	8.2
Strongly in favor of it	5.9	2.0	3.0	0.0	10.1	0.0	5.0

Note: Chi-square statistics were used to test percentages among different groups.

* $p < .05$.
** $p < .01$.
*** $p < .001$.
**** $p < .0001$.

FACTORS ASSOCIATED WITH COMMUNITY-BASED, IN-HOME, HEALTH SERVICES USE

Descriptive statistics of all independent variables were not shown in table form because many of them were reported in the previous chapters. Table 7.3 presents the results of the logistic regression models. All models were significant ($p < .0001$) in predicting Asian American elders' use of community-based, in-home, and health services (physician, emergency room, and hospital services). For the model depicting the use of community-based services, six variables were significantly associated with the likelihood of service use. Comparing the Wald χ^2, enabling factors as a set had the highest predictive power (Wald $\chi^2 = 11.4$), followed by predisposing factors (Wald $\chi^2 = 10.3$). Specifically, older Asian women and elders who had been in the United States for a long time were more likely to use community-based services. Among the enabling factors, having both Medicare Part A and Part B coverage increased the probability of an elder's use of community-based services. Further, Asian elders who reported more medical conditions and more stressful life events were more likely to access community-based services.

In the in-home service model, predisposing factors, as a set, had the strongest impact (Wald $\chi^2 = 14.4$) in explaining in-home services use, followed by enabling factors. None of the need factors made a significant contribution in predicting in-home services use, a counterintuitive finding. Asian American elders who were living alone, who were older, who had lived in the United States longer, who had Medicare Part B, and who expressed a negative attitude toward nursing homes were more likely to use in-home services. In the physician utilization (doctor visits) model, enabling factors, as a set, had the strongest influence (Wald $\chi^2 = 15.0$) in determining physician services use. This was followed by need factors (Wald $\chi^2 = 11.3$). Only one predisposing factor, length of stay in the U.S., was significant in this model. Seven factors were associated with an increased probability of seeking physician services: a longer stay in the U.S. and having Medicare Part A and Medicaid, a positive experience with doctor care, poor self-rated health, fewer stressful life events, and the perception of a small generation gap.

Regarding emergency room use, enabling factors, as a set, had the highest predictive power (Wald $\chi^2 = 16.7$) and five factors (older age, having Medicare Part A and Part B, a higher level of religiosity, and poor self-rated health) influenced the likelihood of using emergency room services. Enabling factors (Wald $\chi^2 = 26$) played the most significant role in explaining hospital utilization, followed by need factors (Wald $\chi^2 = 14.4$). Compared

TABLE 7.3 Logistic Regression Models of Asian American Elders' Service Use

	COMMUNITY-BASED SERVICES[a]	IN-HOME SERVICES[a]	DOCTOR VISIT	EMERGENCY ROOM USE	HOSPITAL USE
	SIGNIFICANT LOGISTIC COEFFICIENTS				
PREDISPOSING FACTORS					
Gender (male=1)	−.89*				
Living alone (yes=1)		.94*			
Age (65–96)		.10*		.08*	.10*
Length of stay in the United States (1–72)	.04*	.09**	.06**		
Wald χ^2 from this set of factors	10.3	14.4	3.2	5.5	6.5
ENABLING FACTORS					
Medicare part A (yes=1)	1.74**		2.28***	.83*	1.08*
Medicare part B (yes=1)	1.28**	2.35**		1.94**	1.24**
Medicaid coverage (yes=1)			.81*		.86*
English proficiency (0–9)[b]					.20*
Religiosity (0–3)[b]				.45*	.62*
Children living within two hours (0–10)					
Assistance from children (0–8)					−.11*
Satisfied with doctor's care (yes=1)			1.07*		−.94*
Attitude toward nursing home (1–5)[b]		−.68**			
Wald χ^2 from this set of factors	11.4	8.2	15.0	16.7	26.0
NEED FACTORS					
Perceived health (1–5)[b]			−.14*	−.19*	−.21**
Number of medical conditions (0–12)	.22*				
Number of stressful life events (0–6)	.29*		−.39**		
Perceived generational gap (0–3)			−.73*		
Depression (0–30)					.15***
Wald χ^2 from this set of Factors	6.0	0	11.3	5.0	14.4
Intercept	**3.85**	**−8.19***	**3.69**	**−8.39****	**−.81**
Model χ^2	**40.88****	**54.59****	**69.03****	**48.83***	**84.79****

[a] Community-based services and in-home services are listed in Table 7.1.
[b] High scores indicate favorable ratings.
* $p < .05$.
** $p < .01$.
*** $p < .001$.
**** $p < .0001$.

to other models, the hospital use model seemed to be a better fit and provide more specificity in terms of the numbers of significant variables. Among the predisposing factors, only older age was a predictor of hospital use. The seven enabling factors of hospital use included having Medicare Part A and Part B, Medicaid, better English proficiency, a higher level of religiosity, less assistance from children, and dissatisfaction with doctors' care. A higher level of medical and mental health needs in terms of poor perceived health and a high level of depression increased the probability of hospital use.

DISCUSSION

SERVICE NEEDS

This chapter examined variances in the use of community-based, in-home, and health services among the six national origin groups. Findings support diversity within and between groups. Our analyses indicate that levels of service use differ by national origin. Filipino and Vietnamese elders used no in-home services, for reasons that are unclear. This may be related to the finding, discussed in chapter 3, that Filipino elders reported the best health indicators. That Vietnamese American elders rarely use in-home services is troublesome, given the previous finding that they have the poorest health; of course, this may be related to language barriers. More research is warranted to examine this disparity in service use.

Most Asian elders had a regular source of medical care by a physician. A striking exception is Indian elders, more than half of whom had no regular doctor, which is surprising given the impressive number of physicians of East Indian ethnicity practicing medicine in the U.S. Indian elders also reported the highest level of dissatisfaction with treatment and care from physicians, which may explain their lower use of physicians. These findings indicate that Asian elders, especially Indian elders, may not be served well by the service delivery system (Kuo and Torres-Gil 2001; Mui and Kang 2006). Compared to the other groups, Japanese elders who were extremely dissatisfied with their physicians reported the highest level of emergency room and hospital use. Dissatisfaction with physicians can lead to a delay in medical treatment among Japanese elders, which may then result in the use of an emergency room and hospital.

CORRELATES OF COMMUNITY-BASED, IN-HOME, AND HEALTH SERVICES USE

Survey results indicate that the dynamics of service use among the Asian American elderly population differ across the various service categories. In the regression analyses, different models showed different predictors, but they also displayed similarities as the models moved from the most discretionary services (community-based services) to the least (hospital admission). Data showed that Asian elders' use of community-based, physician, emergency room, and hospital services were determined more by enabling than need factors. This finding regarding enabling factors is not consistent with the literature, as previous studies have found that the need factors had the most impact in explaining community-based, in-home services, and physician service use (Mui and Burnette 1994). The findings imply that, for Asian American elders, program interventions that target the enabling factors may encourage Asian American elders to use services when necessary.

In terms of predisposing factors, results indicate that more older women than men were likely to use community-based services, which is consistent with the literature (Kuo and Torres-Gil 2001). This gender disparity may be attributed to the fact that community-based services are more acceptable to older Asian women than to older Asian men. For older women, community-based services provide opportunities for socialization and social relationships, which is more important to women than men (Burnette and Mui 1995, 1999). These findings suggest the need for outreach to older men who may not find the existing community-based services attractive. Asian immigrant elders living alone were more likely to use in-home services than were elders who lived with family members, all else being equal. This finding is consistent with past literature (Kuo and Torres-Gil 2001). The data reflect the need and willingness of elders living alone to depend on formal services when family is unavailable.

Old age was another predisposing factor that increased the likelihood of using in-home, emergency room, and hospital services. This finding is also analogous to the conclusions of previous studies (Kuo and Torres-Gil 2001; Mui and Burnette 1994; Burnette and Mui 1995, 1999). Further, since old age is associated with nondiscretionary services use, family may be playing a role in linking these elders with the health care system. A longer stay in the United States is also associated with the increased likelihood of using community-based, in-home, and physician services. Data suggest that long-timers may have more knowledge about the service delivery system and be more receptive to formal service use than newer immigrants. Service providers need to reach out to the new Asian immigrant elders to educate them about the system and the availability of services.

Regarding enabling factors, all these variables are modifiable, and service providers should pay attention to them. Perhaps the most important of these is health insurance coverage. Findings strongly support the influence of both Medicare and Medicaid coverage on the probability of an elder's use of all five categories of services from the most to the least discretionary, which is consistent with the literature (Abe-Kim et al. 2002; Harada and Laurean 2001; USDHHS 2005). Since a significant proportion of Asian elders do not have Medicare because they lack of a U.S. work history, advocates for immigrant elders need to inform lower-income elders to find out if they are eligible for Medicaid.

Among all the services, hospital utilization (the least discretionary service type) was associated with less support from children. Culturally, having less family support may mean psychological distress as Asian elders expect families to help them when they are in need (Mui 1996. 2001). Findings regarding assistance from children point to the need for Asian American elders to develop better social support networks so that family may encourage early physician care to prevent unnecessary hospitalization. A higher level of religiosity was another enabling factor for hospital use. Spirituality may have given the elders courage to get the help they needed when their children were not available. The role of spirituality and positive self-care behaviors is well documented (Mui and Kang 2006). The finding that high religiosity is associated with hospital use points to the importance of health care professionals receiving cultural competence training so that the Asian immigrant elderly can receive holistic care.

Furthermore, community-based service use is associated with more medical conditions and stressful life events. Data highlight the need to develop health education and stress management programs in all elderly services so that their programs can be effective in fostering service use and in improving elders' health and quality of life. Poor perceived health is the only need factor associated with physician, emergency room, and hospital use. This finding is also analogous to the previous studies (Burnette and Mui 1999; Mui and Kang 2006). In the physician use model, Asian American elders who perceived poor health, had more stressful life events, and perceived a wider generation gap were less likely to seek services. Service providers should be aware of the need and vulnerability of Asian American elders who may be overwhelmed by stresses and losses in their lives but are not seeking help in dealing with these life events. In the hospital-use model, that depressed Asian American elders end up in a hospital suggests the issue of comorbidity, which requires further study.

In sum, this chapter has examined the impact of predisposing, enabling, and need factors and their relative importance in predicting the utilization of community-based, in-home, physician, emergency room, and hospital services by elderly Asian Americans. Across all five categories of service use, need factors did not carry as much weight as enabling factors in predicting utilization as found in other studies on white and other minority elders (Burnette and Mui 1995, 1999; Jang et al. 1998; Mui and Burnette 1994). This is a significant finding, because enabling factors (i.e., health insurance, English proficiency, family support, and attitudes toward physician or nursing home care) are extremely modifiable; policy and program planners should pay attention to these issues in order to improve Asian American elders' quality of life.

8

PRODUCTIVE AGING
Grandparent Caregiving and Volunteering

THE MAJORITY OF OLDER ADULTS remain active by helping family members and engaging in volunteer work. Active involvement in one's social surroundings is considered crucial to the psychological well-being of older adults (Wilmoth 2004), as leaving the labor market and having no family responsibilities undermines their social integration. Contributing to family and society by providing formal and informal help offers elders opportunities to maintain social roles and interpersonal connections. The MacArthur Study on Aging concluded that engagement in meaningful activities contributes to health, satisfaction with life, and longevity, and potentially reduces physical and emotional illness in later life (Rowe and Kahn 1998). With the aging of the baby boom generation and the increase in the number of older adults who remain in good health, there has been renewed interest in the contributions elders make through performing socially valued roles (Burr, Caro, and Moorhead 2002). A growing number of studies have examined elders who are involved in civic participation and volunteer work (Burr, Choi, and Mutchler 2005; Holstein and Minkler 2003; Van Willingen 2000).

Remaining socially integrated through group memberships and by performing social roles can be challenging for many adults after retirement age, but this is more so for older adults who immigrate later in life. Very few studies, however, have explored the lives of older immigrants from the perspective of social integration (Wilmoth 2004).

A large number of Asian elders who immigrate to the United States to be reunited with their children contribute to their family by caring for their grandchildren. However, data are sparse regarding grandparenting among Asian American elders (Kataoka-Yahiro, Ceria, and Caulfield 2004; Yoon 2005). To our knowledge, moreover, no studies have examined Asian elders who are involved with social activities such as volunteer work. This chapter addresses this knowledge gap by examining the involvement of Asian American elders with grandparent caregiving and volunteer work, and the characteristics of elders who are involved in these activities.

GRANDPARENT CAREGIVING

According to the 2000 Census, 5.8 million grandparents in the United States live with their grandchildren under the age of eighteen (Simmons and Dye 2003). Considerable variation in ethnicity is seen among adults who co-reside with grandchildren; only 2.5 percent of non-Hispanic whites aged thirty and older lived with their grandchildren, and 6 percent of Asian Americans, 8 percent of blacks, 8 percent of Native American and Alaska Natives, and 8 percent of Hispanics of comparable age lived with their grandchildren. Among those who co-reside with their grandchildren, 2.4 million grandparents are primarily responsible for raising them (Simmons and Dye 2003). Over 50 percent of blacks and American Indian and Alaska Natives, and 40 percent of non-Hispanic whites have responsibility for their co-resident grandchildren.

Caring for grandchildren can range from helping parents who remain the primary parenting figures to sharing parental responsibilities (co-parenting) to acting as surrogate parents. Most grandparents who co-reside with their adult children assume a supportive rather than a primary role in the care of their grandchildren (Hayslip and Kiminski 2005). At the same time, an increasing number of grandparents become surrogate parents by gaining custody of their grandchildren. Households where grandparents are primarily responsible for their grandchildren are known as "skipped-generation households," as the parents are unable to carry out their parenting duties because of substance abuse, teenage pregnancy, incarceration, mental illness, or HIV/AIDS. Grandparents may also be awarded custody of their grandchildren if their adult children are disabled or deceased (Simmons and Dye 2003).

African American grandparents are more likely than grandparents of other ethnicities to become custodial grandparents (Fuller-Thompson and Minkler 2001). Asian and Hispanic grandparents, on the other hand, are the least likely to be responsible for their grandchildren (20% and 35%, respectively). That fewer Asians have primary responsibility for their grandchildren is largely associated with low divorce rates and female-headed households among the Asian population. Only 4.2 percent of Asians are divorced compared to 9.7 percent for the total U.S. population. Although close to 12 percent of U.S. households are headed by women with no spouse present, the rate for Asian households is 8.8 percent. These figures suggest that most Asian elders co-reside with their adult children and their grandchildren because of cultural factors or economic conditions related to immigration rather than the need to assume custody of their grandchildren (Yoon 2005).

A number of studies have examined how grandparent caregiving affects the elder's psychological well-being. Some studies indicate that grandparenting can negatively affect an elder's mental health, as he or she is often socially isolated and thus lacks social support (Hooyman and Kiyak 2002). Grandparent caregivers also may often develop health problems, as they place the physical needs of their grandchildren ahead of their own. Negotiating and balancing their own needs versus their grandchildren's may also lead to role conflicts, which, in turn, adversely affect psychological well-being (Hayslip and Kaminski 2005). On the other hand, grandparenting may enhance the grandparents' morale and given them a sense of satisfaction (Burton, Dilworth-Anderson, and Merriwether-deVries 1995).

GRANDPARENTING AMONG ASIAN AMERICANS

Asian grandparents in the United States are more likely to live in households headed by their adult children than to be the head of skipped-generation households (Kataoka-Yahiro, Ceria, and Caulfield 2004). Thus their role in caring for the grandchildren is usually that of helping their adult children who are dual-wage earners (Treas and Mazumdar 2004) or run their own family business (P.G. Min 1998). Co-residence with adult children is common in traditional Asian cultures. Whereas the rate of multigenerational households has been decreasing in Japan, for example, it is still the norm in China, India, the Philippines, and Vietnam (Kamo 1998), where taking care of grandchildren is a common task for grandparents (Kataoka-Yahiro et al. 2004). In the Philippines, Thailand, and Taiwan, around 40 percent of older adults live in a household with at least one minor grandchild and are involved in their care (Velkoff and Lawson 1998). Some grandparents in traditional Asian societies contribute to their families financially by paying the educational expenses of their grandchildren (Agbayani-Siewert 1994), whereas others contribute by taking an active role in raising them. In patrilineal families, the father's mother is valued for her knowledge of and experiences with raising children and is expected to advise her daughter-in-law. Grandparents in Asian families have traditionally occupied various roles such as acting as family historians, role models, teachers, mentors, nurturers, and mediators (Vo-Thanh-Xuan and Rice 2000).

When Asian elders immigrate in late adulthood their role as grandparents may be intensified because their visas are sponsored by their adult children who need their help with the family (Min, Moon, and Lubben 2005; Treas and Mazumdar 2004). Ikels (1983), who studied Chinese immigrants in Boston, reported that Chinese immigrant elders have made major contributions in helping to run their adult children's households. Korean elders have also made important contributions to the families of their adult children who run small businesses (Min 1998). In Vietnamese families, the provision of child care and maintenance of the household by elders were essential to the survival of refugee families after they arrived in the United States (Yee 1992). Immigrant grandparents also contribute to the ethnic socialization of their grandchildren by using their native language in the families of their adult children. A survey based on 2000 Census data indicated that children who live with their immigrant grandparents have a much higher rate of speaking their native language than children who do not live in multigenerational households (Ishizawa 2004). As Treas and Mazumdar (2004) note, contributing to family life may be a way for immigrant elders to secure positions for themselves in their families. At the same time, there has been a decrease in grandparents' involvement with grandchildren among Asian immigrant families. As families acculturate, they are less inclined to live in three-generation households (Detzner 1996; Kim, Kim, and Hurh 1991). This phenomenon, also observed in many Asian countries, is attributed to the increased emphasis on nuclear families brought about by industrialization and urbanization (Strom and Strom 1999).

VOLUNTEERING

Older adults engage in volunteer work by helping others on a formal basis through organizations as well helping in informal ways (Li and Ferraro 2005). In the United States, approximately 40 percent of elders are involved in formal volunteer work (Hooyman and Kiyak 2002). Factors that motivate older adults to engage in volunteer work include altruism, needing something to do with their time, wanting to socialize with others, and fulfilling their religious beliefs (O'Reilly and Caro 1994). Studies indicate that, compared to elders who do not volunteer, those who do are younger, have higher incomes, are better educated, and are more likely to have volunteered in the past (Morrow-Howell et al. 2003). Furthermore, elders who volunteer function better physically and report better mental health and stronger life satisfaction than elders who do not volunteer (Morrow-Howell et al. 2003; VanWillingen 2000).

A major benefit of volunteering for older adults is that they gain, or retain, a sense of meaning and purpose in life. Being useful and fulfilling multiple roles enhances emotional well-being (Greenfield and Marks 2004). Gaining new roles and becoming embedded in a social network through volunteering also helps older adults adjust to life transitions, such as retirement and widowhood. Research using national data comparing younger and older volunteers indicated that older adults experience greater life satisfaction and report better health than younger adults as a result of engaging in volunteer work (Van Willingen 2000). Other studies among older adults have found that the sense of doing good for others results in fewer depressive symptoms (Musick, Herzog, and House 1999).

VOLUNTEERING AMONG ASIAN AMERICAN ELDERS

Volunteer work in the U.S. is seen as a way for retirees to engage in productive activities that are meaningful and contribute to society. According to Savishinsky (2004), the concept of finding meaningful activities through volunteer work after retirement is culture bound. As he notes, Americans have been encouraged to spend their retirement enjoying leisure and, at the same time, engaging in purposeful activities, becoming "other-directed in pursuit of self-fulfillment." In traditional Asian Indian culture, he points out, the ideal of retirement is not to become other-directed but rather to renounce worldly engagements and pursue spiritual development.

The centrality of the family in Asian culture may also inhibit elders from engaging in volunteer work. As Carstensen and colleagues (1999) note in their theory of socioemotional selectivity, perceptions of a shortened "time left" influence elders to focus on fewer relationships. Their growing awareness that their remaining time is limited may encourage Asian elders to focus on close family relationships and disregard establishing new, distant relationships (Carstensen, Isaacowitz, and Charles 1999).

Volunteer work among immigrant elders must also be considered from a socio-economic perspective. Factors that motivate and enable people to engage in formal and informal volunteer work are often examined from a human, social, and cultural framework. According to Wilson (2000), "human capital" refers to attributes such as education, health, and financial status; "social capital" includes family relationships and social networks; and "cultural capital" refers to ethical values and beliefs about helping others and contributing to society. From the perspective of human capital, recently arrived Asian elders are often struggling to survive and lack the financial means to engage in formal volunteer work. Family life may also be a barrier to volunteering among Asian elders. Intergenerational co-residence and the need to help family members may inhibit elders from venturing outside the family to help others (Kim et al. 2007). The importance that Asian cultural values place on family is another factor that makes it preferable for elders to assist only family members (J. Kim et al. 2007).

The idea of encouraging elders to help non-family members through formal volunteer work is a relatively new phenomenon in Asian societies. Although civic participation has enjoyed a long tradition in U.S. society (Holstein and Minkler 2003), the concept is relatively new in Asian nations. Increased longevity and economic security among elders, however, has started to prompt Asian nations such as China, Japan, Korea, Singapore, and Taiwan to develop programs for elders to engage in volunteer work (Kim et al. 2007; Mjelde-Mossy, Chi, and Chow 2002; Nakano 2000; Yan and Tang 2003). For example, there has been a movement in Hong Kong to encourage older adults to volunteer in the social services sector to facilitate their remaining active and playing a productive role in the community (Mjelde-Mossey, Chi, and Chow 2002; Yan and Tang 2003). Mjelde and colleagues (2002) report a study in Hong Kong which shows that the idea of retired persons doing volunteer work is still a new phenomenon there. According to a survey on the public perception of volunteering, Mjelde and colleagues note that over 83 percent agreed that retired persons do not have a responsibility to serve the community. Yet, their study of professionals aged forty-five and older found that over 40 percent had volunteer experience and the majority of the respondents were interested in volunteering in social services.

A national survey of older adults in Korea indicates that elders there volunteer less than elders in the United States (J. Kim et al. 2007). Volunteering among Korean elders was associated with higher education, good physical health, and homeownership. Religious beliefs also prompted elders to volunteer. Those who identified themselves as Buddhist or Catholic were more likely to volunteer than those who professed no religion. Older adults who lived alone or with a spouse only were also more likely to volunteer than those who lived with both a spouse and children.

In Japan, the word "volunteer" was virtually unknown twenty years ago. However, the term is now a part of everyday vocabulary in Japan and is embraced by policy makers (Nakano 2000). The wide acceptance of volunteer work is thought to be associated with economic security and the growing belief that individuals may chose different lifestyles. For example, the notion that women are obliged to do housework is changing, and society is more accepting of the idea that women may seek fulfillment by volunteering outside the home. As Nakano notes, volunteerism in Japan is a marker for the emergence of a new type of "citizen-oriented society."

Few studies have examined formal volunteer work among Asian Americans. One study by Ecklund and Park (2005, 2007), however, looked at the Asian American community's participation in volunteer work based on religious affiliation. Their findings indicated differences in patterns of volunteering between Asian Americans and other races. Using the Social Capital Community Benchmark Survey (SCCBS), the authors analyzed data involving 711 Asian American respondents. No differences were found in the level of volunteer participation between members of different Asian nationalities. Catholic and Protestant Asian Americans were shown to volunteer more than other Asians who were not affiliated with a religion, but Hindus and Buddhists volunteered less than the nonaffiliated. Although the study was not limited to older adults, the findings pointed to differences between Asian elders who live in their home country and those who immigrate to the United States. Higher education and income is commonly associated with community volunteerism, but this was not the case with Asian Americans, which may indicate that immigrant Asians continue to feel that they must focus on their family in order to survive in the United States and, further, that they have not yet incorporated the American concept of volunteerism (Nakano, 2000). Because of the Asian Americans' minority status, it is also possible that the dominant society may not reach out to them to solicit their volunteer participation.

CONCEPTUAL FRAMEWORK: PRODUCTIVE AGING

This chapter uses the framework of productive aging to examine grandparent caregiving and volunteer work among Asian American elders. The concept of productive aging is gaining increasing recognition in the field of gerontology because it focuses on the positive aspects of aging rather than on disability, illness, and dependency (Holstein and Minkler 2003). The term "productive aging" refers to any activity by an older adult that produces goods or services or develops his or her capacity to produce them regardless of whether the older adult is paid for the activity (Bass and Caro 2001). For older adults, active engagement usually involves unpaid activities that have societal value, most commonly volunteer work and caring for family members (Menec 2003). Bass and Caro (2001) delineate four distinct variables that influence engagement with productive activities among older adults.

Environmental variables include factors such as the economy, cultural norms, and demographic changes.

Situational variables refer to an individual's socioeconomic status, health, roles, and responsibilities.

Individual variables include gender and ethnicity, and personal attributes such as motivation and beliefs.

Social policy determines work, retirement and pension policies, and tax regulations.

MEASURES

Grandparent caregiving was measured by asking elders if they regularly took care of their grandchildren (yes=1, no=0). *Volunteer work* was a composite score measured by asking elders how often they engaged in volunteer work on a 3-point scale (1=often to 3=never). We collapsed the responses and created a dichotomous variable of doing and not doing volunteer work. *Sociodemographic* measures include age, sex, and Medicaid; the latter was used as a proxy for financial status. Two items were used to measure *acculturation*: English proficiency and the number of years living in the United States. To assess English proficiency, elders were asked to report their ability to read, write, and speak English on a 4-point scale (not at all=0 to very well=3). *Health factors* were measured with a 1-item question that asked elders to rate their health on a 5-point scale (excellent=1 to poor=5), and by asking if they had any medical conditions such as heart disease, cancer, stroke, diabetes, and arthritis. *Family and spiritual factors* included life satisfaction, religiosity, living arrangements, and having children who lived close by. *Life satisfaction* was measured with a single-item global measure. Elders were asked to respond to the question, "All things considered, how satisfied are you with life in general these days?" on a 4-point scale (very dissatisfied=1 to very satisfied=4). *Religiosity* was assessed on a 4-point scale by asking respondents their perception of the importance of religion in their lives (not at all important=0 to very important=3). Living arrangements were assessed by asking elders if they lived with their family. Having children who lived nearby was assessed by the number of children living within a two-hour drive.

RESULTS

The majority of elders in the study had grandchildren (*n*=335, 82.9%), and about a third of these elders reported that they took care of their grandchildren regularly (*n*=118, 35.2%). A smaller number of elders than those who took care of their grandchildren engaged in volunteer work (*n*=104, 25.7%). There was very little overlap between elders who cared for their grandchildren and those who worked voluntarily: a very small number reported both caring for their grandchildren and doing volunteer work (*n*=29, 7%). The two groups, therefore, can be considered quite distinct from each other.

GRANDPARENT CAREGIVING

As presented in table 8.1, comparison between grandparent caregivers (*n*=118) and non-grandparent caregivers (*n*=217) indicates that the former are significantly younger and report better health. There were no significant gender differences or differences based on marital status. Grandparent caregivers are also less acculturated than those who do not care for their grandchildren on a regular basis. They have lower English proficiency and have been in the United States for a shorter period. Elders who cared for their grandchildren regularly also scored higher on the religiosity scale (2.5 vs. 2.3 points). Grandparent caregivers had significantly more frequent face-to-face contact with their children than non-grandparent caregivers (90% and 60%, respectively). Grandparent caregivers were also more likely to have closer relationships with their adult children than non-grandparent caregivers. Elders who cared for

TABLE 8.1 Grandparent and Non-Grandparent Caregivers: Demographic and Social Support Network Comparisons

	GRANDPARENT CAREGIVERS N= 118 (35.2%)	NON-GRANDPARENT CAREGIVERS N= 217 (64.7%)
Age [Mean (*SD*)][a]**	**70.9(0.7)**	**73.0(0.5)**
Gender (female vs. male)[b]	59.3 vs. 40.7%	58.1 vs. 41.9%
Marital status (married vs. not married)	51.7 vs. 48.3%	46.1 vs. 53.9%
Medicaid	40%	47%
	Mean (*SD*)	Mean (*SD*)
Perceived health**	**2.8(1.2)**	**2.4(1.1)**
No. of medical conditions	2.6(1.7)	2.8(2.1)
Religiosity*	2.5(0.9)	2.3(0.8)
Length of stay in the U.S****	15.8(1.2)	22.0(0.9)
English proficiency (0-9)*	2.3(0.3)	3.2(0.2)
Children living within 2 hr (0-10)	2.1 (0.2)	2.0(0.1)
No. of neighbors with close friendship*	3.3 (0.3)	2.6(0.2)
Life satisfaction	3.2 (0.1)	3.0(0.1)
Frequency of interaction [Mean (*SD*)]		
Face-to-face contact with children	3.8(1.3)	4.1(1.2)
Phone contact with children	3.9(1.2)	3.7(1.2)
Would like to see children more	2.5(0.5)	2.6(0.5)
Satisfaction with family	3.3 (0.1)	3.3 (0.1)
Assistance to children (%)		
Help when someone is ill****	87.0	39.2
Give advice****	93.8	43.2
Shop or run errands****	69.6	22.6
Help your children with money**	27.9	14.9
Fix things around (their/his/her) house****	58.2	21.1
Keep house for (them/him/her)****	75.9	26.3
Assistance from children (%)		
Help when you are ill****	95.5	77.0
Give advice****	73.2	48.7
Shop or run errands****	87.3	59.5
Fix things around house****	73.4	45.8
Keep or clean house****	67.9	32.8
Prepare meals, but not keep the house****	62.0	31.3
Help out with money****	72.6	40.8
Provide transportation****	84.9	47.5

[a] Differences between means were tested by T-statistics.
[b] Percentage differences were tested by Chi-square statistics.
* $p<.05$.
** $p<.01$.
**** $p<.0001$.

their grandchildren also reported better self-perceived health than non-grandparent caregivers. There were no differences in reported life satisfaction among the two groups.

VOLUNTEER WORK

As presented in table 8.2, comparison between volunteers ($n = 104$) and non-volunteers ($n = 300$) indicates that Asian elders who participated in volunteer activities were significantly younger than their cohorts who did not do so. A significantly greater number of men (54.8%) than women (45.2%) engaged in volunteer work. Volunteers were also less likely than non-volunteers to receive Medicaid (20% vs. 80%). Volunteers reported better health and fewer medical conditions. They also reported significantly higher rates of intergenerational exchanges, as well as a greater number of friends and neighbors, than did non-volunteers. Elders who volunteered were more likely to help ill family members, give advice, run errands, provide financial assistance, and assist with household tasks. They also received more assistance from their adult children and perceived their health as significantly better compared to the responses of non-volunteers. Volunteering elders also reported significantly higher life satisfaction than their non-volunteering counterparts.

FACTORS ASSOCIATED WITH GRANDPARENT CAREGIVING AND VOLUNTEERING

We used logistic regression models to examine factors associated with grandparent caregiving and volunteering. Following the conceptual framework of productive aging, we entered sociodemographic characteristics (age, gender, and income), acculturation, health, life satisfaction, and religiosity in the model. We were not able to enter employment because only 8 percent ($n = 35$) of the respondents had full- or part-time jobs.

Table 8.3 presents the results of the logistic regression models. Both models were significant ($p < .0001$) in predicting factors associated with Asian American elders' involvement in grandparent caregiving and volunteering. In the grandparenting model, English proficiency, length of stay in the United States, religiosity, and co-residence with family were significantly correlated with the likelihood of an elder being a grandparent caregiver. Elders with poor English skills and a short stay in the United States, and who claimed that

TABLE 8.2 Volunteers and Nonvolunteers: Demographic and Social Support Network

	VOLUNTEERS $N = 104$ (25.7%)	NONVOLUNTEERS $N = 300$ (74.3%)
Age [Mean (*SD*)][a] ****	**69.6 (0.8)**	**73.0 (0.4)**
Gender (female vs. male)[b] *	45.2 vs. 54.8%	59.6 vs. 40.4%
Marital status (married vs. not married)*	57.7 vs. 42.3%	46.7 vs. 53.5%
Medicaid*	20%	80%
	Mean (*SD*)	Mean (*SD*)
Perceived health*****	3.1(1.2)	2.4(1.1)
No. of medical conditions*	2.3(1.6)	2.9(2.1)
Religiosity*	2.4(0.8)	2.2(1.0)
Length of stay in the U.S.	21.0(1.2)	20.0(0.8)
English proficiency (0–9)******	4.7(0.3)	2.5(0.2)
Children living within two hr (0–10)	1.8(0.2)	2.0(0.1)
No. of neighbors with close friendship*	3.4(0.3)	2.7(0.1)
Life satisfaction **	3.2(0.1)	2.9(0.0)
Frequency of interaction [Mean (*SD*)]		
Face-to-face contact with children*	3.8(1.3)	4.2(1.2)
Phone contact with children	3.9(1.2)	3.6(1.2)
Would like to see children more	2.5(0.5)	2.6(0.5)
Satisfaction with family	3.3(0.0)	3.3(0.1)
Assistance to children (%)		
Help when someone is ill******	77.4	48.6
Give advice******	79.8	53.5
Shop or run errands******	63.4	33.5
Help your children with money******	44.7	14.4
Fix things around (their/his/her) house******	64.1	24.5
Keep house for (them/him/her)******	63.0	38.7
Assistance from children (%)		
Help when you are ill	90.3	82.3
Give advice ******	74.2	51.2
Shop or run errands	73.4	69.5
Fix things around house******	75.0	51.9
Keep or clean house*	58.1	43.7
Prepare meals but not keep the house*	52.2	39.9
Help out with money	52.1	51.0

[a] Differences between means were tested by *T*-statistics.
[b] Percentage differences were tested by Chi-square statistics.
* $p < .05$.
** $p < .01$.
**** $p < .0001$.

TABLE 8.3 Logistic Regressions Associated with Being a Volunteer or Grandparent Caregiver

INDEPENDENT VARIABLES	BEING A GRANDPARENT CAREGIVER	BEING A VOLUNTEER
	Significant Logistic Coefficients	
Sociodemographic characteristics		
Age (young old=1)		
Sex (male=1)		
Medicaid (yes=1)		−.40*
Acculturation factors		
English proficiency (0–9)	−.18**	.23**
Length of stay in U.S. (1–72)	−.10**	
Health factors		
Perceived health (1–5)		.10*
No. of medical conditions (0–12)		
Family and spiritual factors		
Life satisfaction (1–4)		
Religiosity (0–3)	.13**	.16**
Living arrangement (alone=1)	−1.6**	
Children live within two hr (0–10)		
Model χ^2	**42.91*****	**49.60*******

* $p<.05.$
** $p<.01.$
*** $p<.001.$
**** $p<.0001.$

religion is important in their lives, were more likely to engage in grandparent caregiving. Factors increasing the likelihood of volunteer work included higher income, better English proficiency, better health, and religiosity. Elders who are not on Medicaid, have better English proficiency, better perceived health, and consider religion as important in their lives were more likely to serve as volunteers.

DISCUSSION

The findings indicate important similarities and differences among Asian American elders who cared for their grandchildren and those who engaged in volunteer work. There were no statistically significant differences between the number of men and women who cared for their grandchildren, but more men than women reported doing volunteer work. This differs from the overall pattern of volunteering in the United States, where women are more likely to volunteer than men (Hooyman and Kiyak 2002). Gender differences in volunteering in the United States have been attributed to the fact that women who are widowed tend to volunteer. Among the Asian elders who were volunteers, a higher percentage was married than not married. Married women tend to have other competing demands such as domestic responsibilities, which may explain why more men than women volunteered in our sample. Furthermore, more men than women take on leadership roles in the community and religious organizations in Asian immigrant communities, which may account for the larger number of men reporting that they engage in volunteer work.

Both grandparent caregivers and volunteer elders were engaged in more intergenerational exchanges than grandparents who were not caregivers and did not volunteer. An examination of intergenerational support among grandparent caregivers and volunteer elders reveals that a larger portion of the former group provided assistance to their families in caring for an ill family member, giving advice, and keeping house.

Elders who engage in volunteer work are more likely to be acculturated than elders who care for their grandchildren, for a number of reasons. First, the concept of volunteer work may be foreign to newly immigrated elders, who are less acculturated, and so they may not even consider engaging in such work. Second, less acculturated elders may adhere more closely to the traditional notion of intergenerational solidarity and feel obliged to meet the needs of their adult children. Third, these less acculturated elders are linguistically isolated, which may be a barrier to their engaging in volunteer work. Finally, these elders may be financially dependent on their families and thus feel the need to assist their families rather than people to whom they are not related.

Financial security was associated with volunteering but not with caring for grandchildren, a finding that concurs with other research demonstrating the association between human capital and volunteer work (Musick and Wilson 2003). Elders with financial resources can engage in helping others, whereas those who struggle financially lack the means to do so. Perceived health was also associated with volunteering, which again concurs with other studies indicating an association between good health and volunteerism (Wilson 2000). Health, however, was not significantly associated with grandparent caregiving, which may suggest that caring for grandchildren does not adversely affect the health of elders as previous studies have testified (Hughes et al. 2007). At the same time, Asian elders may be in family situations where they must care for their grandchildren regardless of their health.

Religiosity was significantly associated with both volunteer work and grandparent caregiving, perhaps because of the importance religion places on caring for others. Our findings concur with previous studies that indicated associations between volunteer work and religiosity. Both religious beliefs and engaging in volunteer work provide people with meaning and purpose in life (Koenig, McCullogh, and Larsen 2001). Moreover, religious organizations in the United States, including Christian churches and Buddhist and Hindu temples, provide venues for volunteer work providing elders who are members of a religious organization with more opportunities to engage in such work.

Affiliations with religious organizations also provide a support network (Koenig et al. 2001). At the same time, religiosity is associated with coping. Researchers have found, for example, that people with illnesses are able to find strength in the face of adversity and better cope when they have religious beliefs (Cohen and Koenig 2003; Musick et al. 2000). Being religious may provide an important coping mechanism for elders who may experience stressors from caring for their grandchildren. Life conditions differ between elders who do volunteer work and those who engage in caring for their grandchildren. The former are able to exert choice and control over the nature and amount of their involvement. Elders who care for family members, however, usually have little choice regarding the amount and type of their involvement (Burr et al. 2005). As Rosario and colleagues (2004) note, unlike volunteer work, caring for family members usually comes as an "inevitable responsibility" and is contingent on the needs of the person being cared for and the nature of the preexisting relationship with this person. It is not surprising, therefore, that elders who worked as volunteers reported higher self-satisfaction than those who did not engage in such work.

No significant differences in life satisfaction were found between grandparents who provided care and those who did not, a finding which suggests that elders may not necessarily have a positive experience when caring for their grandchildren. Indeed, doing so can pose a number of challenges for grandparents. Research on long-term relationships between Mexican grandparents and their grandchildren suggests that acculturation of the grandchild generation creates social and emotional distance between young adult grandchildren and their grandparents (Silverstein and Chen 1999). According to Silverstein and Chen, differences in cultural values between grandparents and their young adult grandchildren results in less interaction between them. Although the affection grandparents feel toward their grandchildren does not change, over time young adult grandchildren experience less intimacy toward their grandparents. When grandchildren acculturate into the dominant culture, they usually become more fluent in English and less motivated to speak their native language. These language gaps between grandparents and grandchildren reduce the amount of contact between them and weaken the relationship (Strom, Buki, and Strom 1997).

The traditional role of grandparents to teach cultural values and traditions can be a challenge to Asian immigrant families, as children may no longer want to learn about their culture (Strom and Strom 2000). Differences in cultural values can also create tension in intergenerational relationships (Detzner 1996; Weinstein-Shr and Henkin 1991). In traditional Asian cultures, children were not allowed to question adults' authority. Grandchildren may resent the traditional hierarchical pattern of family relationships, and grandparents may not know how to handle the rebellious behaviors of their grandchildren. The widening distance between grandparents and grandchildren may result in grandparents feeling lonely and disappointed.

Grandparent caregivers need to learn skills that will facilitate rewarding intergenerational exchanges. Support services may include programs to help grandparents adjust to changing family relationships owing to acculturation. Skills training and psychosocial support groups may also help elders cope with intergenerational cultural conflicts (Hayslip and Kiminski 2005; Strom and Strom 2000). Strom and Strom (2000) proposed a curriculum for Chinese grandparents who have had difficulties adapting to rapid sociocultural changes in Taiwan, and it includes teaching communication skills and ways of listening to their grandchildren.

As noted earlier, grandparents in traditional Asian families played many roles, including that of historian, teacher, and mentor. Whereas grandparents were traditionally respected for their accumulated knowledge and wisdom (Vo-Thanh-Xuan and Rice 2000), these qualities may be of little use to immigrant families. As a result, grandparent caregivers may feel they are not appreciated and reap few emotional rewards for the care they provide their families (Vo-Thanh-Xuan and Rice 2000). Grandparents may also need to learn ways to give up their investment in maintaining certain cultural values, such as expecting unquestioning loyalty from their grandchildren. Research suggests that close relationships with grandparents also benefit grandchildren, particularly adolescents struggling with identity issues (Burton et al. 1995). Therefore facilitating positive relationships between grandparents and grandchildren is also to the advantage of grandchildren.

As discussed in previous chapters, evidence suggests that acculturation weakens intergenerational solidarity among Asian immigrant families. A study of Chinese, Korean, and Japanese American families reported that adult children, as they acculturate, tend to move away from ethnic communities and live separately from their elderly parents (Ishii-Kuntz 1997). Some elders, as they settle into life in the United States, prefer their greater independence from their adult children (Yoo and Sung 1997). As Asian elders become more independent, opportunities need to be made available so they can establish relationships with people outside their immediate family. In this respect, formal volunteer work can be a source of social support and in turn mitigate social isolation (Min et al. 2005). Engaging in formal volunteer work, as noted earlier, may be a new concept for immigrant elders. Volunteer organizations that focus on elders, such as those that recruit foster grandparents and senior companions, may not have programs that serve the Asian American community and would therefore not recruit Asian elders as volunteers. Such organizations would also be faced with language barriers. In light of the increasing number of older adults in the Asian American community, programs need to be developed that will facilitate social engagement and opportunities for productive activities among this population.

9

CONCLUSION

Implications for Practice, Policy, and Research

THE AGING OF THE WORLD'S population is a concern for all generations in all nations, all sectors (private, public, nonprofit, business, medical, and social services), and all communities. The dramatic increase in the aging population profoundly impacts the lives of individuals, families, and societies. Governments and local communities must respond to this demographic shift by developing infrastructures and services to meet the needs of their aging members and enable them to "age in place." "Elder-friendly communities"—a term that refers not only to physical surroundings but also to environments that are responsive to elders' social and psychological needs—are based on a culture of inclusion where older adults are validated and respected for their contributions (AARP Public Policy Institute 2007; Ally et al. 2007; Austin et al. 2005).

In developing elder-friendly communities we must address basic and financial needs to foster security; provide culturally sensitive physical and mental health services to promote well-being and life-satisfaction; maximize opportunities to access services in order to facilitate autonomy; and promote social engagement so as to decrease linguistic isolation and enhance social inclusion (Feldman and Oberlink 2003; Successful Aging Initiative 2007). Developing these communities also requires a commitment to cultural competence among service providers as well as the collaboration of stakeholders, government organizations, NGOs, transportation systems, private businesses, and grass-roots organizations. This chapter uses the framework of the elder-friendly community to highlight our research findings and discuss implications for policy, practice, and future research.

THE NEED FOR GREATER UNDERSTANDING OF THE ASIAN AMERICAN AGING EXPERIENCE

Our study shows, overall, that Asian American elders are disadvantaged in almost all the dimensions of quality-of-life indicators. At the same time elders of all six national origin groups are shown to manifest strengths and resilience, and the capacity to adjust to changes in intergenerational relationships, endure life stressors, and find life satisfaction. Our findings also confirm diversity and heterogeneity among elders in English proficiency, educational attainment, economic security, physical and mental health needs, family relationships, and service utilization. This heterogeneity can be best understood from an ecological framework, focusing on four different dimensions of peoples lives and circumstances involving macro-cultural, exo-level, micro-level, and personal factors (Bronfenbrenner 1979) Macro-cultural factors include the socio-historical conditions in the country of origin; diplomatic relationships between the country of origin and the United States; attitudes of the general public toward the country of origin; and public policies toward immigrants at any given time in U.S. history. Exo-level factors include resources that are available within ethnic communities, and micro-level factors include immediate family members and close kin. Personal factors encompass gender, age, social class and socioeconomic status, English proficiency, and length of stay in the U.S. This last factor influences, among other issues, levels of acculturation, knowledge of the U.S. social welfare system, and access to benefits and services.

Quantitative surveys are inadequate to capture the lives and experiences of immigrant elders. Further research will benefit from various other methods (Padgett 2008). For example, narrative methods that examine life stories can contribute to the understanding of pre- and post-immigration experiences; continuities and disruptions; acculturation and adaptation; and hardships and endurance (Cohen et al. 2006; Deci and Ryan 2000). Knowledge obtained from such studies can shed light on risk and resiliency factors over the life course, and elucidate ways that Asian immigrant elders use adaptive strategies to resolve conflict and not only overcome but even benefit from adversity (Cohen et al. 2006). Such studies will also assist practitioners to better serve their clients by appreciating the multifaceted nature of their immigration experience.

THE NEED TO PROVIDE A FINANCIALLY SECURE
ENVIRONMENT FOR ASIAN AMERICAN ELDERS

Poverty is a critical issue for many Asian American elders. The majority of our study respondents live below the national poverty line, and 13 percent reported experiencing severe financial hardship. As reported in chapter 2, more than one-third of the Asian elderly respondents received food stamps and means-tested assistance such as Supplemental Security Income. More than half (52%) were ineligible for Social Security benefits. Financial status differed by national origin. Many Indian and Japanese elders reported income levels above the poverty line, whereas Filipino and Vietnamese elders reported severe economic challenges. Socioeconomic indicators were strongly related to health status, in that Asian American elders living in poverty were susceptible to numerous health problems (Burnette and Mui 1999; Sorlie, Backlund, and Keller 1995). Case management and advocacy services that enable Asian American elders living in poverty to access public benefit programs, health care, and affordable housing will have lasting positive psychosocial effects. Social service and health care providers need to be aware that many Asian elders, though eligible, may not be receiving benefits from either the government or private sector programs simple because they are not aware of these programs.

Significant improvement and changes in existing federal and state policies are required to increase retirement protection for immigrant and other low-wage-earning adults. Elders who earned low wages throughout their lives are likely to receive few Social Security benefits, if they are eligible at all, and are, at best, entitled to minimal pensions and other limited benefits. The lives of older immigrants who do not have U.S. citizenship have become tenuous since the Personal Responsibility and Work Opportunity Reconciliation Act (PRWORA) of 1996, which rendered immigrants ineligible for Medicare, food stamps, and cash assistance. Although New York State responded by implementing programs for disabled immigrants, and Congress subsequently restored food stamp eligibility to the elderly, older immigrants who arrived after August 1996 or who were out of the country for more than ninety days are not eligible to receive food stamps. Furthermore, immigrants who meet the eligibility criteria for food stamps must apply for citizenship within thirty days of filing an application.

Today less than half the Asian elderly respondents in our study have U.S. citizenship. Many who are eligible do not apply because of limited language proficiency; as a result, they do not qualify for means-tested benefits and services (Mui et al. 2007). Programs must not only advocate for the welfare rights of immigrants but must also assist Asian immigrant elders in gaining citizenship. As noted in chapter 7, almost 30 percent of Asian American elders needed information about entitlements and had not obtained it. Policies are needed that target funds to increase entitlement information for Asian and other immigrant elders. Elder employment assistance programs would also create jobs that would enable Asian American elders to become self-reliant, continue to contribute to the local economy, and maintain a decent standard of living.

THE NEED TO CREATE A LINGUISTICALLY FRIENDLY ENVIRONMENT FOR ASIAN AMERICAN ELDERS

Over two-thirds of respondents report no or poor English-language skills and almost one-quarter live in a household in which no one speaks English well. Overcoming language barriers is one of the most difficult cultural adaptations for immigrant elders, since elderly immigrants have trouble learning a new language. The creation of Asian-elder–friendly, English-language programs that are experiential and less formal compared to conventional language programs can help elders overcome their fear of failure and possible loss of face (Chung 2004). Language programs should also be provided at physicians' offices, hospitals, primary schools, child care centers, pharmacies, police precincts, financial institutions, law offices, and grocery stores—all locations frequented by Asian elders.

As noted in chapter 3, people with limited English proficiency also have poor health-related quality-of-life outcomes. Our findings support the literature which indicates that Asian American elders suffer from poor health because of disparities caused by language and cultural barriers (Office of Minority Health 2003). A government report acknowledges that English-language barriers among non–English-speaking patients pose a wide range of problems from access to health care to the quality of care they receive (U.S. Department of Health and Human Services 2005). Language barriers also result in severe communication problems between patients and health care providers, which in turn result in health disparities. English-speaking physicians are less likely to engage in meaningful conversations with patients whose English-language abilities are limited (Woloshin et al. 1995). Poor communication between patients and health care providers results in poor medical outcomes because of medical noncompliance (Woloshin et al. 1995). Asian American elders with limited English proficiency may be discouraged from seeking Western health services, because their inability to express themselves may be embarrassing. Communication and effective use of language are critical not only for proper diagnosis and treatment but also in building doctor-patient rapport.

The Civil Rights Act of 1964 has been interpreted as affording all U.S. citizens equal access to federally funded medical programs, regardless of the patient's language ability or culture (Mui et al. 2007) Barriers to quality communication between health care providers and patients impede this access. In fact, inadequate communication on the part of health care providers can be considered a form of discrimination against patients whose primary language is not English. Language barriers are exacerbated by the government's failure to adequately fund access to medically trained interpreters (Woloshin et al. 1995). Because of the high cost of obtaining interpreters, health care providers may encourage patients to use their adult children, grandchildren, or other relatives as interpreters. Nonprofessional interpreters such as family members are often not able to interpret medical information correctly. Misunderstandings can also occur when children and other relatives simplify information provided by the patient (Sharma and Kerl 2002). Furthermore, using grandchildren or adult children as interpreters can undermine the authority of elderly parents in their families and diminish their sense of self-efficacy and autonomy.

There is an urgent need for bilingual and bicultural professionals in ethnic-specific programs and in all health and social service settings that serve Asian American elders and other ethnic elderly groups. Manpower and workforce preparation in the elder care field is the first priority in all professional training. Strategies and programs are needed to recruit, retain, and train bilingual and bicultural Asian academics and professionals to serve this population. More funding and programs to support bilingual/bicultural physicians, social workers, and other health care providers is desperately needed. The development and mentoring of competent Asian professionals is an effective way to build Asian-elder–friendly service environments.

THE NEED TO DESIGN AN ASIAN-FRIENDLY MENTAL HEALTH SYSTEM FOR ASIAN AMERICAN ELDERS

Depressive symptoms were extensive among the Asian American elders in our study. As reported in chapter 4, 40 percent of respondents were considered depressed based on the Geriatric Depression Scale, a much higher rate of depression than the 19–20 percent observed in most studies of community-dwelling ethnic elders (Ferraro, Bercier, and Chelminski 1997; Hazuda et al. 1998; Shibusawa and Mui 2001; Woo et al. 1994). Depression, of course, is a treatable disease but is more likely to go undetected or be misdiagnosed among Asian American elders because of cultural and language barriers (Mui and Kang 2006).

Depression is associated with suicides, and so mental health service providers must place priority on early screening and assessment, and on the development of culturally appropriate interventions for depression. Moreover, mental health professionals need to understand the complexity of the Asian immigrant aging experience and factors associated with their psychological distress. Because mental health is associated with physical health, professionals must assess for comorbidity (Mui et al. 2007). Mental health providers also need to understand how depression is culturally constructed. Clinically it is a disease with predictable symptoms and treatment responses (Mui 1996b); from a sociocultural perspective, the manifestation of depression, including symptom expression, definition of the illness, and response to the illness is shaped by the belief system and cultural norms of a given culture (Mui 1996a).

Depression screening is crucial given the high prevalence of depression among this population. Early depression screening should be provided in all community-based settings, including senior housing, community centers, physicians' offices, adult day care centers, and other health and social service programs. Mental health education, including information about the relationship between physical and mental health, must be provided in Asian American communities. Counteracting the stigma commonly associated with depression is vital to helping Asian American elders seek services while maintaining a sense of dignity.

THE NEED TO CREATE ASIAN-FRIENDLY SERVICE ENVIRONMENTS FOR ASIAN AMERICAN ELDERS

Our study shows that utilization of community-based service, in-home service, doctors' service, emergency room service, and hospital service among Asian American elders is associated with a number of predisposing, enabling, and need factors. Enabling variables are important to examine because they

are modifiable. Policy or programs targeted at enabling factors will make formal service environments friendlier to Asian elders. An essential issue is
health insurance coverage. Findings confirm that, as with other studies, both
Medicare and Medicaid coverage are associated with the utilization of formal
services (Abe-Kim, Takeuchi, and Hwang 2002; U.S. Department of Health
and Human Services 2005). Clearly Asian elder–friendly, policy-driven interventions must include increased access to health insurance.

According to our data, half the respondents did not have Medicare, but 41
percent had Medicaid. Given the high levels of poverty among this population, the cost of insurance premiums is a major barrier to these elders' use of
medical services. The rapidly rising cost of medication is a national concern
that has special urgency for Asian American elders with acute and chronic
care needs. Developing programs that assure basic physical and mental health
care protection for Asian immigrant elders is an important direction for policy
planners and elder care providers. Moreover, service providers need to pay attention to the danger arising from cultural and linguistic isolation among
Asian American elders. They need to work toward building an Asian-elder–
friendly community by supporting local community building and mutual
aid/empowerment groups, including peer outreach and neighborhood visita-
tion programs in their own ethnic communities. Asian American elders
dissatisfied with their physician's care are less likely to seek medical care. Dissatisfaction with physician care may be related to the physician's inability to
establish rapport with Asian elders. Health care professionals will benefit from
training physicians on how to work with Asian elders.

Understanding cultural and linguistic barriers to the utilization of formal
services is essential in planning approaches that are Asian elder-friendly. Service providers need to understand how elders who seek assistance from a formal service system experience stigma. Strategies that empower Asian American elders to seek help by increasing access to medical information,
interpreters, and entitlements will help decrease their sense of stigma.

Asian American elders who perceived religion as important are more
willing to seek medical help by using hospitals than are their less religious
counterparts. The role of spirituality and positive self-care behaviors is well
documented (Mui and Kang 2006). Asian American elders who have inner
strength may be better able to deal with the hospital system when they need the
care. Religious interpretations of stressful life events may bring Asian elders inner peace or acceptance when faced with a situation beyond their control (Idler
2002). Religion is a powerful spiritual resource for coping (Ai et al. 1998). The

association of religiosity and hospital use points up the importance of religious groups or faith-based organizations collaborating with the health care systems to make holistic care available to Asian American elders. Professionals should be informed about the worldviews and religious practices of Asian American elders.

THE NEED TO STRENGTHEN AND DEVELOP FAMILY-FRIENDLY ENVIRONMENTS FOR ASIAN AMERICAN ELDERS

The majority of Asian American elders in our study valued traditional family responsibility in elder care and filial obligation. At the same time, most elders felt that their opinions regarding family traditions differed from those of their children. It is therefore imperative that professionals observe the different levels of acculturation and possible conflicts that may stem from differences in expectations regarding filial responsibility. Recognizing the potential for intergenerational conflicts between Asian American elders and their children is vital because of the negative impact these conflicts have on mental health.

Our results indicate that adult children provide most of the informal support for Asian American elders. More than half the elders in the study reported receiving help from their children in times of illness, and also with shopping or errands, transportation, making repairs around the house, and dealing with money. Although data indicated that Asian American elders also provide assistance to their adult children, it is important for professionals to assess how intergenerational exchanges are negotiated within Asian families. Adult children may also need support from professionals in finding ways to balance filial obligation and other family responsibilities.

Asian American elders are at risk for becoming overly dependent on their immediate family members, which in turn may lead to family conflicts. Within the Asian community, it is important to integrate peer and family relationships into the larger ethnic community. The benefits include reducing social isolation among Asian American elders, improving their sense of meaning and purpose in life, and reducing the filial burden of younger generations. Service providers need to support efforts to strengthen the full range of social networks available to older Asians and their families. Asian American elders who volunteer in the community are more satisfied with life than those who do not, and thus priority should be given to mobilizing elders to become active participants and contribute to their communities.

FUTURE DIRECTIONS

This book has identified the issues faced by Asian American elders in a number of areas including economic considerations, physical health, mental health, access to formal service utilization, acculturation, linguistic challenges, and family support. The obvious question is what can be done to better serve this population. Our findings point to future directions for more research and practice. Multi-site national studies of Asian American elders should be conducted to develop a more representative knowledge base in the literature. More funding is needed to conduct nationally representative sample surveys of Asian American elders of all subgroups, both cross-sectional and longitudinal and including all Asian American subgroups. Future nationally representative sample surveys of aging, physical health, and mental health need to include a meaningful representation, and not mere tokens, of Asian Americans to allow for consequential analyses of ethnic and racial differences. An overly large number of blacks have routinely been sampled for this purpose in many previous surveys, and the current trend is to do the same with Hispanics in nationally representative sample surveys. Considering that the Asian American population is the most rapidly increasing ethnic group, it is only logical that future surveys include a sufficient number to achieve meaningful outcomes. In addition to investing in large-scale surveys and research projects, public and private funding sources need to continuously encourage small-scale studies of Asian American subgroups by making funds available for these projects. Limited as these studies may be in terms of generalizing their outcomes, they are still useful for increasing the understanding of this population among social service providers and researchers. The accumulated findings of such studies will also contribute to the existing knowledge base and to designing and providing culturally meaningful services. Especially for the Asian American elderly subgroups such as Cambodian, Hmong, Vietnamese, Khmer, Lao, and Indochinese, about whom little research has been done, exploratory studies may be useful both for practical reasons and for laying the foundation for future research of greater scope.

Although our findings highlight the significance of the cultural dimensions in Asian American elders' quality-of-life issues, specific questions related to the attitudes of Asian American elders and their families toward receiving formal help, the nature of cultural barriers to using formal services, and the quality and adequacy of informal and formal supports have not been answered.

Also not tested are the effects of discrimination based on ethnicity and national origin, both contemporaneous and cumulative, on the Asian American elders' and families' psychological well-being and their attitude toward and access to formal service systems. Moreover, because the data were cross-sectional, longitudinal changes in the elasticity of informal support and formal service use in response to Asian American elders' changing health status and the effect of informal and formal support on health-related quality of life could not be assessed. Future research must be done to fill these knowledge gaps. To achieve this effect, however, also needed are longitudinal national surveys that include representative Asian American elderly subgroups large enough for meaningful multivariate analyses of their quality-of-life issues and formal service utilization patterns.

Strong family relationships and personal resilience among Asian American elders are impressive in light of the stressors that mark their daily lives. Understanding the cultural and interpersonal resources that shape their overall outlook and coping abilities as well as their service needs is necessary to sustain multigenerational families in the Asian community. It is important to note that research using quantitative data needs to be augmented with the real voices of the Asian American elders. Studies of cultural differences, life experiences, the impact of discrimination, and coping strategies adopted by Asian and other ethnic minorities often require both qualitative and quantitative research methods. Standardized scales, inventories, and survey questionnaires are convenient and useful, but they have limited utility when it comes to the in-depth presentation of life experiences.

The UN International Plan of Action on Ageing (United Nations 2002a) has confirmed the development of "ensuring and enabling supportive environments" as one of its three priority areas. The Research Agenda on Ageing for the 21st Century, produced by the United Nations Office on Ageing and the International Association of Gerontology for the Second World Assembly on Aging, lists research priorities that address environmental determinants of healthy aging and quality of life (United Nations 2002b). In recent years, the initiative toward developing elder-friendly communities has focused on ensuring that community dwelling elders have a sense of well-being which is brought about by responding effectively to life changes and challenges; sustaining positive, meaningful, and dynamic relationships; and living with a sense of purpose and psychological well-being while remaining in their homes as long as it is safe and practical to do so. Our findings, overall, point to the need to provide an economically, linguistically, and culturally friendly, supportive environment for our Asian American elders so that their psychosocial quality of life will improve. Our goal at the start was to fill the knowledge gaps regarding the quality of life of Asian American elders. Although we hope that we have achieved that aim, clearly much more needs to be done and our findings may well provide a reference point for further studies by researchers, practitioners, and students.

REFERENCES

AARP. 1997. *Depression in Later Life*. Washington, D.C.: Author.

AARP Public Policy Institute. 2007. Consumer-directed home and community-based services [Electronic Version]. Retrieved August 20, 2007, from http://www.aarp.org/research/housing-mobility/homecare/fs128_cons_dir.html#FIRST.

Abe-Kim, J., D. Takeuchi, and W. Hwang. 2002. Predictors of help seeking for emotional distress among Chinese Americans: Family matters. *Journal of Counseling and Clinical Psychology* 70 (5), 1186–1190.

Agbayani-Siewert, P. 1994. Filipino American culture and family: Guidelines for practitioners. *Families in Society* 75 (7), 429–438.

AHA *News Now*. 2005. JACHO standard will require documenting patient communication needs. Chicago: American Hospital Association's Daily *News Now* E-mail Report for Healthcare Executives, June 21 (VocusGR.185.372600@vocusgr.com).

Ai, A. L., R. E. Dunkle, C. Peterson, and S. Bolling. 1998. The role of private prayer in psychological recovery among midlife and aged patients following cardiac surgery. *The Gerontologist* 38 (5), 591–601.

Ally, D., P. Leibig, J. Pynoos, T. Banergee, and I. H. Choi. 2007. Creating elder-friendly communities: Preparations for an aging society. *Journal of Gerontological Social Work* 49 (1/2), 1–18.

Andersen, R. M. 1995. Revisiting the behavioral model and access to medical care: Does it matter? *Journal of Health and Social Behavior* 36, 1–10.

Andersen, R. M., and J. F. Newman. 1973. Societal and individual determinants of medical care utilization. *U.S. Milbank Memorial Fund Quarterly* 51, 95–124.

Anetzberger, G.. 2000. Caregiving: Primary cause of elder abuse? *Generations* 24 (2), 46–51.

Angel, J. L., R. J. Angel, and K. J. Henderson. 1997. Contextualizing social support and health in old age: Reconsidering culture and gender. *International Journal of Sociology and Social Policy* 17 (9/10), 83–117.

Angel, R. J., J. L. Angel, G. Y. Kee, and K. S. Markides. 1999. Age at migration and family dependency among older Mexican immigrants: Recent evidence from the Mexican American EPESE. *The Gerontologist* 39, 59–65.

Antonucci, T. C. 1990. Social supports and social relationships. In R. H. Binstock and L. K. George, eds., *Handbook of Aging and Social Sciences*. New York: Academic Press.

Antonucci, T. C., and H. Akiyama. 1987. Social networks in adult life and a preliminary examination of the convoy model. *Journal of Gerontology* 42, 519–527.

Aroian, K. J., B. Wu, and T. V. Tran. 2005. Health care and social service use among Chinese immigrant elders. *Research in Nursing and Health* 28, 95–105.

Asian American Health Initiatives. 2005. Retrieved April 2006 from http://www.aahiinfo.org/asianAmericans.php.

Austin, C. D., E. Des Camp, D. Flux, R. W. McClelland, and J. Sieppert. 2005. Community development with older adults in their neighborhoods: The elder friendly communities program. *Families in Society* 86, 401–409.

Azen, S. P., et al. 1999. Psychometric properties of a Chinese translation of the SF-36 Health Survey Questionnaire in the Well Elderly Study. *Journal of Aging and Health* 11(2), 240–251.

Bartels, S. J., et al. 2002. Suicidal and death ideation in older primary care patients with depression, anxiety, and at-risk alcohol use. *American Journal of Geriatric Psychiatry* 10 (4), 417–427.

Bass, S., and F. G. Caro, 2001. Productive aging: A conceptual framework. In N. Morrow-Howell, J. Hinterlong & M. Sherraden, eds., *Productive Aging: Concepts and Challenges*, pp. 37–78. Baltimore: Johns Hopkins University Press.

Becker, J. 1996. *Hungry Ghosts: Mao's Secret Famine*. New York: Free Press.

Bengston, V. L., E. O. Burgess, and T. M. Parrott. 1997. Theory, explanation, and a third generation of theoretical development in social gerontology. *Journal of Gerontology* 52 (2), S72-S88.

Bengtson, V. L., and R. E. L. Roberts. 1991. Intergenerational solidarity in aging families: An example of formal theory construction. *Journal of Marriage and the Family* 53, 856–870.

Berkman, L. 1985. The relationships of social networks and social support to morbidity and mortality. In S. Cohen and S. L. Syme, eds., *Social Support and Health*, pp. 241–259. New York: Academic Press.

——. 1995. The role of social relations in health promotion. *Psychosomatic Medicine* 57, 245–254.

Bisconti, T. L., and C. S. Bergeman. 1999. Perceived social control as a mediator of the relationships among social support, psychological well-being, and perceived health. *The Gerontologist* 39 (1), 94–103.

Black, S.A., K. S. Markides, and T. Q. Miller. 1998. Correlates of depressive symptomatology among older community-dwelling Mexican Americans: The Hispanic EPESE. *Journal of Gerontology* 53 (4), S198-S208.

Bond, M.H., and K. K. Hwang. 1986. The social psychology of Chinese people. In M.H. Bond ed., *The Psychology of the Chinese People*, pp. 213–264. Hong Kong: Oxford University Press.

Borden, W. 1991. Stress, coping, and adaptation in spouses of older adults with chronic dementia. *Social Work Research and Abstracts* 27, 14–21.

Borrayo, E.A., J. R. Salmon, L. Polivka, and B. D. Dunlop. 2002. Utilization across the continuum of long-term care services. *The Gerontologist* 42 (5), 603–612.

——. 2004. Who is being served? Program eligibility and home- and community-based services use. *Journal of Applied Gerontology* 23 (2), 120–140.

Brackbill, Y., and D. Kitch. 1991. Intergenerational relationships: A social exchange perspective on joint living arrangements among the elderly and their relatives. *Journal of Aging Studies* 5 (1), 77–97.

Bronfenbrenner, U. 1979. The ecology of human development. *American Psychologist* 32, 513–531.

Browne, C., and A. Broderick. 1994. Asian and Pacific island elders: Issues for social work practice and education. *Social Work* 39 (3), 252–259.

Burnette, D., and A. C. Mui. 1995. In-home and community-based service utilization by three groups of elderly Hispanics: A national perspective. *Social Work Research* 19 (4), 197–206.

——. 1999. Physician utilization by Hispanic elderly: A national perspective. *Medical Care* 37 (4), 362–374.

Burr, J.A., F. G. Caro, and J. Moorhead. 2002. Productive aging and civic participation. *Journal of Aging Studies* 16 (1), 87–105.

Burr, J.A., N. G. Choi, J. E. Mutchler, and F. Caro. 2005. Caring and volunteering: Are private and public helping behaviors linked? *Journal of Gerontology* 60 (5), S247–S256.

Burr, J.A., and J. E. Mutchler. 1993. Nativity, acculturation, and economic status: Explanations of Asian American living arrangements in later life. *Journal of Gerontology* 48 (2), S55–S63.

Burton, L. M., Dilworth-Anderson, P., and Merriwether-deVries, C. 1995. Context and surrogate parenting among contemporary grandparents. *Marriage and Family Review*, 20(3/4), 349–366.

Cabezas, A., L. H. Shinagawa, and G. Kawaguchi. 1986. New inquiries into the socioeconomic status of Pilipino Americans in California. *Amerasia Journal* 13, 1–21.

Cantor, M., M. Brennan, and A. Sainz. 1994. The importance of ethnicity in the social support systems of older New Yorkers: A longitudinal perspective (1970–1990). *Journal of Gerontological Social Work* 22, 95–128.

Caprara, G. V., and P. Steca. 2005. Self-efficacy beliefs as determinants of prosocial behavior conducive to life satisfaction across ages. *Journal of Social and Clinical Psychology* 24 (2), 191–217.

Carstensen, L. L., D. M. Isaacowitz, and S. T. Charles. 1999. Taking time seriously. *American Psychologist* 54 (3), 165–181.

Casado, B. L., and P. Leung. 2001. Migratory grief and depression among elderly Chinese American immigrants. *Journal of Gerontological Social Work* 36 (1–2), 5–26.

Centers for Disease Control and Prevention. 2004. The state of aging and health in America 2004. Retrieved March 6, 2005, from http://www.miahonline.org/resources/speeches/content/sp_nov22_2004.html.

Centers for Disease Control and Prevention, National Center for Injury Prevention and Control, Office of Statistics and Programming. 2006. *Web-based Injury Statistics Query and Reporting System* (WISQARS™). Retrieved April 2006 from http://www.cdc.gov/ncipc/wisqars/default.htm.

Centers for Medicare and Medicaid Services (CMS). 2005. *Medicaid: A Brief Summary*. Retrieved March 6, 2005, from http://www.cms.hhs.gov/publications/overview-medicare-medicaid/default4.asp.

Chao, R. K. 1995. Chinese and European American cultural models for the self reflected in mothers' childrearing beliefs. *Ethos* 23, 328–354.

Chen, C. 2000. Aging and life satisfaction. *Social Indicators Research* 54, 57–79.

Cheng, S., and A. C. Chan. 2006. Relationship with others and life satisfaction in later life: Do gender and widowhood make a difference? *Journal of Gerontology:* 61 (1), S46–S53.

Chi, I., and K.-L. Chou. 2001. Social support and depression among elderly Chinese people in Hong Kong. *International Journal of Aging and Human Development* 52 (3), 231–252.

Chow, J. C., K. Jaffee, and L. R. Snowden. 2003. Racial/ethnic disparities in the use of mental health services in poverty areas. *American Journal of Public Health* 93 (5), 792–797.

Chung, D. K. 1992. Asian cultural commonalities: A comparison with mainstream American culture. In S. Furuto, R. Biswas, D. Chung, K. Murase and E. Ross-Seriff, eds., *Social Work Practice with Asian Americans*, pp. 27–44. Newbury Park, Calif.: Sage.

Chung, I. 2004. The sociocultural reality of the Asian immigrant elderly: Implications for group work practice. *Journal of Gerontological Social Work* 44 (1/2), 81–93.

Chung, R.C. and K. M. Lin. 1994. Help-seeking behavior among Southeast Asian refugees. *Journal of Community Psychology* 22, 109–120.

Cohen, A. B., and H. G. Koenig. 2003. Religion, religiosity, and spirituality in the biopsychosocial model of health and aging. *Ageing International* 28 (3), 215–241.

Cohen, H., R. R. Greene, Y. Lee, J. Gonzalez, and M. Evans. 2006. Older adults who overcame oppression. *Families in Society* 87 (1), 35–43.

Conwell, Y., and D. Brent. 1995. Suicide and aging. I: Patterns of psychiatric diagnosis. *International Psychogeriatrics* 7 (2). 149–164.

Cordova, F. 1983. *Filipinos, Forgotten Asian Americans: A Pictorial Essay, 1763 circa 1963*. Dubuque, Iowa: Kendall/Hunt.

Cowgill, D. O., and L. D. Holmes. 1972. *Aging and Modernization*. New York: Appleton-Century-Crofts.

Damron-Rodriguez, J., S. Wallace, and R. Kington. 1994. Service utilization and minority elderly: Appropriateness, accessibility and acceptability. *Gerontology and Geriatrics Education* 15(1), 45–63

Dannerfer, D. 2003. Cumulative advantage and the life course: Cross-fertilizing age and social science theory. *Journal of Gerontology* 58 (6), S327–S337.

Das, S. 2002. Loss or gain? A saga of Asian Indian immigration and experiences in America's multi-ethnic mosaic. *Race, Gender, and Class* 9 (2), 131–155.

Deci, E. L., and R. M. Ryan. 2000. The "what" and "why" of goal pursuits: Human needs and the self-determination of behavior. *Psychological Inquiry* 11, 227–268.

Detzner, D. F. 1996. No place without a home: Southeast Asian grandparents in refugee families. *Generations* 20, 45–48.

Diener, E., and M. Diener. 1995. Cross-cultural correlates of life satisfaction and self-esteem. *Journal of Personality and Social Psychology* 68, 653–663.

Diwan, S., S. S. Jonnalagadda, and S. Balaswamy. 2004. Resources predicting positive and negative affect during the experience of stress: A study of older Asian Indian Americans in the United States. *The Gerontologist* 44 (5), 605–614.

Doi, M. L. 1991. A transformation of ritual: The Nisei 6oth birthday. *Journal of Cross Cultural Gerontology* 6, 153–163.

Dowd, J. J. 1975. Aging as exchange: A preface to theory. *Journal of Gerontology* 30, S584–S594.

Dugsin, R. 2001. Conflict and healing in family experience of second-generation emigrants from India living in North America. *Family Process* 40 (2), 233–241.

Ecklund, E. H., and J. Z. Park. 2005. Asian American community participation and religion. *Journal of Asian American Studies* 8 (1), 1–25.

——. 2007. Religious diversity and community volunteerism among Asian Americans. *Journal of the Scientific Study of Religion* 46 (2), 233–244.

Elder, G. H. J., M. K. Johnson, and R. Crosnoe. 2003. The emergence and development of life course theory. In J. T. Mortimer and M. J. Shanahan, eds., *Handbook of the Life Course*, pp. 3–22. New York: Kluwer Academic/Plenum.

Espiritu, Y. L. 1997. *Asian American Women and Men*. Thousand Oaks, Calif.: Sage.

Falcon, L.M., and K. L. Tucker. 2000. Prevalence and correlates of depressive symptoms among Hispanic elders in Massachusetts. *Journals of Gerontology*55 (2), S108–S116.

Federal Interagency Forum on Aging-Related Statistics 2004. *Older Americans: Key Indicators of Well-Being.* Washington, D.C.: U.S. Government Printing Office.

Feldman, P. H., and M. R. Oberlink. 2003. The AdvantAge initiative: Developing community indicators to promote the health and well-being of older people. *Family and Community Health* 26 (4), 268–274.

Ferraro, F. R., B. Bercier, and I. Chelminski. 1997. Geriatric Depression Scale–Short Form (GDS–SF) performance in Native American elderly adults. *Clinical Gerontologist* 18 (1), 52–55.

Fiske, A. P., S. Kitayama, H. Markus, and R. E. Nisbett. 1998. The cultural matrix of social psychology. In. D. T. Gilbert, S. T. Eiske, and G. Lindzey, eds., *Handbook of Social Psychology*, pp. 915–981. Boston: McGraw-Hill.

Fitzpatrick, A.L., N. R. Powe, L. S. Cooper, D. G. Ives, and J. A. Robbins. 2004. Barriers to health care access among the elderly and who perceives them. *American Journal of Public Health* 94 (10), 1788–1794.

Fry, P. S. 2001. Predictors of health-related quality-of-life perspectives, self-esteem, and life satisfactions of older adults following spousal loss: An 18-month follow-up study of widows and widowers. *The Gerontologist* 41 (6), 787–798.

Fuligini, A. J., V. Tseng, and M. Lam. 1999. Attitudes toward family obligations among American adolescents with Asian, Latin American, and European backgrounds. *Child Development* 70 (4), 1030–1044.

Fuller-Thompson, E., and M. Minkler. 2001. American grandparents providing extensive child care to their grandparents. *The Gerontologist* 41, 201–209.

Gallo, J. J., and B. D. Lebowitz. 1999. The epidemiology of common late-life mental disorders in the community: Themes for the new century. *Psychiatric Services* 50, 1158–1166.

Gelfand, D. E. 1989. Immigration, aging, and intergenerational relationships. *The Gerontologist* 28, 73–78.

Gelfand, D., and B. W. K. Yee. 1991. Influence of immigration, migration, and acculturation on the fabric of aging in America. *Generations* 15 (4), 7–10.

Gold, S. J. 1992. Mental health and illness in Vietnamese refugees. *Western Journal of Medicine* 157, 290–294.

Gonzalez, H. M., M. N. Haan, and L. Hinton. 2001. Acculturation and the prevalence of depression in older Mexican Americans: Baseline results of the Sacramento Area Latino Study on Aging. *Journal of the American Geriatrics Society* 49 (7), 948–953.

Gottlieb, G. L. 1991. Barriers to care for older adults with depression. Paper presented at the National Institutes of Health Consensus Development Conference on diagnosis and treatment of depression in later life, Bethesda, Md., November.

Greenfield, E. A., and N. F. Marks. 2004. Formal volunteering as a protective factor for older adults' psychological well-being. *Journals of Gerontology* 59 (5), S258–S265.

Gupta, R. 2000. A path model of elder caregiver burden in Indian/Pakistani families in the United States. *International Journal of Aging and Human Development* 51 (4), 295–313.

Gyory, A. 2000. An exchange on the U.S. labor movement and Chinese immigration: A reply to Stanford Lyman. *New Politics* 8 (1), 51–59.

Hagestad, G. O., and B. Neugarten. 1985. Age and the life course. In R. Binstock and E. Shanas, eds., *Handbook of Aging and the Social Sciences*, pp. 35–61. New York: Van Nostrand Reinhold.

Haller, J., R. M. R. M. Weggenmans, M. Ferry, and Y. Guigoz. 1996. Mental health: Mini-mental state examination and geriatric depression score of elderly Europeans in the SENECA study of 1993. *European Journal of Clinical Nutrition* 50 (Suppl. 2), S112–S116.

Harada, N. D., and Laurean, S. K. 2001. Use of mental health services by older Asian and Pacific Islander Americans. In N. G. Choi, ed., *Social Work Practice with the Asian American Elderly*. New York: Haworth Social Work Practice Press.

Harada, N., V. Tsuneishi, S. Fukuhara, and T. Makinodan. 1998. Cross-cultural adaptation of the SF-36 Health Survey for Japanese-American elderly. *Journal of Aging and Ethnicity* 1 (2), 59–80.

Hardy, S. E., J. Concato, and T. M. Gill. 2004. Resilience of community-dwelling older persons. *Journal of the American Geriatrics Society* 52 (2), 257–262.

Hayslip, B., and P. L. Kiminski. 2005. Grandparents raising their grandchildren: A review of the literature and suggestions for practice. *The Gerontologist* 45 (2), 262–269.

Hazuda, H. P., R. C. Wood, M. J. Lichtenstein, and C. V. Espino. 1998. Sociocultural status, psychosocial factors, and cognitive functional limitation in elderly Mexican Americans: Findings from the San Antonio Longitudinal Study of Aging. *Journal of Gerontological Social Work* 30 (1–2), 99–121.

Hertzman, C. 2004. The life-course contribution of ethnic disparities in health. In N. B. Anderson, R. A. Bulatao, and B. Cohen, eds., *Critical Perspectives on Racial and Ethnic Differences in Health in Late Life*, pp. 145–170. Washington, D.C.: National Academies Press

Hing, B. O. 1993. Making and remaking Asian Pacific America: Immigration policy. In P. Ong, ed., *The State of Asian Pacific America: A Public Policy Report*, pp. 127–140. Los Angeles: LEAP Asian Pacific American Policy Institute and UCLA Asian American Studies Center.

Ho, Y. F. 1994. Cognitive socialization in Confucian heritage cultures. In P. M. Greenfield and R. R. Cocking, eds., *Cross-Cultural Roots of Minority Child Development*, pp. 285–313. Hillsdale, N.J.: Lawrence Erlbaum.

——. Filial piety, authoritarian moralism, and cognitive conservatism in Chinese societies. *Genetic, Social, and General Psychology Monographs* 120, 347–365.

Holstein, M. B., and M. Minkler. 2003. Self, society, and the "new gerontology." *The Gerontologist* 43, 787–796.

Hooyman, N. R., and H. A. Kiyak. 2002. *Social Gerontology: A Multidisciplinary Perspective*. 6th ed. Boston, Mass.: Allyn and Bacon.

Horwarth, E., J. Johnson, G. L. Klerman, and M. M. Weissman. 1992. Depressive symptoms as relative and attributable risk factors for first-onset major depression. *Archives of General Psychiatry* 49 (10), 817–823.

Hovey, J. D. 2000. Acculturative stress, depression, and suicidal ideation in Mexican Americans. *Cultural Diversity and Ethnic Minority Psychology* 6 (2), 134–151.

Hu, T.W., L. R. Snowden, J. M. Jerrell, and S. H. Kang. 1993. Public mental health services to Asian American ethnic groups in two California counties. *Asian American and Pacific Islander Journal of Health* 1 (1), 79–90.

Hughes, M. E., L. J. Waite, T. A. LaPierre, and Y. Luo. 2007. All in the family: The impact of caring for grandchildren on grandparents' health. *Journals of Gerontology* 62, S108–S119.

Huh, N. S., and W. J. Reid. 2000. Intercountry, transracial adoption and ethnic identity: A Korean example *International Social Work* 43 (1), 75–87.

Husaini, B. A., R. S. Castor, G. Linn, S. T. Moore, H. A. Warren, and R. Whitten-Stovall. 1990. Social support and depression among the black and white elderly. *Journal of Community Psychology* 18, 12–18.

Ichioka, Y. 1988. *The Issei: The World of the First-Generation Japanese Immigrants, 1885–1924*. New York: Free Press.

Idler, E. L. 2002. The many causal pathways linking religion to health. *Public Policy and Aging Report* 12 (4), 7–12.

Ik Ki Kim and Cheong-Seok Kim. 2003 Patterns of family support and the quality of life of the elderly. *Social Indicators Research* 62 (1), 437–452.

Ingersoll-Dayton, B., C. Saengtienchai, J. Kespichayawattana, and Y. Aungsuroch 2004. Measuring psychological well-being: Insights from Thai elders. *The Gerontologist* 44 (5), 596–600.

Ishii-Kuntz, M. 1997. Intergenerational relationships among Chinese, Japanese, and Korean Americans. *Family Relations* 46, 23–32.

Ishizawa, H. 2004. Minority language use among grandchildren in multigenerational households. *Sociological Perspectives* 47 (4), 465–483.

Jackson, J., et al. 2000. Derivation and pilot assessment of a health promotion program for Mandarin-speaking Chinese older adults. *International Journal of Aging and Human Development,* 50 (2), 127–149.

Jambunathan, S., and K. P. Counselman. 2002. Parenting attitudes of Asian Indian mothers living in the United States and in India. *Early Child Development and Care* 172, 657–662.

Janelli, R. L., and D. Y. Janelli. 1982. *Ancestor Worship and Korean Society.* Stanford, Calif.: Stanford University Press.

Jang, M., E. Lee, and K. Woo. 1998. Income, language, and citizenship status: Factors affecting the health care access and utilization of Chinese Americans. *Health and Social Work* 23 (2), 136–145.

Jenkins, C. N. H., T. Le, S. J. McPhee, S. Stewart, and N. H. Ha. 1996. Health care access and preventive care among Vietnamese immigrants: Do traditional beliefs and practices pose barriers? *Social Science and Medicine,* 43 (7), 1049–1056.

Joffe, C., H. Brodaty, G. Luscombe, and F. Ehrlich. 2003. The Sydney Holocaust Study: Posttraumatic stress disorder and other psychosocial morbidity in an aged community sample. *Journal of Traumatic Stress* 16 (1), 39–47.

Kamo, Y. 1998. Asian grandparents. In M. Szinovacz, ed., *Handbook on Grandparenthood,* pp. 97–112. Westport, Conn.: Greenwood.

Kataoka-Yahiro, M., C. Ceria, and R. Caulfield. 2004. Grandparent caregiving role in ethnically diverse families. *Journal of Pediatric Nursing* 19 (5), 315–328.

Kakar, S. 1978. *The Inner Worlds: A Psycho-analytic Study of Childhood and Society in India.* New Dehli: Oxford University Press.

Kauh, T. 1997. Intergenerational relations: Older Korean-Americans' expectations. *Journal of Cross-Cultural Gerontology* 12, 245–271.

Kemp, C. 1999–2004. *Korean-American Health Care Beliefs and Practices.* Retrieved April 2006 from, http://www.baylor.edu/~Charles_Kemp.htm.

Kerlinger, F. N., and H. B. Lee. 1999. *Foundations of Behavioral Research.* New York: Wadsworth.

Kessler, R. C., C. Foster, P. S. Webster, and J. S. House. 1992. The relationship between age and depressive symptoms in two national surveys. *Psychology and Aging* 7 (1), 119–126.

Kim, J., J. Kang, M.-A. Lee, and Y. Lee. 2007. Volunteering among older people in Korea. *Journal of Gerontology* 62 (1), S69–S73.

Kim, K. C., S. Kim, and W. M. Hurh. 1991. Filial piety and intergenerational relationship in Korean immigrant families. *International Journal on Aging and Human Development* 33 (3), 233–245.

Kim, H. K., M. Hisata, I. Kai, and S. K. Lee. 2000. Social support exchange and quality of life among the Korean elderly. *Journal of Cross-Cultural Gerontology* 15, 331–347.

Kim, I. K., and C.-S. Kim. 2003. Patterns of family support and the quality of life of the elderly. *Social Indicators Research* 62, 437–454.

Kim, U., and S. Choi. 1994. Individualism, collectivism, and child development: A Korean perspective. In P.M. Greenfield and R.R. Cocking, eds., *Cross-Cultural Roots of Minority Child Development*, pp. 227–257. Hillsdale, N.J.: Lawrence Erlbaum.

Koh, J.Y., and W. G. Bell. 1987. Korean elders in the United States: Intergenerational relations and living arrangements. *The Gerontologist* 27 (1), 66–71.

Koyano, W. 1989. Japanese attitudes toward the elderly: A review of research findings *Journal of Cross-Cultural Gerontology* 4, 335–345.

Krause, N. 2004. Lifetime trauma, emotional support, and life satisfaction among older adults. *The Gerontologist* 44 (5), 615–623.

Krause, N., and L. M. Goldenhar. 1992. Acculturation and psychological distress in three groups of elderly Hispanics. *Journal of Gerontology* 47 (6), S279-S288.

Kuo, T., and F. M. Torres-Gil. 2001. Factors affecting utilization of health services and home- and community-based care programs by older Taiwanese in the United States. *Research on Aging* 23 (1), 14–36.

Kwong, P. 1997. *Forbidden Workers: Illegal Chinese Immigrants and American Labor* New York: New Press.

Lan, P.C. 2002. Subcontracting filial piety. *Journal of Family Issues* 23, 812–835.

Le, C.E. 2006. Socioeconomic statistics and demographics. Asian-Nation: The landscape of Asian America. [Electronic Version]. Retrieved April 6, 2000, from http://www.asian-nation.org/demographics.shtml.

Le, Q.K. 1997. Mistreatment of Vietnamese elderly by their families in the United States. *Journal of Elder Abuse and Neglect* 9, 51–62.

Lee, E., and M.R. Mock. 2005. Chinese families. In M. McGoldrick, J. Giordano, and N. Garcia-Preto, eds., *Ethnicity and Family Therapy*, 3rd ed., pp. 302–318. New York: Guilford.

Lee, M.S., K. S. Crittenden, and E. Yu. 1996. Social support and depression among elderly Korean Americans in the United States. *International Journal of Aging and Human Development* 42 (4), 313–327.

Leong, F. T. L. 1994. Asian Americans' differential patterns of utilization of inpatient and outpatient public mental health services in Hawaii. *Journal of Community Psychology* 22, 82–96.

Leung, B.W., G. B. Moneta, and C. McBride-Chang. 2005. Think positively and feel positively: Optimism and life satisfaction in late life. *International Journal of Aging and Human Development* 61 (4), 335–365.

Leung, P.K., and J.K. Boehnlein. 2005. Vietnamese families. In M. McGoldrick, J. Giordano, and N. Garcia-Preto, eds., *Ethnicity and Family Therapy*, pp. 363–373. New York: Guilford.

Liang, J., N. M. Krause, and J. M. Bennett. 2001. Social exchange and well-being: Is giving better than receiving? *Psychology and Aging* 16 (3), 511–523.

Lim, Y., and S. M. Resko. 2002. Immigrants' use of welfare after welfare reform: Cross-group comparison. *Journal of Poverty* 6 (4), 63–82.

Litwin, H. 2005. Correlates of successful aging: Are they universal? *International Journal of Aging and Human Development* 61 (4), 313–333.

Liu, W., and E. Yu. 1985. Asian/Pacific American elderly: Mortality differentials, health status, and use of health services. *Journal of Applied Gerontology* 4 (1), 35–64.

Loo, C., B. Tong, and R. True. 1989. A bitter bean: Mental health status and attitudes in Chinatown. *Journal of Community Psychology* 17, 283–296.

Lowe, L. 1991. Heterogeneity, hybridity, multiplicity: Marking Asian American differences. *Diaspora* 1, 24–44.

Lucaccini, L. F. 1996. The public health service on Angel Island. *Public Health Reports* 111 (1), 92–94.

Lum, O. 1995. Health status of Asians and Pacific Islanders. *Clinical Geriatric Medicine* 11 (1), 53–67.

Luthar, S. S., D. Cicchetti, and B. Becker. 2000. The construct of resilience: A critical evaluation and guidelines for future work. *Child Development* 71, 543–562.

Ma, G. X. 1999. *The Culture of Health: Asian Communities in the United States.* Westport, Conn.: Bergin and Garvey.

Manigbas, M. 2002. Multiservice organization combats elder abuse in Chinese community. *Generations* 26 (3), 70–72.

Markides, K. S., and C. Mindel. 1987. *Aging and Ethnicity.* Newbury Park, Calif.: Sage.

Mason, K. O. 1992. Family change and support of the elderly in Asia: What do we know? *Asia-Pacific Population Journal* 7 (3), 12–23.

Mazumdar, S. 1984. Punjabi agricultural workers in California, 1905–1945. In L. Cheng and E. Bonachich, eds., *Labor Immigration under Capitalism: Asian Workers in the United States before World War II*, pp. 549–578. Berkeley: University of California Press.

McCormick, T., et al. 1996. Attitudes toward use of nursing homes and home care in older Japanese-Americans. *Journal of the American Geriatrics Society* 44, 769–777.

Menec, V. H. 2003. The relation between everyday activities and successful aging: A 6-year longitudinal study. *Journal of Gerontology* 58 (2), S74–S82.

Mills, T. L., and J. C. Henretta. 2001. Racial, ethnic, and sociodemographic differences in the level of psychosocial distress among older Americans. *Research on Aging* 23 (2), 131–152.

Min, J. W., A. Moon, and J. E. Lubben. 2005. Determinants of psychological distress over time among older Korean immigrants and non-Hispanic white elders: Evidence from a two-wave panel study. *Aging and Mental Health* 9 (3), 210–222.

Min, P. G. 1990. "Korean Immigrants in Los Angeles" (April 7) [Electronic Version]. *Institute for Social Science Research. Volume V. 1989–90—California Immigrants in World Perspective: The Conference Papers, April 1990. Paper 2.* Retrieved April 2005 from http://repositories.cdlib.org/issr/volume5/2.

——. 1998. *Change and Conflicts: Korean Immigrant Families in New York.* New York: Allyn and Bacon.

Mitchell, J., and J. A. Krout. 1998. Discretion and service use among older adults: The behavioral model revisited. *Gerontologist* 38 (2), 159–168.

Mitchell, J., H. F. Mathews, and L. W. Griffin. 1997. Health and community-based service use. *Research on Aging*, 19 (2), 199–222.

Mjelde-Mossey, L. A., I. Chi, and N. Chow. 2002. Volunteering in the social services: Preferences, expectations, barriers, and motivation of aging Chinese professionals in Hong Kong. *Hallym International Journal of Aging* 4 (1), 31–44.

Mollica, R., G. Wyshak, and J. Lavelle. 1987. The psychosocial impact of war trauma and torture on Southeast Asian refugees. *American Journal of Psychiatry* 144 (12), 1567–1572.

Moon, A., J. E. Lubben, and V. Villa. 1998. Awareness and utilization of community long-term care services by elderly Korean and non-Hispanic White Americans. *The Gerontologist* 38 (3), 309–316.

Morrow-Howell, N., J. Hinterlong, P. A. Rozario, and F. Tang. 2003. Effects of volunteering on the well-being of older adults. *Journal of Gerontology* 58, S137–S145.

Mui, A. C. 1993. Self-reported depressive symptoms among black and Hispanic frail elders: A sociocultural perspective. *Journal of Applied Gerontology*, 12(2), 170–187.

——. 1996a. Correlates of psychological distress among Mexican, Cuban, and Puerto Rican elders living in the USA. *Journal of Cross-Cultural Gerontology*, 11(2), 131–147.

——. 1996b. Depression among elderly Chinese immigrants: An exploratory study. *Social Work*, 41, 633–645.

——. 1996c. Geriatric depression scale as a community screening instruments for elderly Chinese immigrants. *International Psychogeriatrics*, 8(3), 445–458.

——. 1998. Living alone and depression among older Chinese immigrants. *Journal of Gerontological Social Work*, 30(3/4), 147–166.

——. 2001. Stress, coping, and depression among elderly Korean immigrants. *Journal of Human Behavior in the Social Environment*, 3(3/4), 281–299.

Mui, A.C., and D. Burnette. 1994. Long-term care service use by frail elders: Is ethnicity a factor? *The Gerontologist* 34 (2), 190–198.

Mui, A.C., D. Burnette, and L. M. Chen. 2001. Cross-cultural assessment of geriatric depression: A review of the CES-D and the GDS. *Journal of Mental Health and Aging* 7 (1), 137–164.

Mui A.C., N.G. Choi, and A. Monk. 1998. *Long-Term Care and Ethnicity.* Westport, Conn.: Greenwood.

Mui, A.C., and M.D. Domanski. 1999. A community needs assessment among Asian American elders. *Journal of Cross-Cultural Gerontology* 14, 77–90.

Mui, A.C., and S.K. Kang. 2006. Acculturation stress and depression among Asian American elders. *Social Work* 51 (3), 243–255.

Mui, A.C., S.K. Kang, L.M. Chen, and M. Domanski. 2003. Reliability of the Geriatric Depression Scale for use among elderly Asian Americans in the USA. *International Psychogeriatrics* 15 (3), 253–273.

Mui, A.C., S.K. Kang, D. Kang, and M.D. Domanski. 2007. English-language proficiency and health-related quality of life among Chinese and Korean immigrant elders. *Health and Social Work* 32 (2), 119–127.

Mui, A.C., D. Kang, D. D. Nguyen, and M. D. Domanski. 2006. Demographic profiles of Asian immigrant elderly residing in metropolitan ethnic enclave communities. *Journal of Ethnic and Cultural Diversity in Social Work* 15 (1/2), 193–214.

Mui, A.C., and T. Shibusawa. 2003. Japanese American elders and the Geriatric Depression Scale. *Clinical Gerontologist* 26 (3/4), 91–104.

Mullatti, L. 1995. Families in India: Beliefs and realities. *Journal of Comparative Family Studies* 26 (1), 11–25.

Musick, M.A., J. W. Traphagen, H. G. Koenig, and D. B. Larson. 2000. Spirituality in physical aging and health. *Journal of Adult Development* 7 (2), 73–86.

Musick, M.A., and J. Wilson. 2003. Volunteering and depression: The role of psychological and social resources in different age groups. *Social Science and Medicine* 56, 259–269.

Nagata, D. 1993. *Legacy of Silence: Exploring the Long-term Effects of the Japanese American Internment.* New York: Plenum.

Nakano, L.Y. 2000. Volunteering as a lifestyle choice: Negotiating self-identities in Japan. *Ethnology* 39 (2), 93–107.

National Alliance for Caregiving and the American Association of Retired Persons. 1997. *Family Caregiving in the U.S.: Findings from a National Survey.* Washington, D.C.: National Alliance for Caregiving and the American Association of Retired Persons.

National Cancer Institute. 2000. *The Nation's Investment in Cancer Research: A Plan and Budget Proposal for Fiscal Year.* Washington, D.C.: National Institutes of Health.

Ng, S. H. 1998. Social psychology in an aging world: Ageism and intergenerational relations. *Asian Journal of Social Psychology* 1 (1), 99–116.

Ngo, D., T. Tran, J. Gibbons, and J. Oliver. 2001. Acculturation, premigration traumatic experiences, and depression among Vietnamese Americans. *Journal of Human Behavior in the Social Environment* 3 (3/4), 225–242.

Ngo-Metzger, Q., E. P. McCarthy, R. B. Burns, R. B. Davis, F. P. Li, and R. S. Phillips. 2003. Older Asian Americans and Pacific Islanders dying of cancer use hospice less frequently than older white patients. *American Journal of Medicine* 115, 47–53.

Nguyen, Q. C. X., and L. P. Anderson. 2005. Vietnamese Americans' attitudes toward seeking mental health services: Relation to cultural variables. *Journal of Community Psychology* 33 (2), 213–231.

Office of Minority Health. 2003. Why companies are making disparities their business: The business case and practical strategies [Electronic Version]. Retrieved April 27, 2005, from http://www.omhrc.gov/inetpub/wwwroot/cultural/business_case.pdf.

Okihiro, G. Y. 2001. *The Columbia Guide to Asian American History*. New York: Columbia University Press.

Ong, A. D., and C. S. Bergeman. 2004. Resilience and adaptation to stress in later life: Empirical perspectives and conceptual implications. *Aging International* 29 (3), 219–246.

O'Reilly, P., and F. G. Caro. 1994. Productive aging: An overview of the literature. *Journal of Aging and Social Policy* 6 (3), 39–71.

Ou, Y. S., and H. P. McAdoo. 1993. Socialization of Chinese American children. In H. P. McAdoo, ed., *Family Ethnicity: Strength in Diversity*, pp. 245–270. Newbury Park, Calif.: Sage.

Oyserman, D., H. M. Coon, and M. Kemmelmeier. 2002. Rethinking individualism and collectivism: Evaluation of theoretical assumptions and meta-analyses. *Psychological Bulletin* 128, 3–72.

Padgett, D. K. 1998. *Qualitative Methods in Social Work Research: Challenges and Rewards*. Thousand Oaks, Calif.: Sage.

——. 2008. *Qualitative Methods in Social Work Research: Challenges and Rewards*. 2nd ed. Thousand Oaks, Calif.: Sage.

Palmore, E., and D. Maeda. 1985. *The Honorable Elders Revisited: A Revised Cross-cultural Analysis of Aging in Japan*. Durham: Duke University Press.

Pang, E. C., M. Jordan-Marsh, M. Silverstein, and M. Cody. 2003. Health-seeking behaviors of elderly Chinese Americans: Shifts in expectations. *The Gerontologist* 43 (6), 864–874.

Pang, K. Y. C. 1998. Symptoms of depression in elderly Korean Americans: Narration and the healing process. *Culture, Medicine, and Psychiatry* 22, 93–122.

Park, I. H., and L.-J. Cho. 1995. Confucianism and the Korean family. *Journal of Comparative Family Studies* 26 (1), 117–127.

Park, K. (1997). *The Korean American Dream: Immigrants and Small Business in New York City*. Ithaca, N.Y.: Cornell University Press.

Park, S.-J., and S.-Y. Kang. 2007. Korean American elders. In P. J. Kolb, ed., *Social Work Practice with Ethnically and Racially Diverse Nursing Home Residents and Their Families*, pp. 162–190. New York: Columbia University Press.

Pettys, G. L., and P. R. Balgopal. 1998. Multigenerational conflicts and new immigrants: An Indo-American experience. *Families in Society* 79 (4), 410–424.

Phan, T. (2000). Investigating the use of services for Vietnamese with mental illness. *Journal of Community Health* 25 (5), 411–425.

Phillips, K. A., K. R. Morrison, R. Andersen, and L. A. Aday. 1998. Understanding the context of health care utilization: Assessing environmental and provider-related variables in the behavioral model of utilization. *Health Services Research* 33, 571–596.

Phua, V. C., G. Kaufman, and K. S. Park. 2001. Strategic adjustments of elderly Asian Americans: Living arrangements and headship. *Journal of Comparative Family Studies* 32 (2), 263–281.

Piercy, F. P., A. Soekandar, C. D. M. Limansubroto, and S. D. Davis. 2005. Indonesian families. In M. McGoldrick, J. Giordano, and N. Garcia-Preto, eds., *Ethnicity and Family Therapy*. 3rd ed., pp. 332–338. New York: Guilford.

Pillari, V. 2005. Indian Hindu families. In M. McGoldrick, J. Giordano, and N. Garcia-Preto, eds., *Ethnicity and Family Therapy*, pp. 395–406. New York: Guilford.

Portes, A., D. Kyle, and W. W. Eaton. 1992. Mental illness and help-seeking behavior among Mariel Cuban and Haitian refugees in South Florida. *Journal of Health and Social Behavior* 33 (4), 283–298.

Posadas, B. 1999. *The Filipino Americans*. Westport, Conn.: Greenwood.

President's Advisory Commission on Asian Americans and Pacific Islanders. 2003. Asian Americans and Pacific Islanders addressing health disparities: Opportunities for building a healthier America. Retrieved April 2006 from http://www.mbda.gov/?section_id = 9andbucket_id = 620andcontent_id = 6207andwell = entire_page. http://www.mbda.gov/?section_id=9&bucket_id=620&content_id=6207&well=entire_page.

Proctor, E. K., N. Morrow-Howell, E. Rubin, and M. Ringenberg. 1999. Service use by elderly patients after psychiatric hospitalization. *Psychiatric Services* 50 (4), 553–555.

Pyke, K. 2000. "The normal American family" as an interpretive structure of family life among grown children of Korean and Vietnamese immigrants. *Journal of Marriage and the Family* 62 (1), 240–255.

Rastogi, M., and S. Wadhwa. 2006. Substance abuse among Asian Indians in the United States: A consideration of cultural factors and treatment. *Substance Use and Misuse* 41, 1239–1249.

Ren, X., and K. Chang. 1998. Evaluating health status of elderly Chinese in Boston. *Journal of Clinical Epidemiology* 51 (5), 429–435.

Root, M. P. P. 2005. Filipino families. In M. McGoldrick, J. Giordano, and N. Garcia-Preto, eds., *Ethnicity and Family Therapy*, 3rd ed. New York: Guilford.

Rosenstock, I. M., V. J. Strecher, and M. H. Becker. 1988. Social learning theory and the health belief model. *Health Education Quarterly* 15 (2), 175–183. Retrieved April 2006 from http://www.pubmed.gov.

Rowe, J. W., and R. L. Kahn. 1998. *Successful Aging*. New York: Pantheon Books.

Ryan, A. S., A. C. Mui, and P. Cross. 2003. *Asian American Elders in New York City: A Study to Assess Health, Social Needs, Quality of Life, and Quality of Care*. New York: Asian American Federation of New York.

Ryff, C. D. 1999. Psychology and aging. In W. R. Hazard, J. P. Blass, W. H. Ettinger, J. B. Halter, and J. G. Ouslander, eds., *Principles of Geriatric Medicine and Gerontology*, 4th ed., pp. 159–169. New York: McGraw-Hill.

Ryff, C., et al. 1998. Resilience in adulthood and later life: defining features and dynamic processes. In J. Lomranz, ed., *Handbook of Aging and Mental Health: An Integrative Approach*, pp. 69–96. New York: Plenum Press.

Savishinsky, J. 2004. The volunteer and the "sannyasin": Archetypes of retirement in America and India. *International Journal of Aging and Development* 59 (1), 25–41.

Schaller, J., R. Parker, and S. B. Garcia. 1998. Moving toward culturally competent rehabilitation counseling services: Issues and practices. *Journal of Applied Rehabilitation Counseling* 29 (2), 40–48.

Schnurr, P. P., A. Spiro, III, M. J. Vielhauer, M. N. Findler, and J. L. Hamblen. 2002. Trauma in the lives of older men: Findings from the normative aging study. *Journal of Clinical Geropsychology* 8 (3), 175–187.

Segal, U. A. 1991. Cultural variables in Asian Indian families. *Families in Society* 72, 233–241.

——. 2002. *A Framework for Immigration: Asians in the United States*. New York: Columbia University Press.

Shapiro, J., K. Douglas, O. de la Rocha, S. Radecki, C. Vu, and T. Dinh. 1999. Generational differences in psychosocial adaptation and predictors of psychological distress in a population of recent Vietnamese immigrants. *Journal of Community Health* 24 (2), 95–112.

Sharma, P., and S. B. Kerl. 2002. Suggestions for psychologists working with Mexican American individuals and families in health care settings. *Rehabilitation Psychology* 47 (2), 230–239.

Shen, B. J., and D. T. Takeuchi. 2001. A structural model of acculturation and mental health status among Chinese Americans. *American Journal of Community Psychology* 29 (3), 387–418.

Shibusawa, T. 2001. Japanese American parenting. In N. B. Webb, ed., *Culturally Diverse Parent-Child and Family Relationships: A Guide for Social Workers and Other Practitioners*, pp. 282–303. New York: Columbia University Press.

Shibusawa, T., J. Lubben, and H. Kitano. 2001. Japanese Americans. In L. K. Olson, ed., *Through Ethnic Lenses: Caring for the Elderly in a Multi-Cultural Society*, pp. 33–44. Boulder, Colo.: Roman and Littlefield.

Shibusawa, T., and A. C. Mui. 2001. Stress, coping, and depression among Japanese American elders. *Journal of Gerontological Social Work* 36 (1–2), 63–81.

Siegel, P., E. Marin, and R. Bruno. 2001. *Language Use and Linguistic Isolation: Historical Data and Methodological Issues.* Paper presented at the FCSM Statistical Policy Seminar, Bethesda, Md., November 8–9, 2000.

Silverstein, M., and X. Chen. 1999. The impact of acculturation in Mexican American families on the quality of adult grandchildren-grandparent relationships. *Journal of Marriage and the Family* 61, 188–198.

Silverstein, M., and E. Litwak. 1993. A task-specific typology of intergenerational family structure in later life. *The Gerontologist* 33, 258–264.

Silverstein, M., X. Chen, and K. Heller. 1996. Too much of a good thing? Intergenerational social support and the psychological well-being of older parents *Journal of Marriage and the Family* 58, 970–982.

Silverstein, M., T. M. Parrott, and V. L. Bengtson. 1995. Factors that predispose middle-aged sons and daughters to provide social support to older parents. *Journal of Marriage and the Family* 57 (2), 465–476.

Simmons, T., and J. L. Dye. 2003. *Grandparents Living with Grandchildren: 2000.* Retrieved June 4, 2007, from www.census.gov/prod/2003pubs/c2kbr-31.pdf

Simpson, C. C. 1998. "Out of an obscure place": Japanese war brides and cultural pluralism in the 1950s. *differences: A Journal of Feminist Cultural Studies* 10 (3), 47–81.

Snowden, L. R. 2003. Bias in mental health assessment and intervention: Theory and evidence. *American Journal of Public Health* 93 (2), 239–243.

Snowden, L. R., and F. K. Cheung. 1990. Use of inpatient mental health services by members of ethnic minority groups. *American Psychologist* 45(3), 347–355.

Soldo, B. J., D. Wolf, and E. Agree. 1990. Families, households, and care arrangements of frail older women: A structural analysis. *Journals of Gerontology* 45, S238–S249.

Sorlie, P. D., E. Backlund, and J. B. Keller. 1995. U.S. mortality by economic, demographic, and social characteristics: The National Longitudinal Mortality Study. *American Journal of Public Health* 85, 949–956.

Spencer, M.S. and J. Chen. 2004. Effect of discrimination on mental health service use among Chinese Americans. *American Journal of Public Health* 94 (5), 809–814.

Stokes, S.C., L. W. Thompson, S. Murphy, and D. Gallagher-Thompson. 2001. Screening for depression in immigrant Chinese-American elders: Results of a pilot study. *Journal of Gerontological Social Work* 36 (1–2), 27–44.

Strom, R. D., L. P. Buki, and S. K. Strom. 1997. Intergenerational perceptions of English-speaking and Spanish-speaking Mexican American grandparents. *International Journal of Aging and Development* 45, 1–2.

Strom, R. D., and S. K. Strom. 1999. Education for grandparents in Taiwan and the United States. *Journal of Intercultural Studies* 26, 119–166.

——. 2000. Intergenerational learning and family harmony. *Educational Gerontology* 26, 261–283.

Successful Aging Initiative. 2007. *Elder Friendly Communities*. Retrieved August 27, 2007, from http://www.successfulaging.org/page7784.cfm.

Sue, S., D. C. Fujino, L. T. Hu, D. T. Takeuchi, and N. W. S. Zane. 1991. Community mental health services for ethnic minority groups: A test of the cultural responsiveness hypothesis. *Journal of Consulting and Clinical Psychology* 59 (4), 533–540.

Sung, K. T. 1995. Measures and dimensions of filial piety in Korea. *The Gerontologist* 35, 240–247.

——. 1998. An exploration of filial piety. *Journal of Aging Studies* 12 (4), 369–386.

Takaki, R. 1989. *Strangers from a Different Shore: A History of Asian Americans*. Boston: Little, Brown.

Thomas, S. B. 2001. The color line: Race matters in the elimination of health disparities. *American Journal of Public Health* 91 (7), 1046–1048.

Tompar-Tiu, A., and S. Sustento-Seneriches. 1995. *Depression and Other Mental Health Issues: The Filipino American Experience*. San Francisco: Jossey-Bass.

Tran, T. V. 1991. Family living arrangement and social adjustment among three ethnic groups of elderly Indochinese refugees. *International Journal of Aging and Human Development* 32 (2), 91–102.

——. 1993. Psychological traumas and depression in a sample of Vietnamese people in the United States. *Health and Social Work* 18 (3), 184–194.

Tran, T. V., T. Fitzpatrick, W. R. Berg, and R. Wright. 1996. Acculturation, health, stress, and psychological distress among elderly Hispanics. *Journal of Cross-Cultural Gerontology* 11 (2), 149–165.

Treas, J., and S. Mazumdar. 2004. Kinkeeping and caregiving: Contributions of older people in immigrant families. *Journal of Comparative Family Studies* 35, 105–122.

Triandis, H. C., et al. 1993. An etic-emic analysis of individualism and collectivism. *Journal of Cross-Cultural Psychology* 24 (3), 366–383.

Tsai, D.T., and R. A. Lopez. 1997. The use of social supports by elderly Chinese immigrants. *Journal of Gerontological Social Work* 29, 77–94.

Tseng, M.H., J.F.R. Lu, and B. Gandek. 2003. Cultural issues in using the SF-36 Health Survey in Asia: Results from Taiwan. *Health and Quality-of-Life Outcomes* 1 (72). Retrieved June 2006 from http://www.hqlo.com/content/1/1/72.

Tucker, G.R. 1998. A global perspective on multilingualism and multilingual education. In F. Cenoz and F. Genesee, eds., *Beyond Bilingualism: Multilingualism and Multilingual Education*, pp. 3–15. Clevedon, England: Multilingual Matters.

Underwood, A., and J. Adler. 2005. When cultures clash. *Newsweek*, April 25, 68–72.

United Nations. 2002a. International plan of action on ageing. Adopted by the Second World Assembly on Ageing, Madrid, April 8–12, 2002 [Electronic Version]. Retrieved March 29, 2007, from http://www.un.org/esa/socdev/ageing/ageipaa4.htm.

——. 2002b. Office on Ageing and the International Association of Gerontology. Research agenda on ageing for the 21st century. Second World Assembly on Ageing, Madrid, April 8–12, 2002 [Electronic Version]. Retrieved March 29, 2007, from http://www.un.org/esa/socdev/ageing/agerraa.htm.

——. 2007. Towards a society for all ages. Retrieved August 29, 2007, from http://www.un.org/esa/socdev/ageing/society.html.

U.S. Census Bureau. 1990. 1990 census of population: Asian and Pacific Islanders in the United States (1990 CP-3–5) [Electronic Version]. Retrieved March 19, 2005, from http://www.census.gov/prod/cenl990/cp3/cp-3–5.pdf.

——. 2000. Census 2000 Summary File 2 (SF2) 100-Percent Data. Retrieved January 10, 2005, from http://factfinder.census.gov/servlet/DTGeoSearchByListServlet?ds_name=DEC_2000_SF2_Uand_lang=enand_ts=112893145481.

——. 2001. *Total Population by Age, Race, and Hispanic or Latino Origin for the United States: 2000* (Census 2000 Summary File 1). Retrieved March 19, 2005, from http://www.census.gov/population/cen2000/phc-t9/tab01.pdf.

——. 2002. The Asian population: Census 2000 Brief [Electronic Version]. Retrieved April 2005 from http://www.census.gov/prod/2002pubs/c2kbr01–16.pdf.

——. 2004. *We the People: Asians in the United States (Census 2000 Special Reports)*. Retrieved December 2004 from http://www.census.gov/prod/2004pubs/censr-17.pdf.

U.S. Department of Health and Human Services (2001). *Mental Health: Culture, Race, and Ethnicity—A Supplement to Mental Health: A Report of the Surgeon General*. Rockville, Md.: U.S. Department of Health and Human Services, Public Health Service, Office of the Surgeon General.

——. 2005a. *Disparities/Minority Health (No. 295)*. Silver Spring, Md.: Author.

——. 2005b. Sociodemographic factors affect receipt of preventive care services among women aged 65 and older. Retrieved April 27, 2005 from http://www.ahrq.gov/RESEARCH/apr05/0405RA17.htm.

U.S. Department of Health and Human Services, Office of Minority Health. 2003. *Why Companies Are Making Disparities Their Business: The Business Case and Practical Strategies.* Retrieved April 27, 2005, from http://www.omhrc.gov/inet-pub/wwwroot/cultural/business_case.pdf.

U.S. Department of Health and Human Services, Office of the Surgeon General. 2001. Retrieved April 2005 from http://www.mentalhealth.org/cre/ch5_introduction.asp.

Van Willingen, M. (2000). Differential benefits of volunteering across the life course. *Journal of Gerontology* 55B (5), S308–S318.

Velkoff, V.A., and V. A. Lawson. 1998. *International Brief: Gender and Aging.* Washington, D.C.: U.S. Department of Commerce, Economics, and Statistics Administration, Bureau of the Census.

Virnig, B., Z. Huang, N. Lurie, D. Musgrave, A. M. McBean, and B. Dowd. 2004. Does Medicare managed care provide equal treatment for mental illness across races? *Archives of General Psychiatry* 61, 201–205.

Vo-Thanh-Xuan, J., and P. R. Rice. 2000. Vietnamese-Australian grandparenthood: The changing roles and psychological well-being. *Journal of Cross-Cultural Gerontology* 15, 265–288.

Wallace, S. P., K. Campbell, and C. Lew-Ting. 1994. Structural barriers to the use of formal in-home services by elderly Latinos. *Journal of Gerontology* 49, S253–S263.

Walsh, F. 2004. A family resilience framework: Innovative practice applications. *Family Relations* 51 (2), 130–138.

Ware, J. E., Jr. 1993. *SF-36 Health Survey: Manual and Interpretation Guide.* Boston: Health Institute, New England Medical Center.

Ware, J. E., M. Kosinski, and J. E. Dewey. 2000. How to score version two of the SF-36 Health Survey. Lincoln, R.I.: QualityMetric.

Weinstein-Shr, B., and N. Henkin. 1991. Continuity and change: Intergenerational relations in Southeast Asian refugee families. *Marriage and Family Review* 16 (351–1367).

Wethington, E., and R. C. Kessler. 1986. Perceived support, received support, and adjustment of stressful life events *Journal of Health and Social Behavior* 27, 45–54.

Wilmoth, J. M. 2001. Living arrangements among older immigrants in the United States. *The Gerontologist* 41 (2), 228–239.

——. 2004. *Social Integration of Older Immigrants in 21st Century America.* Syracuse, N.Y.: Center for Policy Research, Maxwell School, Syracuse University.

Wilmoth, J. M., G. F. DeJong, and C. L. Himes. 1997. Immigrant and non-immigrant living arrangements among America's White, Hispanic and Asian elderly population. *International Journal of Sociology and Social Policy* 17 (9/10), 57–82.

Wilson, J. 2000. Volunteering. *Annual Review of Sociology* 26, 215–240.

Wolf, D. A. 1997. Family secrets: Transnational struggles among children of Filipino immigrants. *Sociological Perspectives* 40 (3), 457–482.

Woloshin, S., N. A. Bickell, L. M. Schwartz, F. Gary, and H. G. Welch. 1995. Language barriers in medicine in the United States. *Journal of the American Medical Association* 273 (9), 724–728.

Wong, M. G. 1986. Post-1965 Asian immigrants: Where do they come from, where are they now, and where are they going? *Annals of the American Academy of Political and Social Science* 487, 150–168.

Wong, P. T. P., and K. V. Ujimoto. 1998. The elderly: Their stress, coping and mental health. In L. C. Lee and N. W. S. Zane, eds., *Handbook of Asian American Psychology*, pp. 165–209. Thousand Oaks, Calif.: Sage.

Wong, R. 2007. Chinese American elders. In P. J. Kolb, ed., *Social Work Practice with Ethnically and Racially Diverse Nursing Home Residents and Their Families*, pp. 72–105. New York: Columbia University Press.

Wong, S. T., G. J. Yoo, and A. L. Stewart. 2006. The changing meaning of family support among older Chinese and Korean immigrants. *Journals of Gerontology* 61 (1), S4–S10.

Woo, J., et al. (1994). The prevalence of depressive symptoms and predisposing factors in an elderly Chinese population. *Acta Psychiatrica Scandinavica* 89, 8–13.

——. 1995. The status of health assessment 1994. *Annual Review of Public Health* 16, 327–354.

World Health Organization. 2004. Health promotion. Retrieved August 30, 2006, from http://www.who.int/topics/health_promotion/en/.

——. 2005. *WHO Study on Global Ageing and Adult Health.* Retrieved August 30, 2006, from http://www.who.int/healthinfo/systems/sage/en/index.html.

Wu, S.-J. 2001. Parenting in Chinese American families. In N. B. Webb, ed., *Culturally Diverse Parent-Child and Family Relationships: A Guide for Social Workers and Other Practitioners*, pp. 235–260. New York: Columbia University Press.

Yan, E. C., and C. S. Tang. 2003. The role of individual, interpersonal, and organizational factors in mitigating burnout among elder Chinese volunteers. *International Journal of Geriatric Psychiatry* 18, 795–802.

Yap, J. 1986. Philippine ethnoculture and human sexuality. *Journal of Social Work and Human Sexuality* 4(3), 121–134.

Yee, B. W. K. 1992. Markers of successful aging among Vietnamese refugee women. *Women and Therapy* 13, 221–238.

Yee, B. W. K., L. N. Huang, and A. Lew. 1998. Families: Life-span socialization in a cultural context. In L. C. Lee and N. W. S. Zane, eds., *Handbook of Asian American Psychology*, pp. 83–135. Thousand Oaks, Calif.: Sage.

Yesavage, J.A., et al. 1983. Development and validation of geriatric depression screening scale: A preliminary report. *Journal of Psychiatric Research* 17 (1), 37–49.

Ying, Y. W., P. D. Akutsu, X. Zhang, and L. N. Huang. 1997. Psychological dysfunction in Southeast Asian refugees as mediated by sense of coherence. *American Journal of Community Psychology* 25 (6), 839–859.

Yoo, S. H., and K. T. Sung. 1997. Elderly Koreans' tendency to live independently from their adult children: Adaptation to cultural differences in America. *Journal of Cross-Cultural Gerontology* 12, 225–244.

Yoon, S. M. 2005. The characteristics and needs of Asian-American grandparent caregivers: A study of Chinese-American and Korean-American grandparents in New York City. *Journal of Gerontological Social Work* 44 (3-4), 75–94.

Yu, E.-Y., P. Choe, and S. I. Han. 2002. Korean population in the United States, 2000. *International Journal of Korean Studies* 6 (1), 71–107.

Zhou, M., and J. V. Gatewood. 2000. *Contemporary Asian America: A Multi-Disciplinary Reader.* New York: New York University Press.

Zhou, M., and J. Lee. 2004. Introduction: The making of culture, identity, and ethnicity among Asian American youth. In J. Lee and Z. Min, eds., *Asian American Youth: Culture, Identity, and Ethnicity*, pp. 1–32. New York: Routledge.

INDEX

Page numbers in italics refer to figures and tables.